SEALs

T.L. Bosiljevac

SEALS

UDT/SEAL Operations in Vietnam

PALADIN PRESS
BOULDER, COLORADO

SEALs
UDT/SEAL Operations in Vietnam
by T.L. Bosiljevac

Copyright © 1990 by T.L. Bosiljevac

ISBN 0-87364-531-6
Printed in the United States of America

Published by Paladin Press, a division of
Paladin Enterprises, Inc., P.O. Box 1307,
Boulder, Colorado 80306, USA.

CONTENTS

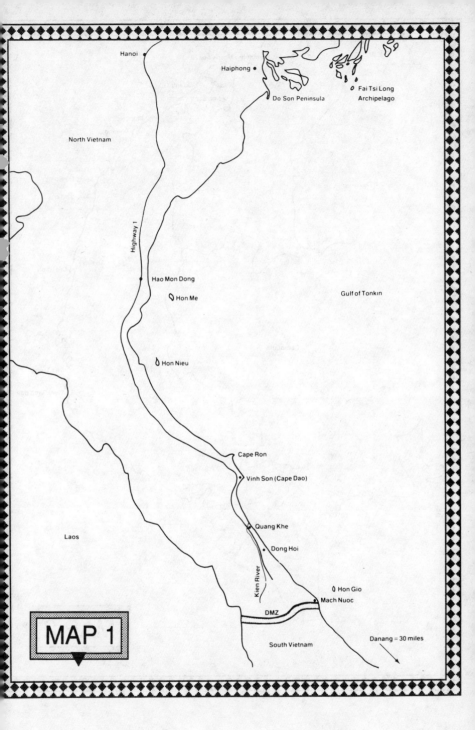

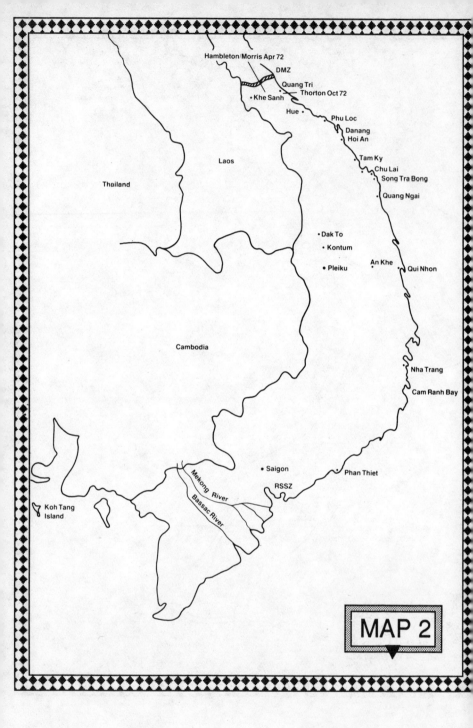

Hambleton/Morris Apr 72
DMZ
Quang Tri
Thorton Oct 72
Khe Sanh
Hue
Phu Loc
Danang
Hoi An
Tam Ky
Chu Lai
Song Tra Bong
Quang Ngai

Laos

Thailand

Dak To
Kontum
Pleiku
An Khe
Qui Nhon

Cambodia

Nha Trang
Cam Ranh Bay

Saigon
RSSZ
Phan Thiet
Mekong River
Bassac River
Koh Tang Island

MAP 2

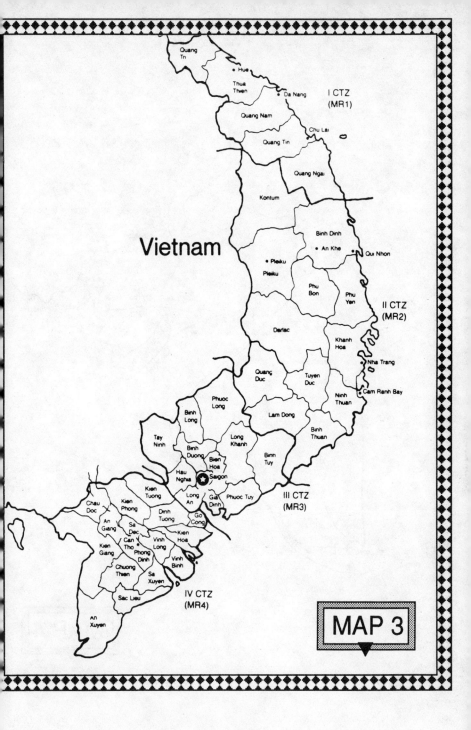

Vietnam

Quang
Tri
• Hue
Thua
Thien
• Da Nang
I CTZ
(MR1)
Quang Nam
Chu Lai
Quang Tin
Quang Ngai
Kontum
Binh Dinh
• An Khe
Qui Nhon
• Pleiku
Pleiku
Phu
Bon
Phu
Yen
II CTZ
(MR2)
Darlac
Khanh
Hoa
• Nha Trang
Quang
Duc
Tuyen
Duc
• Cam Ranh Bay
Phuoc
Long
Ninh
Thuan
Binh
Long
Lam Dong
Binh
Thuan
Tay
Ninh
Long
Khanh
Binh
Duong
Bien
Hoa
Binh
Tuy
Hau
Nghia
★ Saigon
Kien
Tuong
Long
An
Gia
Dinh
Phuoc Tuy
III CTZ
(MR3)
Chau
Doc
Kien
Phong
Dinh
Tuong
Go
Cong
An
Giang
Sa
Dec
Kien
Hoa
Kien
Giang
Can
Tho
Phong
Dinh
Vinh
Long
Chuong
Thien
Sa
Xuyen
Vinh
Binh
Bac Lieu
IV CTZ
(MR4)
An
Xuyen

MAP 3

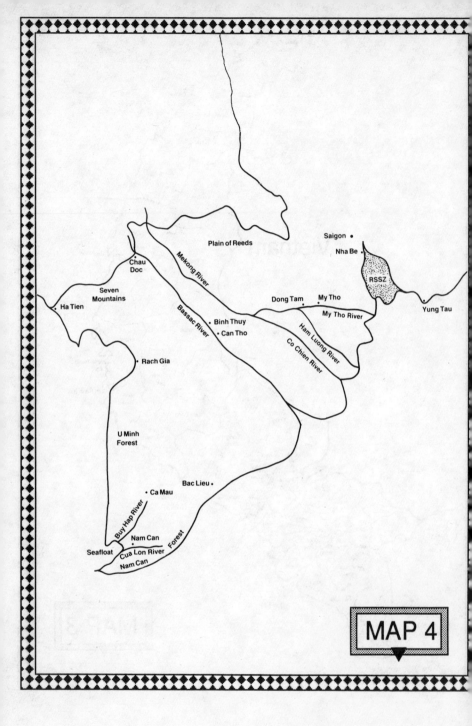

x

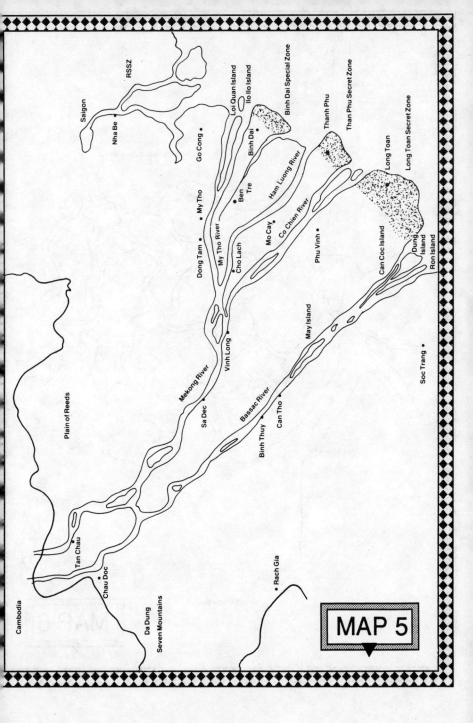

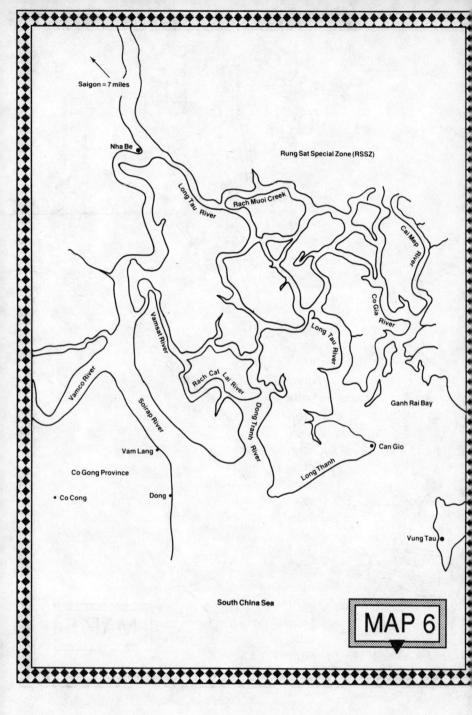

Saigon = 7 miles

Nha Be

Rung Sat Special Zone (RSSZ)

Long Tau River

Rach Muoi Creek

Cai Mep River

Co Gia River

Long Tau River

Vamsat River

Vamco River

Soirap River

Rach Cat Lai River

Dong Tranh River

Ganh Rai Bay

Can Gio

Vam Lang

Co Gong Province

Dong

Long Thanh

Co Cong

Vung Tau

South China Sea

MAP 6

ACKNOWLEDGMENTS

I wish to express my deepest thanks to all those who have assisted me in the completion of this work. My sincere thanks to Dr. Loren E. Pennington for his tremendous guidance and help throughout this venture. Additionally, I extend my appreciation to the other members of my thesis committee, professors Glenn E. Torrey and Randall C. Anderson.

My deepest thanks to Capt. Thomas E. Murphy and Cdr. Daley T. Coulter for originally inspiring me to begin the project and providing me ample support to complete it. Capt. Ronald E. Yeaw allowed me to sift through the volumes of the Special Warfare historical data he has so carefully accumulated over the years. Mr. G. Wesley Pryce provided me with invaluable assistance at the Naval Historical Center, Washington Navy Yards, without which my work would be meaningless.

I also wish to thank the countless officers and men who provided me with information and assisted by proofreading my rough drafts. Finally, my deepest thanks to my wife for her assistance, patience, and considerable support in this endeavor. To my family, who experiences sacrifices daily for my profession, I am forever indebted.

INTRODUCTION

The concepts expressed in this work are the views and opinions of the author alone. These ideas do not reflect the official views of any branch of the U.S. government, including the Defense Department and the U.S. Navy, nor any individual who serves in an official capacity.

During the Vietnam War, the U.S. Navy Special Warfare community (NAVSPECWAR, or, more commonly, SPECWAR) was composed mainly of Sea, Air, Land Teams (SEAL Teams), Underwater Demolition Teams (UDT), and supporting units. The purpose of this book is to detail the unclassified operations of the SPECWAR units, concentrating mostly on UDT and SEAL operations and accomplishments (the distinction between the UDT and SEAL units will be defined later in this introduction).

Prior to the invasion of North Africa in November 1942, the U.S. Navy had organized a 17-man detachment to cope with the problem of maritime and beach obstacles faced by amphibious landing forces. In July 1943, an additional 21-man detachment was established and became known as Naval Combat Demolition Unit One (NCDU 1), whose mission was to assist in the invasion of Sicily. The future need for these units was recognized by planners, and in the summer of 1943, a formal training program was established at Fort Pierce, Florida, to raise 6-man NCDUs.

During November 1943, U.S. Marines secured the Tarawa Atoll in the Pacific following a very bloody and costly three-day battle. The initial amphibious landing became an unexpected bloodbath when landing craft became stranded hundreds of yards offshore on a submerged coral reef. The reef, which was known to exist, forced the marines to wade ashore from many of their trapped landing craft. Intense enemy small-arms fire cut down a large number of leathernecks as they struggled through deep water laden with full combat gear. Under such loads, other men drowned after falling into underwater holes. The casualties were heavy even before the marines were able to make it ashore to press their attack.

These difficulties greatly troubled planners of future amphibious operations. Tactical planning for the Normandy Invasion was already in high gear at the time of the amphibious landing at the Tarawa Atoll, while the planning for the attack on Kwajalein in the Pacific was in its final stages. The navy decided to place additional emphasis on the new group of NCDUs, who would be totally devoted to scouting and marking beach approaches; demolishing landing obstacles, be they manmade or natural; and providing initial tactical cover to the first wave of landing forces. It was hoped that the new units would provide the opening in an enemy beach for Allied forces to rapidly establish a beachhead. The idea was to send these men ashore on the very first landing craft. Under fire, they would be called upon to clear a path for the invading forces.

Initial volunteers were taken from the Navy Seabees, the famous combat engineers, and the Marine Raiders, the rugged Marine assault unit of World War II. The first cadre at Fort Pierce approached training with the concept that the human body could perform ten times more work than was normally believed possible. In addition to an extremely rigorous physical training regimen, the men were subjected to long hours of exposure to the worst physical environment, such as mud, cold water, rain, swamp, and pounding surf. Selection criteria emphasized those who were strong swimmers, while the training concentrated on small boat handling and the use of explosives in demolishing targets and obstacles.

Those who survived the initial training composed the early NCDUs, which were employed during the Normandy Invasion. For the invasion, the NCDUs were expanded to 13-man teams. Casualties ran 70 percent at Omaha Beach, while those at Utah Beach were 30 percent. Despite their losses, the navy men were able to accomplish their mission and greatly assisted the invasion force. The survivors of Omaha Beach were returned to Fort Pierce, while those from Utah Beach took part in the invasion of southern France. The NCDUs who took part in that invasion were the last of the demolitioneers who did not swim to their objectives.

Many NCDUs became the nucleus of even newer units and were shipped to the Pacific theater for additional operations that were being planned. These new 100-man units, christened Underwater Demolition Teams (UDTs), remained under the navy's operational control. The more colorful and common name earned by these early amphibians was frogmen. Their insignia consisted of a stalky-looking frog with a Dixie cup sailor cap cocked to one side of its head. Its face registered a Popeye snarl, with a cigar stub poking out of the corner of the mouth. The insignia caught the frog in the middle of a bold stride and carrying a stick of lighted dynamite in one hand. It seemed to be an appropriate symbol of the bold, professional UDT attitude in the face of a demanding mission.

Throughout the Pacific theater, UDTs proved their worth during numerous island operations. Eight days after the Normandy Invasion, Saipan was invaded. The vanguard of that amphibious assault, UDTs participated in every major amphibious action for the remainder of the war. As their experience grew, they modified their tactics and techniques to take advantage of the lessons learned when fighting the Japanese. Specifically, their mission was defined as the reconnaissance and clearance of the area from the 6 1/2-fathom curve (twenty-one feet of depth) to the high-water mark on a prospective landing beach.

A basic preassault operation during World War II was much the same as such operations conducted today. A day or two prior to launching a marine amphibious landing, frogmen would be transported to the vicinity of the prospective beachhead in fast-moving boats. Once in the area of operations, the UDT would exit the craft in pairs as the boats paralleled the shoreline. These pairs would form a long line several meters apart and swim toward the beach. Soundings and other hydrographic data were recorded, as were any obstacles that could hinder a landing.

If at all possible, the frogmen would attempt to remain undetected so as not to give away their intention. In other instances, they were sent in under Allied covering fire from offshore naval ships and aircraft as the enemy fired at them from the beach. Sometimes many groups were sent forward not only to reconnoiter all possible avenues of approach, but also to deceive the enemy as to the exact location of a future landing so that he might spread his defenses much thinner. The combat surveys would often terminate at the beach or above the high-water line. Commanders would be most interested in a sample of beach sand to determine if the beach could support the heavy amphibious vehicles without engineer support. Enemy defenses, natural obstacles, and routes leading from the beach and into the hinterland would also be of great interest.

Once their job was completed, the frogmen would slip away from the beach and swim to sea to await pickup by small craft. Not only did they have to successfully elude the enemy forces, but in all instances, they had to battle such elements as heavy surf and strong currents. A particularly alert enemy might cause the frogmen to tow a wounded buddy to the pickup point far out to sea.

Their compiled data, along with aerial photography and other information, would provide planners with an excellent idea of the target area. Their job half done, the UDT would be reintroduced back into the area of operations just prior to the main assault. As they again jumped from high-speed boats, the frogmen now swam toward shore towing haversacks of explosives. These charges would be secured to all obstacles within the assault lanes, whether they were underwater or exposed. Sometimes assault lanes would be marked by buoys or lights. All the explosives would then be connected together by means of an explosive cord. The UDTs would detonate the entire explosive field by using a time fuse or electrical means ("command detonation").

As often as possible, the demolitions were rigged to the seaward side of the obstacles. When detonated, much of the debris would be sent toward the enemy on shore. The effect on the barriers would be devastating, while the psychological effect on the enemy was no less substantial. In most situations, before the smoke could clear and as the debris rained from the sky, the marine force would be speeding toward the shoreline for the main assault under cover of air strikes and naval gunfire.

By the end of World War II, there were approximately thirty-four Underwater Demolition Teams holding about 3,500 frogmen. Their post-World War II training added the conduct of limpet mine attacks, in which combat swimmers would attach specially prepared charges to the hull of an enemy ship moored or anchored in a harbor. As explosives specialists, they also trained to conduct demolition raids on harbor facilities or targets near maritime approaches. They were also called upon to perform civil or administrative functions, such as the demolition of obstacles to improve harbor facilities and channels.

After World War II, most of the Underwater Demolition Teams were decommissioned, but a handful remained in active roles. The outbreak of the Korean War put the frogmen back into the reconnaissance and raiding business. UDTs were called upon to demolish tunnels, railroads, bridges, and other inland targets. Within a matter of years, frogmen were also training to parachute and honing patrol skills for inland raids. During World War II, their most common weapon was a mere knife.[1] They now became experts with a variety of small arms.

By 1961, President John Kennedy was highly impressed with the abilities of the U.S. Army's Special Forces. In numerous brushfire wars around the globe, they had proved invaluable in projecting U.S. foreign policy while remaining diplomatically low-key. With the advent and buildup of large nuclear forces, it was reassuring to have such small units to bridge the gap in foreign policy. Particularly successful in Laos in stemming insurgency up until that time, the Green Berets, as they came to be known, were expanded with presidential blessing and publicly praised.

The air force and navy were pressured to form special warfare units of their own to be used in counterinsurgency, counterguerrilla, and unconventional operations. The Southeast Asian arena appeared to warrant this expansion with the escalation of U.S. advisors to countries there. The air force responded by creating the Air Commandos (now known as Air Force Special Operations). These men carried out a variety of operations involving specially equipped aircraft and navigational control equipment for counterguerrilla operations and special missions.[2]

The navy decided to commission its own special warfare unit. In January 1962, two Sea, Air, Land Teams were formed. Called SEALs for short, after the well-known maritime mammal, the unit drew its name from the elements by which they infiltrate, operate, and melt away. Formed from UDT volunteers, these men were assigned a different mission. While UDTs normally operated up to the high-water mark, SEALs were tasked to operate beyond the high-water line and into the enemy's hinterland (normally defined as up to twenty miles inland). There they would act as naval commandos, whose functions were to gather intelligence, raid, ambush, capture prisoners, and create havoc in the enemy's rear areas. They could be used to instruct the forces of other nations in these same techniques, much like the Army Special Forces.

A normal SEAL Team was composed of numerous platoons, the basic operating SEAL element. The 14-man platoons consisted of two officers (an Officer-in-Charge, or OIC, and a Second-in-Charge, or 2IC) and twelve enlisted men. Each platoon could be deployed and operate independently; it could further be split to patrol as half a platoon (called a squad) or less.

The initial training of frogmen varied slightly over the years, but the basics remained the same. UDT members and SEALs both underwent the same basic training in order to qualify as frogmen. Upon graduation, the recruits were assigned either to an Underwater Demolition Team or SEAL Team, depending upon the needs of the Special Warfare community. The present Basic Underwater Demolition/SEAL Training Course (BUD/S) is twenty-five weeks in duration. The officers and men who comprise the classes are given identical treatment.

The initial two weeks involves an Indoctrination Phase in which volunteer candidates must qualify under set standards in order to be formally accepted into the course. Physical training is stressed, utilizing running, swimming, and extensive exercise. Hair is shaved to a stubble, and discipline is demanded. The students find that a high degree of both discipline and motivation is required in order to continue. Classes are also given in first aid and water survival. During the course, which is both rugged and dangerous, such knowledge in basic skills proves quite valuable.

Those who successfully complete the indoctrination phase are fully accepted into training. Now called "Tadpoles" by the cadre, they find they must continually run and swim further and are pressed to their physical breaking points. Instant reaction to orders is expected. On a UDT or SEAL combat operation, a man who hesitates an instant could be killed or cause the death of others, as well as the failure of the mission. Although the instructors apply intense pressure to the students, they attempt to produce a positive training environment. The accomplishment of training tasks is left to the individual's will and his ability to work with his comrades as a team. These seven weeks are called Phase One.

In the middle of the first phase is a five-day physical marathon called "Motivation Week." The term most commonly used in describing this ordeal is "Hell Week." The students undergo a whirlwind test of their abilities and will. From around midnight on Sunday night, the instructors take the men from one cycle to another. To complete each cycle, the men must call upon every reserve of strength and stamina and, above all, teamwork. About eight hours of sleep are allowed for the entire week if the student crews make no mistakes along the way. Chances are that the students will get considerably less sleep, and even then only in periods of about fifteen minutes most of the time. Up until this week, an average class may have swum up to twenty miles and run 150 more.

During Hell Week, the days and nights blur together, as do the additional miles traversed. The stress and fatigue cause many aspiring frogmen to quit. The final day is spent crawling among exploding charges detonated by the cadre. In reference to the first Pacific missions carried out by frogmen under enemy fire, the instructors holler, "so solly!" as the charges blow. Just as UDT men discovered during World War II when fighting the Japanese, the exhausted students are reminded that to quit is to fail and possibly die. No matter how exhausted, they must remain alert and push forward. The alternative in combat could cost one his life. Hell Week has remained a frogman institution since those earliest days at Fort Pierce. The men who survive Hell Week are lucky. They finish the first phase by learning how to conduct beach reconnaissance utilizing several different techniques.

The second phase of BUD/S concentrates on land warfare. It is in this phase that the students learn the tactics of raiding and ambushing from the sea, as well as target reconnaissance. Field skills, such as patrolling, are also taught, as are such insertion methods as rappelling (sliding down a rope from a helicopter). Emphasis is placed on the characteristics and employment of explosives and demolitions. The entire phase comes to a climax during a twenty-one-day exercise on San Clemente Island, where students put all their skills to the test. Many of the operations they conduct utilize live ammunition and explosives for realism.

The third phase of BUD/S concentrates mainly on the use of various scuba rigs in the application of Special Warfare diving. Additional instruction is provided on various maritime operations the men will be called upon to accomplish. Physical requirements increase. Runs stretch out until the students can negotiate fourteen miles in the last phase. The longest open ocean swim is about five and a half miles. Academic coursework in diving physics and diving medicine also provide challenges. Attrition rates of 50 to 80 percent within a class are not uncommon, but one further evolution awaits them.[3]

Upon graduation from BUD/S, the entire class is shipped off to U.S. Army Airborne School at Ft. Benning, Georgia. It is there that the future frogmen are taught the insertion method of static-line parachuting. Although rigorous physical training is involved, the BUD/S graduates normally are overqualified at this point, running circles around the rest of their Airborne classmates. Still, there is something unnatural about hurling yourself from a perfectly good aircraft while in flight. The stress can be substantial, but the navy men rarely wash out. As a general rule, they normally receive a considerable amount of additional attention for their overzealous, nonconformist motivation.

Following this intensive initial training program, the graduates were then assigned to a UDT or SEAL Team for a six-month probationary period. Any man who failed to meet the standards of his unit during that period was reassigned to the fleet. At the end of the six months, the men were all officially accepted as frogmen; however, their training never ceased. UDT men furthered their skills with specially designed equipment and on extended operations worldwide while deployed on surface fleet assets and submarines. SEALs also participated in various exercises worldwide and were sent to various land warfare schools, such as Ranger, Pathfinder, and HALO.[4] When considering the scope of their qualifications, it becomes clear that these men often performed well beyond all expectations. Simply to gain acceptance into a UDT or SEAL unit required uncommon ability. Those who made the grade were further trained to an exceptionally high standard.

The ability of these men to drive their wills and unharness physical endurance unknown to most men has become, at times, legendary. They have done amazing things, and are infamous for perpetuating outrageous tales about their own feats. In actuality, many of the outrageous tales are based on fact. One author who wrote about these navy men included the following in part of his title: "Some of what you heard may even be true!"[5]

While sightseeing on a glacier in Greenland with other navy men and several airmen, one UDT member was injured with his group as a portion of the glacier collapsed. Several men were seriously hurt. The frogman rendered first aid to the injured and then ran as hard as he could for help. He covered seven miles in rugged terrain, but never would have been able to make it had he not been in top condition. Because of his ability, all the men survived and were evacuated.[6]

Another group of UDTs were abandoned on an arctic ice field while their ship fought to escape from a sudden closing ice flow. Without food, shelter, or other equipment, they reported back to their base in Virginia two weeks later. How they made it back remains a UDT secret.[7] Other frogmen accompanied Admiral Richard Byrd on Antarctic expeditions.

During the early days of the U.S. Manned Space Program, NASA scientists were shocked when astronauts broke down under gravity simulation in giant centrifuges. Assuming they had miscalculated what limits a man could endure, they called upon several SEALs to undertake the same tests. Over voice communications, the scientists asked one SEAL if he'd had enough. Under the force of all those Gs, his face was contorted, but through clenched teeth he barely managed to say, "More! Screw it on!"[8] Incidentally, it was a UDT that assisted in the recovery of all the manned Mercury, Gemini, and Apollo spacecraft directly after splashdown in the 1960s and 1970s.

Special equipment was also developed for UDTs that was to be utilized in a wide range of missions. Left many times to their own initiatives to complete an assignment, these men were given wide latitude when selecting weaponry and equipment. For example, small submersible vehicles (swimmer delivery vehicles, or SDVs) were developed to extend the underwater range in scuba operations and to provide a means to haul heavier loads. With an extensive repertoire of skills, training, and equipment, UDT and SEAL teams could perform a very wide variety of operations anytime, anywhere. They were routinely assigned to the numbered fleets of the U.S. Navy and cruised the world, both above and below the ocean surface. During times of international crisis requiring the attention of the U.S. Navy, frogmen were always close at hand. When the conflict in Southeast Asia flared up, it was not surprising that frogmen were among the first navy men to go into action.

Notes

1. The type of knife used by UDTs is termed a K-Bar and is much sought after as a status symbol. One SEAL said of this knife: "Other people can get 'em; we get to use 'em!" Richard Hill, "Mean Mothers With Dirty Faces," *Esquire* (May 1974), p. 148.

2. Such men were involved in the unsuccessful attempt to rescue American hostages in Iran in 1980. They were again called to serve during the Grenada crisis in 1983.

3. One class graduated no one!

4. Ranger school teaches small-unit leadership and field tactics, such as raids, ambushes, and reconnaissance. Pathfinder school teaches terminal guidance of army aircraft in isolated field environments. HALO (high altitude, low open) is the military freefall school where men train to free-fall parachute with full combat equipment in order to clandestinely infiltrate an operational area. They exit the aircraft at extreme altitudes and must breathe oxygen while falling.

5. Fred Reed, "Gutting it Out," *Times Magazine* (September 4, 1978), magazine cover.

6. Erick Berry, *Underwater Warriors* (New York, 1967), p. 88.

7. Ibid., pp. 88-89.

8. Hill, "Mean Mothers," p. 91.

CHAPTER ONE

The Early Years (1954–1964)

Following their defeat in the French Indochina War, French forces began a withdrawal from their former Asian colony of Vietnam. At the same time, thousands of Vietnamese refugees fled to the South as the North came under communist rule. This migration was dubbed "The Passage To Freedom." The United States moved to assist the French forces and Vietnamese civilian refugees in hopes of easing the transition of the newly formed nations in any way possible.

The Geneva Accords that ended hostilities with the French divided North and South Vietnam at roughly the 17th parallel. Laos and Cambodia were also formed as separate nations. U.S. Naval Amphibious Forces were ordered to relocate into the Gulf of Tonkin in 1954 in order to provide transport and security. The majority of the amphibious task force arrived from Korea on 14 and 15 August 1954. Under the direction of Commander A. E. Teal, the head of the control unit for the Amphibious Control Division, a detachment from Underwater Demolition Team 12 conducted surveys of potential landing sites for naval amphibious vessels. Of primary interest was a beach landing area on the Do Son Peninsula located about twenty-five miles below the North Vietnamese port of Haiphong[1] (see Map 1). With this small activity, Naval Special Warfare first began direct involvement in the U.S. effort in Indochina. That effort would eventually escalate into a major conflict that would not end for nearly twenty more years.

The U.S. efforts in the years directly following the French disengagement concentrated mostly on replacing the French presence. At that time, the United States saw the rising tide of communist expansion and chose to attempt to contain the threat in many areas of the world. Korea was an unpleasant study in warfare on the Asian continent for the United States; it was apparent that limited warfare would prove costly indeed against communism in Asia. U.S. conventional forces were trained to fight in an unrestrained but orthodox manner where front lines were definitively drawn. Now, however, guerrilla warfare became the new order of the day, and communist support of brushfire wars around the world became commonplace. Against a backdrop of the McCarthy hearings, the threat of communism, in a monolithic form and directed by Moscow, seemed to have permeated the American conscience.

In September 1954, the Southeast Asia Treaty Organization (SEATO) was formed. Its function was to serve as a NATO-type collective of nations in the region against communism. The same month, the Nationalist Chinese gained the full support of the United States in defending the islands of Quemoy and Matsu against the Red Chinese. This was followed in February 1955 by the evacuation of the Tachen Islands, which were also threatened by the Chinese communist mainland. In July 1958, marines landed in Lebanon to stifle a communist-inspired rebellion. Around the world, the United States maneuvered to counter the communist threat of expansion. In Indochina, the United States moved to draw the line and succeed where the French had failed. To do so in the nuclear age, however, would take a different approach. There had to be an increase in unconventional warfare capability.

The first major effort in Indochina came in Laos, rather than in South Vietnam. In 1959, the North Vietnamese Central Executive Committee issued its Resolution 15, which called for a change in strategy in the South. The political struggle now became an armed struggle. In order to support the insurgency in the South, North Vietnam realized that control of at least certain areas of Laos would be essential. Not only would such areas provide a more comfortable buffer to the communist state, but, more importantly, they would serve as a medium for lines of communication and resupply to the communists fighting in the South; thus, the establishment of the Ho Chi Minh Trail came to pass. U.S. Army Special Forces moved into both Laos and South Vietnam during the late 1950s to advise and assist the young forces of those countries. In Laos, the fighting grew in scale by the day, and control of the terrain changed by the season.

One small piece of support provided by the U.S. Navy at the time was to give the Royal Lao government five LCVP (landing craft, vehicle, and personnel) and five LCM (landing craft, medium; commonly called "Mike" boat) to bolster its riverine forces. For a landlocked country, the Lao needed little in the way of naval assets; once delivered, however, the LCVPs and LCMs would serve to help their security forces patrol the long Mekong River. The small flotilla assembled in Saigon in early June 1960 to begin the trip up the Mekong for the delivery. Commander C. W. Westergaard was assigned to command the team. He was joined by Detachment Mike of UDT 12, then located out of Yokosuka, Japan. Lt. David Del Giudice was the officer-in-charge (OIC) for the 10-man frogmen force, which would help guide the craft through the river during the tremendous snow runoff from the Tibetan Mountains in July, while also providing a minimal security force. The men reported aboard the USS *Okanogan* (APA 220) for the transit to Saigon. By mid-June, the flotilla began its riverine voyage. The 430-mile journey was successfully completed on the afternoon of 4 July. Their mission complete, the UDT and navy men boarded an aircraft in Pakse and returned to Saigon, the first stop in their trip back.[2]

In Vietnam, senior Vietnamese naval officer Ho Tan Quyen proposed the formation of a Vietnamese frogman unit to remove underwater obstacles, protect harbor and port facilities, and conduct special operations in a maritime environment. Conventional U.S. naval advisors did not support the idea initially, believing that the Vietnamese marines were responsible for such missions. But, in late 1960, the Vietnamese turned to another source, requesting assistance from Taiwan in the training and establishment of the unit. One officer and seven enlisted men completed this initial training and formed the first Vietnamese frogman unit, later known as the Lien Doc Nguoi Nhia (LDNN), or the "soldiers who fight under the sea." The Vietnamese UDT unit was formally established in July 1961, having an authorized strength of forty-eight officers and enlisted men.[3]

The guerrilla war in Laos proved to be another diplomatic dilemma, but the U.S. Army's Special Forces detachments proved invaluable in the fight. The new Kennedy administration saw the handwriting on the wall for Southeast Asia, as well as the value of such men as the Green Berets. Kennedy moved to expand their numbers and active role throughout the world in order to bridge the U.S. response between nuclear and conventional warfare and diplomatic measures. April 1961 was a dark moment for the Kennedy administration; the Bay of Pigs defeat only accentuated the need for unconventional forces and an ability to fight insurgencies and guerrillas.

In March 1961, the Plans and Policy Office under the Chief of Naval Operations (CNO) supported a proposal put forth by its Strategic Plans Division. With the administration's affection for the Green Berets, the other services felt pressured to respond by establishing their own units for similar tasks. In March, the proposal to the CNO recommended establishing Sea, Air, and Land Teams within the navy which were to be known by the acronym SEAL. Their responsibility would be to develop a naval guerrilla/counterguerrilla capability, develop elements of a tactical doctrine, and help to develop special equipment to support those roles. At the time, emphasis was on direct action raids and missions on targets in close proximity to bodies of water. The name SEAL was to indicate an all-around environmental capability.[4] Before being formally established, their role was expanded to include advisory assignments to friendly nations in the conduct of maritime special operations. Additionally, the SEALs were to be drawn from experienced frogmen of the navy's Underwater Demolition Teams.[5]

Late in 1961, CINCPAC (Commander in Chief, Pacific) recognized that the conflict in Southeast Asia could flare without warning. Very little hydrographic information had been collected regarding the various areas along the South Vietnamese coastline of interest to U.S. naval forces. CINCPACFLT (Commander in Chief, Pacific Fleet) was authorized to conduct an administrative data-collection operation at the beginning of 1962. On 4 January, USS *Cook* (APD 130) began the hydrographic reconnaissance mission, utilizing a small West Coast UDT detachment. The frogmen charted beaches in the vicinity of Quang Tri, Danang, Nha Trang, Cam Ranh Bay, Vung Tau, and Qui Nhon. Such information as beach gradients, obstacles, accesses, and tides were collected for future reference. At this early stage of the conflict, the frogmen were fortunate. They met no resistance and completed their work uneventfully on 27 January.

Vice President Lyndon Johnson visited South Vietnam in May to further demonstrate U.S. resolve in the area. In the wake of the Berlin Crisis, President Kennedy requested an additional $3.25 billion dollars for the defense budget and called for an increase in defense manning. At the beginning of 1962, the Military Assistance Command, Vietnam (MACV) was formed, and the advisory role of U.S. forces continued to increase. Almost immediately after the establishment of SEAL Teams One and Two on 1 January 1962, their active role in Vietnam began.

SEAL Team One, assigned to the Pacific Fleet, drew most of its 60-man force from Underwater Demolition Teams 11 and 12. The first assigned commanding officer was David Del Giudice, the young naval officer who had escorted the Mekong River Flotilla into Laos two years earlier while assigned to UDT 12. Two officers from Team One were dispatched in January 1962 to survey the support the unit could provide to the Vietnamese and other U.S. forces advisors. Through that month and part of February, they determined that they could best help advise Mobile Training Team 7, which was scheduled for Riverine Advisory Duty in the near future.[6] Back in the States, the navy's first SEALs dispersed to a wide variety of military schools to train for their immediate missions. The SEALs of Team One, anticipating deployment to Vietnam, would be part of the navy's immediate future Vietnam involvement.

On 10 March 1962, two SEALs arrived in-country to begin a six-month tour instructing the Vietnamese in clandestine maritime operations. After this mission was completed, another one was initiated from January to December 1963. At the same time, Mobile Training Team (MTT) 10-62 began training Biet Hai commandos (Junk Force Commando Platoons) of the South Vietnamese navy in April 1962. The MTT was composed of one officer and nine men from both SEAL Teams One and Two. In their six-month assignment, they conducted a frogman-style course of rugged training for their allies. Sixty-two Vietnamese were graduated from the course in October 1962. An additional six-month course was conducted by MTT 4-63 that ran from 20 September 1962 to 30 January 1963, and those indigenous cadres assumed the responsibility of instructing other Vietnamese. The U.S. advisory team consisted of men from both U.S. Navy SEAL teams.[7]

The Kennedy administration had nearly intervened with direct military force in Laos in May 1962. A task force that included 5,000 marines and 50 jet fighters sat on naval vessels in the Gulf of Thailand during the crisis. The marines did not land, but political tensions between the Americans and communists continued under strain throughout the year.

In October, Kennedy faced the Soviets in a direct confrontation over the installation of medium-range ballistic missiles in Cuba. A naval blockade of the island was established, and the Soviets backed down. It seemed as if nuclear war could erupt overnight, and the ability of the United States to use restraint increased in significance. The value of unconventional capabilities doubled overnight.

By January 1963, the United States had nearly 12,000 military personnel in Vietnam. Unrest against the U.S.-backed Diem regime in Saigon grew until Diem was removed from power and murdered in a coup in November 1963. Following the coup, the new South Vietnamese leadership seemed more open to U.S. advice. It was also in November that President Kennedy was assassinated and Lyndon Johnson stepped into the White House. Just prior to his assassination in 1963, President Kennedy wrote the Chief of Naval Operations:

"When I was in Norfolk in 1962, I noted particularly the members of the SEAL Teams. I was impressed by them as individuals and with the capability they possess as a group. As missiles assume more and more of the nuclear deterrent role and as your limited war mission grows, the need for Special Forces in the Navy and the Marine Corps will increase."

He ended the note by asking directly about the present state of Naval Special Warfare forces.[8]

The transition of both the U.S. and Vietnamese governments now created new leadership that was even more conducive to further U.S. involvement in Vietnam. From January to December 1963, another SEAL detachment of two officers and ten enlisted men continued to train Vietnamese in the conduct of maritime commando operations from a base in Danang. This team of men followed the first two SEAL officer advisors who had departed South Vietnam in the fall.[9]

During the Kennedy administration, the United States conducted a wide variety of operations to further national policy goals. Most of these operations were overt military assistance, while a small portion were covert operations. The results of these actions, and especially the communist response to them, were definitely related. In 1961, President Kennedy had authorized the operating arm of the CIA, known as the Combined Studies Group, to assist the South Vietnamese in running covert operations against the North. This action was taken in response to North Vietnamese support of the insurgencies in Laos and South Vietnam. In support of this policy, the navy and other services submitted potential responses or courses of action from which the administration could choose. The responses could be selected to fit political intentions and thereby provide a specific degree of appropriate counteraction.

One particular course recommended by the navy included UDT and/or SEAL personnel conducting commando raids into North Vietnam. It was proposed that the teams would attack the vulnerable rail and highway lines that ran south through the North Vietnamese panhandle and connected to the Ho Chi Minh Trail. Preparations were also made to use Vietnamese frogmen to destroy the Swatow class gunboats used by the North Vietnamese navy. The operations would be launched from Vietnamese motorized sampans.

Senior U.S. naval officers hardly felt that missions of this magnitude could be successfully accomplished utilizing such modest assets. Although they fully supported the CIA-directed campaign, the navy felt a drastic improvement was in order. Finally, on 27 September 1962, an Administration Special Advisory Group formally recommended the use of high-speed PT boats and SEALs to conduct covert operations against the North Vietnamese.[10]

The high-speed patrol craft proposal was accepted, but it was only to be used with indigenous personnel. Two old mothballed U.S. boats originally built in 1950, Fast Patrol and Torpedo or PTFs, were refurbished and prepared on the East Coast of the United States. Two other PTFs were purchased from a Norwegian shipbuilding company and arrived in the United States in early 1963. Dubbed a "Nasty" boat, after the Norwegian "Nasty" class PT boats, these Norwegian-built, aluminum-hulled boats were more modern than the two U.S. boats taken out of mothballs. Their original two Napier Deltic engines could reach speeds over forty knots with a range of about one thousand miles. Their armament included machine guns and, later, mortars. In August, the PTFs were shipped to San Diego. During their stay on the West Coast, the boats were tested in two days of exercises with UDT and SEAL personnel in a variety of raid and insertion/recovery operation profiles.[11] They left San Diego for Hawaii in the middle of September in preparation for operations in Vietnam.[12]

UDTs had been active during this period as well. It was recognized that commando and survey teams would need clandestine transport to forward areas to conduct operations. Such missions had seen success during the Korean War when British Royal Marine Commandos and U.S. UDT frogmen from submarines were used.[13] One of these subs, the *Perch* (APSS 313), and a sister vessel, *Sealion* (APSS 315), were recommissioned in the fall of 1961. Training in the Pacific arena followed, using UDT/SEAL units as well as marine reconnaissance forces. After March 1963, the *Perch* was home-ported in Subic Bay in the Philippines to directly support UDT and unconventional operations.[14] The *Perch* would remain available for potential missions in Southeast Asia.

During early 1963, the Saigon government decided to disband the Biet Hai commandos and dissolve funding. Forty-two of the remaining South Vietnamese raiders, trained by U.S. SEALs, were transferred to the regular navy's LDNN frogmen.[15] Late in 1962, the Pacific Fleet had again wanted to gain more intelligence on areas in Vietnam for contingency operations. It had been a year since the last hydrographic reconnaissance operations were conducted along the coast, and current data was again required to provide planners with up-to-date intelligence. USS *Weiss* (APD 135) was called upon to conduct surveys of the South Vietnamese beaches at Danang, Qui Nhon, Cape Vung Tau, and Bac Lieu (see Maps 2 and 4). Coordination was conducted in January 1963 for the upcoming operations. Although risks were considered minimal, the UDT men would carry small arms ashore for self-defense. It was determined that UDT would not recon beyond the high-water mark, allowing the U.S. Marine Corps 3rd Reconnaissance Battalion to support in that respect.

The operations began on 21 February 1963 near Danang, utilizing the five officers and twenty-nine enlisted frogmen from UDT 12's Detachment Bravo (Det Bravo). Sniper fire was encountered by the beach party on several occasions.

It became obvious to the frogmen that the guerrilla forces were more active in their resistance than previously expected. *Weiss* proceeded with its operations and moved south along the coast. At midday on 12 March, the survey party came under light attack from about a dozen insurgents, five miles east of Vinh Chau on the coastline of the Mekong Delta. No casualties were sustained, but withdrawal from the beach was tricky. Naval commanders determined that sufficient data had been obtained during the operations, and no further risks were necessary to complete the work. *Weiss* returned to Subic Bay.[16]

In January 1964, a U.S. survey team was established to study the depth of the communist insurgency in the Mekong Delta and the effectiveness of the Saigon government to fight it. The original head of the commission fell gravely ill, and Captain Phillip H. Bucklew was appointed in his place. Bucklew was highly respected for his insight into unconventional warfare. A very senior and experienced frogman, he had been very highly decorated for his UDT exploits during World War II.[17] Following the Korean War, he was again called upon, this time to assist the ROK (Republic of Korea) Naval Intelligence in monitoring North Korean naval activity and assist in the infiltration of agents into North Korea. Captain Bucklew's knowledge and experience in naval special warfare operations was recognized as considerable. Included in his 9-man Delta Infiltration Survey Team was a representative from SEAL Team One and other naval officers. The group traveled to Southeast Asia in January 1964. The findings and recommendations of the Bucklew Report were seriously examined by the Joint Chiefs of Staff and acted upon throughout the following years. Included in the recommendations was the suggestion to deploy SEALs in an active combat role in Vietnam.[18]

Meanwhile, the SEAL advisory role continued. By early 1964, LDNN strength stood at one officer and forty-one enlisted. On 4 January 1964, a small Vietnamese raiding operation was conducted in the Mekong Delta. The LDNN utilized on the mission were responsible for destroying six

Viet Cong junks.[19] On 20 March, the LDNN officer and most of the enlisted men were transferred to Danang to support special operations (see Map 2). The few men remaining were called upon at times for only minor support.

The USS *Card*, a small, old U.S. aircraft carrier anchored on the Saigon waterfront, was mined on 2 May 1964 by guerrilla maritime sappers. The vessel had just delivered a number of tactical aircraft to the South Vietnamese military. It now took on water and settled the few feet to the muddy bottom of the waterway. An LDNN survey team sent to examine the damage determined that the VC had used several small electrically detonated mines to blow a gaping hole in the ship.[20]

During the spring, political and military leaders from both Vietnam and the United States agreed to establish a small naval facility along the coast. Extensive surveys were conducted in several areas by various naval forces to determine the most suitable area. Cam Ranh Bay was finally selected as the best site, and construction began during the summer. Instrumental in the survey process was a detachment of UDT men who provided valuable hydrographic information to their superiors.

It was during the spring that the North Vietnamese first began to introduce some of their regular army units into the fighting in the South. A SEAL advisor who arrived in-country in July found only eleven men remaining in the South's LDNN unit. This did not include the special operations missions the Vietnamese were running from their base in Danang. A three-month intensive screening process augmented the depleted LDNN unit with an additional sixty Vietnamese. A sixteen-week training course was established in Nha Trang for these men. Patterned after the UDT/SEAL course, training began on 25 September and ended in January 1965. On the average, each graduating student paddled 115 miles, ran 75 miles, carried a rubber boat 21 miles, and swam 10 miles during the single period called Hell Week, much the same as their U.S. counterparts. Even prior to graduation, the students participated in a handful of operational missions.

The thirty-three men who completed the course were stationed at Vung Tau and began operations[21] (see Map 4).

By April 1964, the U.S. military took control of covert military operations under the Military Assistance Command, Vietnam-Studies and Observations Group (called MACV-SOG), under operation Switchback. At the same time, the South Vietnamese established an organization known as the Special Exploitation Service (SES). This unit took control of all Vietnamese covert military operations from the Vietnamese Special Forces Command, which had been established in 1963. Prior to that time, the Vietnamese Secret Special Service had conducted such programs. Up until 1964, the CIA was responsible for supporting the Vietnamese covert effort. It was hoped that open military hostilities could be avoided, but communist infiltration of Laos and Cambodia and the continued assistance of the North Vietnamese to the communist forces throughout the region forced the U.S. to raise support efforts. Overt aid was provided by U.S. military forces under MACV. Under SOG, MACV assumed responsibility for covert actions as well. It was hoped that MACV could efficiently organize and coordinate the U.S. effort if it controlled the entire spectrum of the U.S. support, both overt and covert.

SOG stood for Studies and Observation Group as a cover. Established on 24 January 1964 as a joint force, it drew men from all branches in the U.S. military.[22] Additionally, it employed indigenous personnel from many areas of Southeast Asia. Finally, a number of employees of the Central Intelligence Agency worked on the staff. The organization became divided into several specialty areas. OPS 31 ran all maritime operations; OPS 32, the air operations; OPS 33 provided psychological operations (PSYOPS); OPS 34 dealt with the penetration of North Vietnam by trained agents and other means, and OPS 35 involved direct action and strategic reconnaissance into North Vietnam, Laos, and Cambodia.[23]

Navy Special Warfare personnel were involved throughout the history of SOG. The maritime element was located at Danang in the northernmost portion of South Vietnam (see Map 2). The South Vietnamese attached to the unit utilized the cover of a coastal survey service, while the Americans were known to be a part of the Naval Advisory Detachment (NAD). The NAD included SEAL officers and enlisted men whose role was similar to the advisors sent to Danang in 1962 and 1963 to prepare indigenous frogmen for their forays into the North. Also assigned were one officer and three enlisted leathernecks from Marine Reconnaissance Units.[24] SOG had been erroneously informed that Marine Force Recon Units were comprised of one officer and three enlisted (instead of the usual 14-men platoon). This number fit their desired proposal for marine augmentation, and from that time in early 1964, Marine Recon involvement in SOG remained at one and three. While the SEAL and Recon officers mainly worked the operational planning, SEAL and Recon enlisted men trained numerous 6-man teams to be utilized as the commando forces.

Formed into units called "action teams," these forces, according to a 1969 NAD historical document, were capable of the following operations:

    A. Capture of adult male prisoners.
      1. Capture of predesignated prisoners.
    B. Combat patrols.
      1. Limited scale raids.
      2. Limited scale ambushes.

Action Teams were employed mainly in over-the-beach operations from the afloat assets of SOG located in Danang, but they also received limited training in helicopter and parachuting insertion and extraction operations. Rehearsals and training were conducted in the actual combat environment of South Vietnam. It was from Camp Tien Sha at the base of Monkey Mountain in the harbor at Danang that the Nasty boats were scheduled to operate in 1964. The boats would also operate out of Phoenix Island off Danang during the war. Additionally, a second, smaller-class gunboat was at times utilized for operations. In early 1964, there were only three fifty-foot, aluminum-hulled "Swift" boats, which were armed with an 81mm mortar and light machine guns. These high-performance PCF (Patrol Craft, Fast) boats would drop and recover commando teams at sea as well as conduct coastal raids.

Due to the long infiltration and exfiltration distances, radio communications became a vital link for the missions. One hour prior to launch, radios would be tuned to peak performance by technicians. During operations, an Operations Section Liaison Team (call sign Halsey) would monitor the progress of the mission. Each Action Team would report with a specific team call sign, (e.g., "Buffalo," "Atilla"). The PTFs utilized the call sign "Moonshine," followed by a numerical designation. Returning from a mission up north, the PTFs would call ahead to advise Danang of the number and condition of any prisoners (code-named "potatoes") that may have been taken, thereby allowing an intelligence and interrogation team from the SOG Security Section to be standing by at dockside.

Logistical support was established at Danang in the early months of 1964; by March, the facility was ready to receive the PTFs from Subic Bay. The first two Nastys arrived in Danang in late February, followed by several others in about a month. Throughout the spring, the vessels were tested and modified by dropping their 40mm guns and adding larger fuel tanks to give the craft better range. Capt. Bucklew, now the commander of Naval Operations Support Group in the Pacific, and others felt more armament was necessary, and thus the addition of 81mm mortars was advanced. On the American political side, it was felt that the program was progressing much too slowly.[25]

As hostilities grew in South Vietnam, the United States moved to raise the cost of the communist insurgency. Operations were mounted in retaliation for guerrilla bombings and attacks by the communists in the South. In January 1964, President Johnson finally approved the "34 Alpha" raids under the code name "Timberlake." As a variation of the OPS 34 penetrations, 34A was designed as Swift and Nasty boat strikes into the North. The first operations were executed on 16 February 1964. LDNN were sent into the North Vietnamese naval base at Quang Khe to destroy the Swatow patrol craft and the ferry on Cape Ron. That attempt, as well as a subsequent one, was unsuccessful. Two other missions to blow up bridges along the Route One Highway in the North Vietnamese Panhandle, thereby cutting the road, were aborted[26] (see Map 1).

The slow pace of 34A operations and the lack of real mission success up to this point frustrated political and military leaders. Admiral Ulysses S. Grant Sharp, Commander in Chief of the Pacific Fleet, and other officials also had reservations about the LDNN capabilities under indigenous leadership at this point, after the initial poor results. Finally, in June and July, success was achieved. On 12 June, a storage facility was demolished and about two weeks later, the Route One bridge near Hao Mon Dong was destroyed (see Map 1). Another operation on the night of 30 June dropped a team from two Nastys at the mouth of the Kien River (see Map 1). The men boarded rubber boats and moved toward shore. The group was spotted by North Vietnamese fishermen, but continued its mission. Two scout swimmers did a recon of the beach, and the force moved in. A five-man security element was left to hold the beach landing site, and the commandos moved inland. At the objective, they illuminated the area with mortar flares and destroyed a reservoir pump house with 18 57mm recoilless rifle rounds just after 0215. The North Vietnamese, reacting to the report by the fishermen, found the beach security team and attacked it. The Nasty boats moved in toward shore and provided fire support, holding the North Vietnamese at bay. The raiding party fought a running gun battle to the beach, at times engaging in hand-to-hand combat. The force was able to launch its rubber boats and link up with the Nastys to return to Danang. Two men were missing and believed killed in the action, while the North Vietnamese had twenty-two dead and lost the pump station.[27]

Missions were now normally successful, and several operations were conducted in July. Additionally, numerous North Vietnamese fishermen were captured, detained for short periods to gain intelligence, and released after a few days. The only aborted mission since May occurred on 15

July on a security post on Cape Ron (see Map 1). Two men were lost in the attempt.[28] At the end of July, other plans and targets were finalized. CINCPAC recognized that the raiding parties were encountering ever-stronger defenses in the North. With the number of communist insurgents in the South at over 30,000, CINCPAC also realized that the SOG base at Danang was almost certainly under observation. The departures and arrivals of the Nastys and Swifts could easily be viewed, and the North Vietnamese almost certainly remained vigilant. It was even thought that some of the LDNN and indigenous boat crews might be agents of the North.[29] In late July, North Vietnamese gunboats made their first unsuccessful attack against two Nastys and two Swifts that were operating off their coast.[30] The North Vietnamese were undoubtedly stiffening at the hit-and-run strikes. On 31 July, four Nasty boats struck a radar site on Hon Me Island and a radio transmitter on Hon Nieu located near Vinh, about 115 miles north of the DMZ (see Map 1). Encountering North Vietnamese gunboats in the area, the raiding parties' landing was aborted, and standoff weaponry was used to bombard the targets. The communist boats unsuccessfully attempted to interdict the faster Allied vessels.[31]

This event was followed on the night of 3 August by the shelling of another radar site at Cape Vinh Son, south of Vinh, and a security post on the south bank of the Ron River (see Map 1). The Nastys successfully completed their mission and arrived back in Danang around dawn on 4 August.[32] Apparently convinced that the craft were operating from or related to larger U.S. naval vessels offshore, the North Vietnamese attacked an intelligence ship that was there on an unrelated operation. The mission of the USS *Maddox* was to steam along the North Vietnamese coastline, intercept communist radio transmissions, and collect data on the North Vietnamese coastal defense network. Indeed, *Maddox* had even sighted the Nastys as they were returning to Danang after their attack on 31 July. The attack on *Maddox* was initiated by North Vietnamese gunboats in broad daylight. Following the attack, *Maddox* was ordered back into the area, along with the USS *Turner Joy.* On 4 August, both reported a second attack at night under poor weather conditions. The initial afteraction assessment left the assault in question. It appeared as if it may have been a series of mistaken readings under poor conditions by nervous sailors, yet official evidence today supports the finding that an attack did indeed occur.[33] There is little doubt, however, that the Nasty and Swift commando attacks precipitated a dramatic escalation of hostilities. This Gulf of Tonkin Incident, as it came to be called, decidedly brought Congress to enact the Tonkin Gulf Resolution, thus considerably deepening involvement of U.S. forces in Vietnam.

The raiding continued, with trained Vietnamese being used as frogmen. On 11 August, one proposal by the Commander of U.S. Military Assistance Command in Vietnam (COMUS-MACV) suggested another approach. The plan recommended infiltrating a team of 80 frogmen onto the islands in the Fai Tsi Long Archipelago using submarine assets (see Map 1). Located at the northern end of the Gulf of Tonkin, this target was outside the range of the Swifts and Nastys. CINCPAC disapproved the plan believing it to be too drastic an escalation of overt U.S. participation at that time.[34] In early August, authorization for eight additional Nasty boats was given, and negotiations with the Norwegians for the purchase of the boats were concluded late in the month. The new boats would be quieter, have a greater range, and incorporate important design changes recommended from lessons learned from previous raids. The first new boats were due to arrive at Subic Bay in late spring 1965.[35]

In September 1964, one commando team reportedly was inserted by rubber boat to destroy a section of the Hanoi-Vinh railroad. Guards were eliminated by South Vietnamese using silenced weapons.[36] Two other bridge destruction missions were scheduled to be carried out on Route One during the same month.[37] A variety of other raids was scheduled to be executed by U.S.-trained frogmen, such as the destruction of the Phuc Loi Pier, before the end of the year. That mission was carried out the following month. All together, nearly twenty operations were carried out by the PTFs and seaborne raiders during September and October, most of which were offshore bombardments.[38] Later in October, two more intelligence destroyers were preparing to conduct operations off North Vietnam. As part of their exercises, mock day and night assaults were staged by small, high-speed boats to prevent a repeat of any possible blunders like those of 4 August. The boats utilized for the mock attacks were the Nastys staged out of Danang.[39]

On 30 October, the Vietcong struck the U.S. air base at Bien Hoa, killing five servicemen and destroying six bombers. The Johnson administration responded with additional raids along the North Vietnamese coast. Escalation continued, especially in unconventional warfare. The Fifth Special Forces Group was sent into Vietnam during the same month. Raiding during the latter part of the year switched mainly to standoff bombardment by the high-speed vessels. This successful tactic was a very quick form of a hit-and-run raid that lessened the threat of casualties among the commandos. On 3 October, the boats probed Vinh Son (see Map 1). Rough seas forced the action to be aborted, but the mission was completed a few nights later. Another mission on 25 October was cancelled due to weather. On 28 October, installations near Vinh Son and Cape Dao were hit (see Map 1).

The following month, Lyndon Johnson defeated Barry Goldwater in the presidential election, assuring a continuance of the policy regarding Vietnam. Bad weather cancelled most of the operations for most of the month, but on 25 November, targets on Gio Island just north of the DMZ were bombarded (see Map 1). Installations on Cape Ron were hit on 27 November (see Map 1). The last operation of the year was conducted on 8 December; that night, four boats attacked the radar facility at Mach Nuoc[40] (see Map 1).

Seaborne raids did not significantly alter North Vietnam's military capability. They did, however, create a disruption along the coastline; rather than just create a national fear, the disruption helped strengthen the North's resolve and defensive readiness. On 24 December, the North Vietnamese-backed Vietcong struck U.S. billets in Saigon, killing two servicemen. Following additional guerrilla attacks in the South, the White House ordered "tit-for-tat" raiding against the North. Between 19 January and 2 February 1965, numerous raids were conducted against the North, including nine maritime operations. Five targets were hit in the attacks, one of them twice.[41] Now, the White House was ready to move into a new dimension beyond the Nasty boat raids. Operation Flaming Dart (aerial bombing against the North) was initiated in February 1965, utilizing U.S. tactical air assets against targets in the North Vietnamese panhandle in reprisal for the Vietcong attacks.

The United States was now increasing the pressure against the North Vietnamese in a major way. Regardless of the political rhetoric, the Americans were now unquestionably at war. By 1965, the United States had launched into a strong commitment in Southeast Asia. The fight for South Vietnam was on.

Notes

1. Edwin B. Hooper et al., *The United States Navy and the Vietnam Conflict*, vol. I (Washington, D.C., 1976), pp. 274-276.

2. Edward J. Marolda et al., *The United States Navy and the Vietnam Conflict*, vol. II (Washington, D.C., 1986), pp. 43-45.

3. Ibid., p. 148.

4. Ibid., pp. 103, 112.

5. Ibid., pp. 115, 121.

6. Ibid., p. 189.

7. Ibid., p. 190; Unclassified Command History for SEAL Team Two for the Year 1966, Enclosure 1, p. 1.

8. Marolda, *The United States and The Vietnam Conflict*, vol. II, p. 217.

9. Ibid., p. 190.

10. Ibid., pp. 202-203.

11. Ibid., pp. 204-205.

12. Ibid., p. 206. For details of the development and performance of the Nasty Class PTFs, see Norman Friedman, *U.S. Combatants* (Annapolis, Maryland, 1987), pp. 243-277.

13. Burke Wilkinson, *Cry Sabotage!* (New York, 1972), pp. 215-223; Francis D. Fane et al., *The Naked Warriors* (New York, 1956), pp. 236-269; John B. Dwyer, "UDTs In Korea," *Soldier of Fortune* (September, 1986), pp. 70-73, 86-93.

14. Marolda, *The United States Navy and The Vietnam Conflict*, vol. II, pp. 216-217.

15. Ibid., p. 238.

16. Ibid., pp. 182-183.

17. Marc Huet, "SEALs Are Navy's Elite," *Pacific Stars and Stripes*, 25 June 1967, p. A-7; Blaine Taylor, "Before Invasions Commence," *Military History* (October 1987), pp. 43-49; David Masci and Michael McKinley, "Behind Enemy Lines—The Life of a 'True Warrior'," *All Hands* (December 1987), pp. 32-34.

Captain Bucklew was a former professional football player who began his naval career as an instructor in the navy and marine corps rugged Scout/Raider course in Florida during early World War II. He moved up through the conventional naval officer ranks the hard way, mostly as a result of his vast combat experience. He slipped ashore alone into North Africa to gather intelligence and survey possible beach landing sites for Operation Torch, the Allied invasion of North Africa, returning with a bucket of sand for planners to study to determine if the beaches could support Allied landing craft.

In July 1943, he won the Navy Cross (second only to the Medal of Honor) when he led a team of frogmen from a submarine onto the beaches of Sicily. Although discovered and attacked, he and his men completed their mission to guide the first waves of the invading Allied forces ashore. Two months later, he conducted a similar mission during the invasion of Italy, a mission that earned him the Silver Star. He performed another beach reconnaissance in France six months before the Normandy Invasion, at one point hiding in a swamp from German soldiers who had surrounded him. On D-Day, he returned to support the invasion, earning a second Navy Cross for valor. Finally, he completed an extremely long reconnaissance of Japanese forces on the Chinese mainland north of Hong Kong. The Americans had anticipated invading the Chinese mainland during the period prior to the atomic bombing of Japan. At well over six feet tall, Bucklew traveled four hundred miles with a small guerrilla band while disguised as a coolie. He evaded the Japanese at one point by hiding in a haystack, and was again recommended for a Navy Cross. Bucklew's reputation lives strongly today within SpecWar. In January 1987, the Naval Special Warfare Center in Coronado, California, was dedicated to this senior frogman for his pursuit of excellence in Naval Special Warfare throughout his career. The Center houses BUD/S and several advanced SEAL training schools.

18. Marolda, *The United States Navy and The Vietnam Conflict*, vol. II, pp. 303-305.

19. Ibid., p. 327.

20. Ibid., p. 355.

21. Ibid., p. 310.

22. Ibid., pp. 338-339.

23. Shelby L. Stanton, *Vietnam Order Of Battle* (Washington, D.C., 1981), pp. 251-253.

24. Marolda, *The United States Navy and The Vietnam Conflict*, vol. II, p. 339. It is interesting to note that U.S. Navy frogmen were also training Cuban exiles in seaborne raiding tactics at about this same time, according to one author. The instruction was provided to the exiles in the Florida Keys from where the raids were launched under CIA direction. For details see Bradley E. Ayers, *The War that Never Was* (New York, 1976), pp. 98-137.

25. Marolda, *The United States Navy and The Vietnam Conflict*, vol. II, pp. 335-338; J. D. Gray, "The Forgotten Warriors," *Gung Ho* (June, 1986), pp. 27-28.

26. Ibid., p. 341.

27. Ibid., p. 343.

28. Ibid., p. 343.

29. Ibid., p. 406.

30. Ibid., pp. 406-407.

31. Ibid., pp. 408-410.

32. Ibid., pp. 423-424.

33. Ibid., pp. 426, 436.

34. Ibid., p. 467.

35. Ibid., p. 467.

36. J. David Truby, *The Quiet Killers* (Boulder, Colorado, 1972), p. 54.

37. Neil Sheehan et al., *The Pentagon Papers* (New York, 1971), pp. 301-302.

38. Ibid., p. 303; Gray, "The Forgotten Warriors," pp. 27-28.

39. John Prados, *Presidents' Secret Wars* (New York, 1986), p. 250.

40. Marolda, *The United States Navy and The Vietnam Conflict*, vol. II, p. 468.

41. Prados, *Presidents' Secret Wars*, p. 257.

CHAPTER TWO

The United States Buildup (1965–1966)

On 26 January 1965, ten PTFs were released to the South Vietnamese for use in seaborne raids against the North Vietnamese coastline. The vessels continued to launch and recover out of the base at Danang. While at Danang, the boats fell under the control of U.S. advisors. Once launched on a mission, the vessels were manned and controlled by South Vietnamese commandos. As the North continued to support the insurgency in the South, the South continued to ensure the communists paid for their actions through the maritime raids.

The North Vietnamese made a dramatic increase in arms shipments and personnel infiltrations into South Vietnam during 1964, but large-scale evidence of the communist support was not available to the Americans. Early in 1965, the proof was seized. On 16 February, a U.S. Army helicopter discovered a communist trawler at Vung Ro Bay, a small bay on the central South Vietnamese coast south of Qui Nhon, and Allied forces were called into action. The trawler was attacked by air assets and finally capsized. Follow-up forces met stiff resistance from guerrillas over the next few days as the forces surrounded the bay and closed in on the trawler. After they finally secured the area, they discovered a huge shipment of Soviet and Chinese-made arms and ordnance that was to be delivered to the Vietcong forces in the area even though the VC were able to spirit much of the shipment away during the fighting. Accompanied by a U.S. SEAL advisor, fifteen LDNN were some of the men called upon to salvage and recover this evidence, which played a large part in substantiating U.S. intelligence reports regarding the North's active support of the insurgency.[1]

On 8 March 1965, the first U.S. combat units were committed to Vietnam. On that date, U.S. Marines of the Third Marine Regiment, Third Marine Division, were sent ashore near Danang (see Map 2). Their mission was to provide protection for the U.S. air base at Danang against Vietcong attack. In their traditional manner, the marines stormed ashore in full combat gear from amphibious landing craft. On the beach, they were met by newsmen, who recorded the dramatic U.S. commitment. Additionally, a group of U.S. frogmen from UDT 12 stood by. They had come ashore well in advance of the main forces to provide reconnaissance and secure the beach for the marines. In the tradition of their World War II fathers, they emplanted two rubber boat paddles blade down into the sand, with a frogman greeting stretched between the paddles. The sign read, "Welcome U.S. Marines - UDT 12 -."[2]

The role of U.S. ground forces did not remain defensive for long. In April, the marines and other ground units began to conduct offensive operations to interdict enemy guerrillas. With the introduction of marines and their operations, UDT detachments began to chart much of the South Vietnamese coastline for future reference. Such hydrographic surveys, even at this early stage in the war, often encountered armed resistance. On 23 April 1965, a group of Force Recon Marines was attempting to execute such a survey at Song Tra Bong on the coast between Quang Nam and Quang Tin provinces, about 370 miles north of Saigon (see Map 2). The group came under fire from an estimated twenty-five Vietcong, who were well-entrenched. The Americans were forced to evacuate the area while trying to break contact with the enemy. A rescue team was dispatched from the USS *Cook* (APD 130) to help the besieged men. One marine (Lowell Merrell) and two sailors (EN2 Richard Langford and TM3 William Fuhrman) who were manning an evacuation boat were all mortally wounded in the action. Merrell thus became the first Vietnam fatality of the marine's elite Force Recon units.[3]

Because of the nature of hydrographic reconnaissance operations, frogmen remained lightly armed. To conventional planners, these first casualties reinforced the inherent danger of the UDT mission and the consequent importance of providing internal security. In May, the Army's 173rd Airborne Brigade arrived in-country to begin operations, and the combat role of U.S. forces continued to expand. As hostilities grew in Southeast Asia, the west coast UDTs began deploying as entire commands to the Philippines. Each UDT would spend a six-month tour in the western Pacific (WESTPAC), supporting fleet operations before being rotated back to the West Coast for additional training and re-manning.

Utilizing Subic Bay as a base of operations, UDT detachments were dispersed to various positions in WESTPAC to cover their commitments. The headquarters in Subic Bay supported the deployed elements and was designated Detachment Alfa (Det Alfa). Headquarters assisted by providing administrative support, training other detachments, and providing maintenance for operational equipment. Det Bravo was deployed on an APD, a high-speed transport ship, as part of the Far East Amphibious Squadron (Phibron) for Seventh Fleet operations. This group of frogmen provided beach recons and surveys where necessary.

Det Charlie operated from the USS *Perch*, and later from the USS *Tunny* and USS *Grayback*, conventional fleet submarines that were refitted to carry small teams of combat swimmers for a variety of combat operations. Their primary mission of beach recon was accomplished using two basic methods. In the first method, the swimmers were "locked out" of the submarine by means of a swimmer escape trunk as it lay on the ocean floor (termed "bottomed out") or at a specific depth. The frogmen would surface from a 36-foot depth by means of free buoyant ascent to conduct their hydrographic survey. They would return to the submarine by reversing the process. In the second method, the UDT men would sit in small rubber boats on the deck of the submarine as the vessel lay on the surface. The submarine would then submerge and literally fall away from the rubber boats, allowing the frogmen to paddle to their operational area and complete their mission. They would recover by intercepting the submerged submarine and snagging the periscope with a line. In this manner, they could be towed to an area deemed safe for boarding, or reverse the "locking out" process by diving down and "locking in."

Det Delta was stationed at Camp Tien Sha near Danang, along the northern shore of South Vietnam (see Map 2). The men of Delta were called upon to demolish hundreds of captured enemy bunkers throughout the war. The camp also served as a rest and recuperation (R & R) center for other deployed UDT detachments. Dets Echo and Foxtrot were embarked as part of the Amphibious Ready Group (ARG) and served in the classical UDT hydrographic recon missions. Dets Golf, Hotel, and India served with the riverine forces in the southernmost areas of the Ca Mau Peninsula of South Vietnam later in the war (see Map 4). Their operations consisted not only of bunker destruction, but the detachments also served as a supplemental commando and recon force throughout the canals, rivers, and swamps of the peninsula.[4]

UDT 11 was awarded the Navy Commendation Medal for operations it had conducted between 28 January 1964 and 5 September 1966. The citation stated that elements of the team had participated in eight major amphibious assaults in Vietnam. The team also conducted overt and clandestine hydrographic reconnaissance of over 110 miles of coastline, rivers, and harbors.[5] Other UDT operations covered the entire scope of reconnaissance along the South Vietnamese coast. UDT 12's Det Bravo participated in every major amphibious operation of the year, including Operation Piranha in August, Operation Starlight (September), Operation Dagger Thrust (October), and Operation Blue Marlin (November).[6]

Each of these operations projected the Marine Corps and its amphibious capability deeper into the Vietnam conflict. As more U.S. conventional forces were fielded, the United

States also welcomed support from other SEATO allies in the war. Before the end of the year, armed forces from Australia, New Zealand, and Korea had joined U.S. military forces against the communists in Vietnam. The largest military presence by far was that of the U.S. armed forces.

By late 1965, USS *Perch* (APSS 313) was being utilized as a platform to launch UDT men on clandestine coastal reconnaissance. The first official action took place on the coast of South Vietnam. Amphibious assaults under the code name Operation Dagger Thrust were coordinated by the Seventh Fleet's amphibious commander, Rear Admiral D. L. Wulzen. The clandestine predawn recon fell upon *Perch* and the men of Det Charlie from UDT 12 who were embarked aboard.

The team of frogmen, along with the deck crew, inflated their rubber boats on the afterdeck of the submarine as it lay on the surface. Lines were connected to the periscope. When all was ready, the frogmen boarded the boats, and the submarine dove just below the surface. Still attached, the boats were slowly towed toward the target beach and released. The UDT men paddled ashore quietly and carefully to complete their mission. Meanwhile, *Perch* stood by in the area to assist in vectoring the craft and to provide any support necessary. The required hydrographic data and valuable intelligence was collected and transmitted back to navy assets. The frogmen remained ashore to provide security for the Marine assault at dawn, which was accomplished successfully.[7]

Clandestine surveys such as this were a key reason marine amphibious units were able to successfully conduct seaborne assaults, and these operations were the primary role of the frogmen. UDT 12's Det Alfa was commended for similar overt and clandestine hydrographic reconnaissance work between 1 December 1964 and 29 May 1965. Det Bravo from the same team was commended for similar actions between 21 May and 3 July 1965.[8]

Besides their combat operations, UDT members were also utilized for other important work. The initial shortage of trained divers in Vietnam caused frogmen to become a hot commodity. As a result, they were sometimes called upon to conduct salvage and recovery work. Two UDT men were used in late 1965 to assist in repairing a 4,200-foot underwater fuel line at Chu Lai (see Map 2). Though diving conditions were extremely poor, with rough surface conditions and very murky water, the repair to the valuable fuel line was completed with the divers' expert assistance.[9]

South Vietnamese commandos continued launching their raiding operations into the North from a base at Danang. Although the base utilized a cover operation and had normal security, it was suspected that it fell under the watchful eye of the Communists, as other U.S. installations did. On 28 October, the Officer-in-Charge of MAROPS was killed by a mortar round while riding in a jeep as he inspected the base's security. Commander Robert J. Fay was an experienced frogman who had entered the navy during World War II. He began his career as a frogman in 1951 and had served with a number of units including UDT 2. His UDT experience had been an important factor in his assignment as an advisor to MACV-SOG in April 1965. He thus became the first frogman to be killed in the Vietnam War. The main SOG base at Danang which berthed U.S. Navy personnel and those from the Monkey Mountain Forward Operating Base was named Camp Fay in his honor.

In December 1965, the White House continued to apply military pressure while attempting to induce the North Vietnamese into peace negotiations with an offer of aid. The North flatly rejected the offer. As a result, the limited aerial bombing of North Vietnam by the United States resumed in January 1966. Operations by conventional forces continued to expand in the South. Additionally, raiding parties continued to strike the North Vietnamese coast. On 1 December 1965, the first Nasty gunboat fell victim to the combat operations and was lost. Together with the special operations units of all the service branches, the total U.S. commitment grew daily.

By the beginning of 1966, Vietnam duty was a definite goal for many of the men who completed BUD/S back in the States. Among the graduates, it would have been difficult to describe an average frogman. They came in all shapes and sizes, but many endured the hardships in order to get into the Southeast Asian conflict. One young naval officer who graduated from training on 3 December 1965, Ensign Theodore Roosevelt IV, was the great grandson of President Teddy Roosevelt. The twenty-three-year-old Harvard graduate did not plan to make the navy a career, but he indicated that Vietnam was definitely in his assignment requests. His instructors were noted for exploiting any small personality characteristic while he and others were in the initial UDT/ SEAL training. In remembrance of his great grandfather's foreign policy ("walk softly, but carry a big stick"), he was ordered to shoulder a three-foot tree branch everywhere he went during the course.[10]

UDT 11's Det Charlie conducted surveys of some of the major coastal areas near Phan Thiet, Cam Ranh, Nha Trang, and Qui Nhon from 3 to 21 January 1966[11] (see Map 2). Between 21 and 28 January 1966, another large amphibious operation was undertaken. On the beaches near Quang Ngai and Tam Ky in I Corps of South Vietnam, the navy planned to send the largest force ashore into combat since the Inchon landing during Operation Double Eagle in the Korean War (see Map 2). The USS *Perch* again received the call to conduct a clandestine beach recon, this time using Det Charlie from UDT 11.

Employing a different technique, the submarine bottomed out about one thousand yards offshore. Support divers then locked out of the vessel by exiting the forward escape trunk. Utilizing scuba rigs, the men prepared lines and equipment outside the sub. When all was ready, the crew inside the sub was signaled. The UDT men then exited the sub in a similar manner, and breathing from equipment rigged underwater by the support divers. Rubber boats were sent to the surface and inflated. The frogmen ascended and boarded the craft, and then broke out weaponry, radios, and equipment that had been specially protected for the lock-out process. Once on the surface, the frogmen proceeded toward the target beachline while the lead boat hung an acoustic pinger device in the water. *Perch* picked up the pinger signals and thus vectored the craft to the exact beach landing site, where their clandestine recon began. Such a locking-out process required considerable expertise and long hours of rehearsal. The teamwork displayed by both the crew of *Perch* and the UDT men began to pay off at this early juncture in the war.

Following the successful recon, the frogmen paddled back out to sea, attached a line between the rubber boats, and signaled the sub. *Perch* homed in on the signal and used the periscope of the submerged vessel to snag the line and take the boats in tow. Further out to sea, in an area safe from a shoreline observer, the submarine surfaced and recovered the frogmen and their equipment.[12]

In February, the First Marine Regiment of the First Marine Division deployed to Vietnam. Its operations would include numerous amphibious missions supported by frogmen from the UDT. Also in February 1966, a small group of U.S. SEALs from SEAL Team One in San Diego (consisting of three officers and fifteen enlisted) was sent to South Vietnam for direct-action operations under the control of Commander, U.S. Naval Forces, Vietnam (COMUSNAVFORV). Most naval planners were not sure what to do with the group and did not have any immediate employment plan for it. It had taken all of two years for the recommendation of the Bucklew Report to employ SEALs in the Delta to be implemented.

The SEALs were targeted against Vietcong guerrillas operating in the Rung Sat Special Zone (RSSZ) near Saigon (see Map 4). This muddy mangrove swamp was some four hundred square miles, and the swift four-knot current ran four feet deep. Alive with wildlife, the swamp had long been used by the VC as an operational haven within easy striking distance of Saigon. Saigon's shipping channels ran directly through the VC haven, allowing frequent shelling and ambush of merchant vessels.

The small group of SEALs worked from the naval facility at Nha Be and was identified initially as Detachment Delta. Employing ambush as their main tactic, initial results accumulated by these SEALs warranted deployment of other platoons to Vietnam. Their introduction disrupted the local Vietcong forces, which had been virtually unchallenged to date. The VC could no longer fire freely at shipping and escape. The locations of the SEAL ambushes were determined many times by current intelligence concerning enemy movements gained through infrared detection devices located on spotter aircraft, code named "Red Haze". The Vietcong soon realized that some new and different threat had been turned loose in their backyard, but they were unable to counter until the threat was fully revealed. In the meantime, the VC's effectiveness in the RSSZ was diminished.

For the moment, the exact operational role of the SEALs remained ill-defined, thereby allowing them a great deal of flexibility in the interpretation of their general instructions. One SEAL described an example of their early operation's orders: "Patrol until contact is made. Kill as many enemy as possible. Extract after mission is complete."[13] Problems were encountered in establishing Areas of Operation (AOs) and Standard Operating Procedures (SOPs) within the platoons, but the SEALs did their best to work these out on their own. Naval planners later put together what was termed a "SEAL Package." This group consisted of other elements, such as Boat Support Units (BSUs), Mobile Support Teams (MSTs), and navy Seawolf helicopter gunships. On a typical mission, SEALs would be inserted by these support units, which would pull back and wait. After enemy contact was made, these forces would add fire support to the SEAL contact, oftentimes extracting them under fire from a largely superior force.[14]

An example of such a mission can be seen in an operation in which seven men were inserted onto an island that contained a VC encampment. The SEALs were carried to the location by a riverine boat in the predawn hours, but the boat ran aground approximately five hundred meters offshore. The SEALs hopped out to wade ashore, but encountered deep mud under foot. It took over four-and-a-half hours for them to make it ashore, where they established security and quietly cleaned their weapons. The men then set out to patrol the muddy island for eight hours, but found nothing. As they were returning to their rendezvous with the hidden riverine boat, they found a fresh trail that paralleled a canal to a dry portion of the island. The SEALs slipped into a rapidly moving canal current and quietly moved with the water, keeping concealed in the bank foliage.

The point man halted the team and moved ahead. He then encountered two huts and six Vietnamese gathered in a small group. Stacked nearby were six weapons, some of which were of communist make and design. Returning undetected to report his findings, the SEAL commander split his force in two in order to cut off any VC attempting to escape. As one SEAL group flanked the huts, the other lined up among the sampans in the canal opposite the Vietcong. Suddenly, one of the Vietnamese spotted the group in the canal. Before he could sound the alarm, the SEALs opened fire. Five VC were killed immediately, while one dove into the hut, only to be followed by a frogman's grenade.

While securing the area, the SEALs discovered a large pile of documents. The papers, which were waterproofed in plastic bags, were placed aboard the VC sampans. Since the boats were too small to hold the large Americans, they were used solely to float the documents down the canal while the SEALs swam and guided them in the water. Before they could link up with their patrol craft, the SEAL team came under attack by a large VC force. The riverine boats arrived just in time to add fire support and extract the team. Captured documents were almost always an important bonanza to intelligence personnel, and SEAL patrols such as this one provided a steady flow of current raw information.[15]

On a typical mission, the Seawolf helicopter gunships were used to provide fire support, as were fixed wing aircraft, artillery, and naval gunfire from ships offshore. The SEALs attempted to fight the guerrillas in their own environment, taking the battle to them in their own backyard. Small-unit commando tactics proved to be an effective means to nullify the communist effort. Ambushes at unexpected locations created hardships and psychological stress for the guerrillas. The SEALs capitalized on any innovative method or technique to make the war costly for the insurgents. On one mission, SEALs reportedly killed a high-ranking communist officer. Shortly after, intelligence was able to pinpoint the exact location, date, and time of the officer's funeral. The SEALs returned in force with helicopter gunships, killing several other high-ranking communist officers who were on hand to attend their comrade's funeral.[16]

From 26 March to 7 April 1966, both UDT 11 and SEAL Team One elements were involved in Operation Jackstay. The operation included the landing of U.S. Marines at the mouth of the Saigon River. UDT 11 personnel from both Det Charlie and Delta slipped ashore at 0300 on the dark, rainy morning of the landing and emplanted beacons to guide landing craft through dangerous and shallow portions of the river. They then conducted surveillance operations and swept the area for mines. UDT also set up four-man blocking positions about five hundred to eight hundred meters apart to prevent the escape of fleeing enemy forces, while SEALs and Marines combed the area and set up ambushes. Some of these blocking postions stayed in place for up to eighteen hours. One UDT position ambushed a VC junk and became engaged in a fierce firefight with its six occupants. The Vietcong suffered five killed and one wounded in the fight. Later, the frogmen were called upon to demolish a Vietcong rest camp that had been captured. Jackstay marked the first Vietnam operation in which elements from UDT, SEALs, Marine Recon Teams, and regular marine and naval forces were joined for a large-scale combat operation. Additionally, the Vietnamese LDNN and their U.S. advisor were sent to the RSSZ during the operation to assist the Vietnamese Marines. Their participation included three river reconnaissance missions. The operation was considered successful due to the superb teamwork of the diverse units and the interdiction of a considerable number of guerrillas.[17]

Up until this time, SEAL ambush teams staging out of Nha Be were forced to depart on their missions using riverine craft in full view of the local populace. Launching operations in this manner allowed the Vietcong to receive word of impending operations, and many of these early ambushes therefore failed to make contact. One method used to counter VC intelligence was to load mission equipment into the boats at Nha Be and have the team members driven to Saigon, where they would embark on the craft. When this technique was first used on 18 and 19 April, breaking the normal routine, a SEAL patrol killed three Vietcong soldiers in a sampan in the RSSZ. Early problems still continued, however. The South Vietnamese closely guarded their intelligence sources, and on 13 April, a SEAL squad killed a Vietnamese intelligence agent in an ambush in the RSSZ as the man moved alone in an unlighted sampan in the RSSZ at night. The U.S. Navy similarly held the SEAL ambush operations closely, and better coordination between the two allies was thereafter deemed necessary to prevent such mistakes.[18]

UDT 11 augmented Det Charlie with Det Delta on 25 March, marking the first time all elements of a full Underwater Demolition Team were employed in Vietnam at the same time. UDT 11's Det Delta conducted a recon of the Phu Loc area, twenty miles north of Danang, in support of Operation Osage on 27 April (see Map 2). Osage was one of many marine amphibious thrusts into guerrilla territory designed to catch the enemy forces by surprise. This operation was followed by the first of a series of "Deckhouse" operations that began in the summer. During Deckhouse I, which lasted from 16 to 18 June, UDT 11 conducted clandestine surveys operating from the USS *Cook* on beaches in the Song Cua and Song Cai river areas. The frogmen also worked as a blocking force from Vietnamese junks from Junk Force 21 to stop escaping Vietcong. From 16 to 18 July as part of Deckhouse II, UDT 11 participated in missions designed to support Operation Hastings. This operation was executed to stem the flow of infiltration across the DMZ, but the North Vietnamese were not willing to cease their support of the insurgency in the South.[19] As a result, during June, President Johnson ordered the bombing of oil installations in both Hanoi and Haiphong to increase political pressures once again. U.S. fighting continued to escalate, and the North Vietnamese continued to resist proposals for peace talks.

A SEAL patrol ambushed three VC in a sampan on the Co Gia River on the eastern edge of the RSSZ early on the morning of 15 June (see Map 6). One communist soldier was killed and one wounded, while the third escaped.[20] During July, the commitment of SEAL Team One in Vietnam expanded to include a total of five officers and twenty enlisted for the RSSZ detachment. On 27 July, three SEAL Team One six-man squads were inserted by riverboat west of Can Gio village at midday (see Map 6). As the three units silently patrolled the area, one group followed a well-concealed trail with fresh prints. Just before 1530, the point man came face-to-face with three enemy soldiers; he fired his M-79 grenade launcher, killing one Vietcong. While sweeping the area, the frogmen discovered a base camp that had housed an enemy platoon. The mess hall alone was capable of housing eighty men. Over five hundred rounds of ammunition were captured, along with weapons, equipment, two hundred pounds of rice, sampans, and documents. The camp and material were all destroyed by the Americans. The captured documents, which indicated the camp had based a 24-man platoon, also revealed defensive and mine positions emplaced by the VC in the Long Thanh Peninsula[21] (see Map 6).

With the increase in manpower, the SEAL detachment for the RSSZ, operating from Nha Be, was now identified as Det Golf. The patrols of Det Golf continued to sting the VC throughout the entire RSSZ. Three sampans, two of which were motorized, were captured at dawn on 5 August, along with six thousand pounds of rice, sixteen miles southeast of Nha Be. An enemy soldier in the lead sampan sensed the danger and fired a warning shot. Three enemy soldiers then leaped into the water and fled toward the mangrove swamp. The SEALs pursued, but the communists managed to escape the patrol. A six-man SEAL Team One squad ambushed a junk and two sampans on 7 August, killing seven Vietcong. On the morning of the 18th, a patrol discovered two huge, well-concealed silos containing over 306,000 pounds of rice. An air strike and naval gunfire were called in on the area to destroy the cache. The SEALs later reinserted to evaluate the damage and finish the job.[22]

On 19 August 1966, SEAL Team One suffered its first combat fatality in Vietnam. While on a recon mission, a patrol had discovered a series of bunkers and weapons positions along the Dinh Ba River, thirteen miles southeast of Nha Be. They were extracted and reinserted further upriver to pinpoint two reported camouflaged sampans that had been spotted by a helicopter. Fresh tracks were discovered, and the sampans were then sighted about five hundred meters from the SEALs' position. Petty Officer Billy W. Machen was acting as point man. Coming to a clearing in the jungle growth, he halted the unit and moved ahead into the opening to reconnoiter. As he paused and searched the surrounding area, he suddenly realized the VC were lying in ambush and he was in the middle of the kill zone. Rather than make a futile attempt to seek cover or retrace his steps and thereby pinpoint the patrol's exact location, Machen initiated fire and attacked the enemy unit, forcing them to trigger their ambush prematurely. Immediately after, automatic weapons fire from both banks of the river erupted. The SEAL patrol was alerted to the danger and was able to gain cover, return fire, and engage to suppress the VC attack. Machen was killed in the initial fusillade. He was posthumously awarded the Silver Star, the nation's third highest medal for valor.[23]

UDT 11 frogmen played another important role in Deckhouse III from 15 to 21 August in Binh Thuy Province (see Map 3). One group, operating from the USS *Cook*, conducted two clandestine recons, marking approaches and finally leading forces ashore. On 20 August 1966, the USS *Perch* was again called into action. The objective of operation Deckhouse III was to attack a Vietcong stronghold north of Qui Nhon in II Corps (see Map 2). UDT 11's 14-man Det Charlie, aboard the *Perch*, was given the mission to conduct other clandestine beach surveys. As was true of many operations during the war, the enemy gained advance warning of the operation. Although communist forces might be laying in ambush on the beach, the mission was not cancelled.

On the night of 20 August, three rubber boats filled with

frogmen were able to slip ashore and conduct their work unopposed. The following night, another UDT recon group was launched. This time, the VC were waiting. They knew the team was ashore conducting a survey, yet they could not pinpoint the frogmen's position in the darkness. Enemy fire was ineffective to the small team of commandos. The two-man scout swimmer team became separated in the confusion of the gunfire, and soon a search party from the *Perch* was launched to look for them. Before long, the entire UDT recon group, including the scout swimmers, was recovered by the sub, which now lay on the surface about two thousand yards offshore. The original search party, however, had failed to return.

The UDT commander took two men and launched yet another rubber boat to attempt to find the missing men. About halfway to shore, the UDT officer took a chance and ignited a signal flare. The action was intended to assist the lost men by orienting them and to help in their recovery. The lost men were immediately located, and the Vietcong force on shore fired small arms toward the flare. *Perch* immediately closed in on the boats, and the deck crews manned .50 caliber machine guns and a 40mm cannon to engage the enemy. Fortunately, all hands were recovered.

The first two recons for Deckhouse III had an 85-man South Vietnamese Army force (ARVN) further inland off the beach for protection. The battle on the night of 21 August significantly disturbed the small ARVN element. They could not return to a friendly base before dark, and therefore requested permission to sleep aboard the *Perch*. The commanding officer of the vessel, already cramped for space, could not grant permission. However, he did tell the force that he would ferry them to the site for the third recon the following day. He also anchored the vessel five hundred yards offshore to provide protection for the ARVN as they camped on the beach. As darkness fell, the VC were observed moving into positions around the beach force. *Perch* opened fire on the enemy, causing several secondary explosions as the VC ordnance was ignited. The following morning, the sub evacuated the force, along with some local villagers who were threatened by the Vietcong. These civilians were transferred to U.S. Navy Swift boats for evacuation.

Meanwhile, the *Perch* approached the beach on the surface and called in fire support. The VC were forced from their positions, and the UDT commander, using rubber boats, led a group of ARVN and frogmen on a small assault of the beach. After securing the area and capturing two prisoners, they completed a survey of the site, as planned.[24] This is believed to have been the last surface combat action fought by a U.S. submarine.

A converted Regulus I Missile submarine replaced the *Perch* as the special operations's Pacific Fleet subsurface asset in September 1966. It arrived in the Philippines and transferred 80 percent of *Perch's* crew aboard. The small missile hangar on her afterdeck was converted so as to transport up to seventy frogmen with all their combat equipment, including six IBSs (Inflatable Boat, Small). The USS *Tunny* (APSS 282) had several of her crew trained to accomplish deck rigging, thereby freeing all the UDT men to perform only the combat missions. Also, some of the crew were trained as a ready reaction force to assist an endangered frogman team under fire on a beach or to repel an enemy vessel.[25]

Before the *Perch* left the coast of Vietnam, she worked in support of Operation Deckhouse IV. During the first two weeks of September, two UDT 12 platoons operated from her decks. One other platoon operated from the USS *Diachenko*, a surface vessel. The three platoons conducted two separate clandestine recons in support of amphibious operations.[26] In late 1966 and early 1967, the *Tunny* and UDT groups from Team 11 and Team 12 rehearsed for operations along the Vietnamese coastline. Most of those missions were clandestine surveys, which were to provide information to the National Intelligence Survey. The classified data produced was utilized by the Special Assistant for Counter-Insurgency and Special Activities (SACSA) for the Joint Chiefs of Staff.[27]

Trained by U.S. SEAL advisors in Danang, South Vietnamese frogmen continued their Nasty boat raids into the North. During 1966, five of the fast attack vessels became combat losses in the raids. In the United States, Sewart Seacraft was contracted to produce a newer PTF for SEAL-type operations. Called the Osprey, this new boat was slightly larger with a 95-foot aluminum hull. It utilized the same Deltic engines as the Nastys and could achieve around forty knots speed. The first Osprey was later delivered for action in 1968.

SEALs continued their small commando operations in the RSSZ. Two SEAL ambushes on 1 and 13 September made contact on the Tac Ba and Bai Tien rivers, respectively, killing two Vietcong. An enemy rest camp, previously discovered and destroyed in July, was found to be reactivated. A SEAL patrol again destroyed the base on 18 September.[28] A squad-size SEAL ambushed a sampan between the Go Gia and Nga Bay rivers on 3 October. In two-man positions, the SEALs waited until the VC were eight yards from the ambush location at nearly point-blank range and then opened fire. The three enemy soldiers riding in the boat were killed.[29] On 6 October, a Vietnamese minesweeper came under attack six miles from Nha Be. A small support team, including a SEAL force, was dispatched to the area to drive the enemy from the site.

On 7 October 1966, two SEAL Team One squads of about seven men each were moving to be inserted into the RSSZ via a Medium Landing Craft (LCM). An enemy battalion lay waiting for riverine traffic, and the VC opened fire as the boat entered the ambush. One mortar round made a direct hit on the boat. The men aboard sustained heavy casualties; sixteen of the nineteen were wounded from the initial fire. The SEALs jumped into action and began to return a devastating hail of ordnance. Two SEALs who were manning a .50 caliber machine gun were returning such a heavy volume of fire that the barrel turned white hot and shipmates afterwards swore they could see projectiles moving down the barrel. So aggressive was the return fire that the VC battalion broke and ran after having over forty men killed (not to mention the wounded). The VC battalion had been making a clandestine night movement; it had taken on the SEALs and suffered heavily for the action, causing the communists to retreat and lay low in the RSSZ for the next two weeks. Although no SEALs were killed, three were medically discharged from the navy due to the extensive wounds they sustained in the ambush.[30] The U.S. Navy noted the continued positive results of the operations of the small group of men from SEAL Team One. Their forces were increased to seven officers and thirty enlisted during the month of October.[31] Overall, the White House continued its strong backing of the U.S. fight against the communist insurgency. In late October, President Johnson visited U.S. forces in Vietnam as a show of support. The U.S. buildup would continue.

UDT 12 conducted surveys in the Mekong Delta during November 1966, from the Rung Sat Special Zone all the way to the Cambodian border. The commander of UDT 12, Lt. Commander Robert E. Condon, and eight men flew into Vietnam in November for riverine surveys. They located channels into the Co Chien and Ham Luong rivers for the Operation Deckhouse V landings (see Map 5). In addition, the team conducted reconnaissance in the Thanh Phong Secret Zone to collect intelligence on enemy forces. The Deckhouse V amphibious landing was executed 6 January 1967.[32]

On the East Coast of the United States, SEAL Team Two had been alerted in September for a commitment of five officers and twenty enlisted for duty in Vietnam.[33] Meanwhile, the continuation of intelligence collection during operations by SEAL Team One men proved most valuable. A SEAL ambush team killed the VC paymaster for the RSSZ on one mission and netted "wallets, diaries, pay records, and a small fortune in North Vietnamese money" in the process.[34] SEAL advisors also produced results. Seven SEAL-trained LDNN were selected as bodyguards for the South Vietnamese prime minister during the national day celebrations.[35]

Typical of other captures was a large weapons cache found on 3 December 1966, eleven miles south southeast of Nha Be. It included 57mm recoilless rifles, German and U.S. automatic weapons, and 10,000 rounds of ammunition. The men on this operation had been conducting a recon patrol in the RSSZ in support of Operation Charleston when they captured the arms. The SEALs also destroyed several enemy facilities on the 13th and 21st, as well as hundreds of thousands of pounds of rice in caches that had been used by the VC during 1966.[36] The SEAL squads used helicopters for both insertion and extraction on these missions, a procedure that was generally uncharacteristic of operations at that point in the war. On most of these early operations, riverine craft were mainly utilized.

The final statistics for SEAL Team One operations during 1966 resulted from 153 combat operations in the RSSZ:

VC killed (confirmed) 86
VC killed (probable) 15
Sampans destroyed 21
Junks destroyed 2
Huts/Bunkers destroyed 33
Rice captured/destroyed 521,600 lbs. [37]

The above statistics were compiled by a force of SEALs from Team One that had not exceeded more than forty men in-country at any time up until the end of 1966. Detachment Delta from both UDTs 11 and 12, meanwhile, received the Navy Unit Commendation for operations between 16 August 1966 and 15 December the following year.[38]

The war for control of South Vietnam was just beginning, and the men of Naval Special Warfare had already learned valuable lessons in fighting the guerrillas in their environment. The amphibious recons of UDT would continue at a steady pace and prove invaluable to the successful execution of marine amphibious operations. The results of the freestyle SEAL ambushes in these early years earned the attention of conventional planners at this stage in the war. The navy soon realized that employing the SEALs in the Delta region was a valuable, if modest, method of projecting offensive naval power ashore in an unconventional war that seemed not to require the full potential of a huge, powerful open-ocean fleet. With such huge potential, it may have been difficult for naval planners to watch large army and marine units employed into the thick of the war while the navy's biggest contributions seemed to be through its air components and riverine and coastal patrols. The UDT and SEAL teams had been bloodied and had stung back in kind. More importantly, they had produced concrete results. Like the larger conventional commitment of U.S. forces, the operational buildup had only begun.

Notes

1. Edward J. Marolda and Oscar P. Fitzgerald, *The United States Navy and the Vietnam Conflict*, vol. II (Washington, D.C., 1986), p. 513.

2. Ibid., p. 527; *All Hands* (June 1965), p. 35.

3. *Pacific Stars and Stripes*, 25 April 1965; Ray W. Stubbe, *Aarughu!* (Washington, D.C., 1981), p. 143.

4. *U.S. Naval Special Warfare Handbook* (Millington, Tennessee, 1974), p. xii.

5. *All Hands* (July 1967), p. 11.

6. Unclassified command history for UDT 12 for the year 1965.

7. John B. Dwyer, "Surface Action," *Soldier of Fortune* (May 1987), p. 45.

8. *All Hands* (April 1967), p. 57.

9. *Pacific Stars and Stripes*, January 1966, p. 2.

10. Ibid., 5 January 1966.

11. Unclassified command history for UDT 11 for the year 1966.

12. Dwyer, "Surface Action," pp. 45, 46.

13. Dana Drenkowski, "America's Underwater Elite: U.S. Navy SEALs," *Soldier of Fortune*, Part I (April 1979), p. 49.

14. *U.S. Naval Special Warfare Handbook*, p. xiv.

15. Drenkowski, "America's Underwater Elite," *Soldier of Fortune*, Part II (March 1979), pp. 38-40.

16. Richard Hill, "Mean Mothers With Dirty Faces," *Esquire* (May 1974), p. 150.

17. Unclassified command history for UDT 11 for the year 1966; *Pacific Stars and Stripes*, 28 March 1966, p. 6 and 8 April 1966.

18. COMUSNAVFORV monthly summary, April 1966, pp. 22-23.

19. Unclassified command history for UDT 11 for the year 1966, Enclosure I, p. 4.

20. COMUSNAVFORV monthly summary, June 1966, p. 25.

21. Unclassified command history for SEAL Team One for the year 1966, Enclosure I, p. 3; COMUSNAVFORV monthly summary, July 1966, pp. 27-28.

22. Unclassified command history for SEAL Team One for the year 1966, Enclosure I, p. 3.

23. Ibid., Enclosure I, p. 2; COMUSNAVFORV monthly summary, August 1966, pp. 19-20.

24. Unclassified command history for UDT 11 for the year 1966, Enclosure I, p. 5; Dwyer, "Surface Action," pp. 44, 45.

25. Unclassified command history for USS *Tunny* for the year 1966.

26. Unclassified command history for UDT 12 for the year 1966.

27. Dwyer, "Surface Action," p. 46.

28. COMUSNAVFORV monthly summary, September 1966, p. 14.

29. Ibid., October 1966, pp. 31-32.

30. Unclassified command history for SEAL Team One for the year 1966; John G. Hubbell, "Supercommandos of the Wetlands," *Reader's Digest* (June 1967), p. 54.

31. Unclassified command history for SEAL Team One for the year 1966, Enclosure I, p. 2.

32. Unclassified command history for UDT 12 for the year 1966.

33. Unclassified command history for SEAL Team One for the year 1966, p. 14.

34. Hubbell, "Supercommandos of the Wetlands," p. 53.

35. COMUSNAVFORV monthly summary, November 1966, p. 65.

36. Unclassified command history for SEAL Team One for the year 1966, Enclosure I, p. 2; COMUSNAVFORV monthly summary, December 1966, p. 31.

37. Unclassified command history for SEAL Team One for the year 1966, Enclosure I, p. 2.

38. *All Hands* (November 1967), p. 56.

CHAPTER THREE

SPECWAR Support

UDTs and SEALs characteristically worked in the enemy's backyard, normally beyond large-scale support. The teams did, however, receive a tremendous amount of forward support from other naval and allied units, as well as several special and developmental activities. Operating out front in the canals and mangrove swamps, the independent small squads owed a tremendous amount of their success, and many of their lives, to the support that was provided to them by others.

The U.S. Navy's riverine forces were commonly referred to as the "Brown Water" Navy in contrast to the Blue Water forces of the open ocean, such as aircraft carriers, submarines, and battleships. The riverine forces centered around a fleet of diverse, small craft that could navigate and operate along the near coast and into the narrow inland waterways of South Vietnam. Particularly in the areas southwest of Saigon, the boats were highly effective amid the vast network of rivers and canals. The vessels were also used to insert, extract, and support UDT and SEALs during their forays ashore. Boat Support Unit 1 was established on 1 February 1964 to specifically lend support to and work with Navy Special Warfare units. Its skill provided tremendous assistance to SEAL operations throughout the war. Not only did Boat Support Unit 1 work in the Mekong Delta after December 1966, it also assisted in supporting the thirty-four Alpha missions as early as February 1964 out of Danang.

Several of the most commonly utilized boats are the following:

- River Patrol Boats (PBRs). Thirty-one feet long, with a jacuzzi jet propulsion system, this craft could reach speeds of up to twenty-eight knots. Armament included several .50 caliber and M-60 machine guns and 40mm grenade launchers.

- Fast Patrol Craft (PCF). Commonly called "Swift" boats, these larger boats also carried .50 caliber machine guns and mortars.

- Medium Landing Craft (LCM). The "Mike" boat was utilized for numerous operations by SEALs and UDT.

- Light SEAL Support Craft (LSSC). Twenty-six feet long, this boat was powered by two 300 HP gasoline engines that provided a top speed of about twenty-six knots with a full combat load. It could carry a fully equipped SEAL squad (seven men), and its shallow draft of eighteen inches allowed it good maneuverability on the inland waterways of the Delta.[1] There were two significant complaints about the LSSC that were continually addressed by SEALs during the war. The first was that the pumps on the craft would clog too frequently in the dirty riverine waters of the Delta. The second was that many of the replacement parts for the craft were of substandard quality and therefore caused additional breakdowns. Overall, the LSSC was a highly used boat, considering that most SEAL direct-action patrols were of squad size.

- The Boston Whaler and STAB (SEAL Team Assault Boat), initially dubbed the Bismark. Both were small, high-speed craft used in riverine ambushes.[2] The STAB was twenty-six feet in length and could carry a squad-sized element. It had a speed of between thirty and forty-five knots.

- Medium SEAL Support Craft (MSSC). Thirty-six

feet in length, this craft could carry a full SEAL platoon (fourteen men) while pulling a shallow four-foot draft. Numerous weapons systems were tested and used on this craft, including 7.62mm miniguns.[3] The MSSCs were generally reliable, but they had a high failure rate in very shallow water because the cooling systems could not fully cool the muddy raw water of the Delta waterways. The .50 caliber machine guns sometimes cracked the gunnels due to their heavy stress when fired. Overall, the MSSC proved to be another valuable boat for SEAL river operations. It had a speed of between twenty-five and thirty knots.[4]

Without the assistance and support of the Brown Water fleet, SEAL and UDT patrols would have found it impossible to move into the enemy's rear areas. More importantly, they would never have been able to leave those areas following a patrol.

Many operations were also launched from a series of specially altered submarines. Each transition throughout the period increased the operational capabilities of the frogmen. The USS *Perch* (APSS 313), USS *Tunny* (APSS 282), and USS *Grayback* (LPSS 574) all strongly supported Navy Special Warfare missions throughout the war.[5]

The naval air components most frequently used in support of SEAL and riverine forces were helicopters and fixed-wing close air support aircraft of HAL-3 and VAL-4. HAL-3 (Helicopter Attack, Light) contained the UH-1 gunships, dubbed "Seawolves", which were used for armed transport and close air support. Armament included .50 caliber machine guns, miniguns, rockets, and a variety of ordnance. Officially commissioned in April 1967, the helos increasingly came into play as the war progressed. The utilization of helos meant greatly increased mobility, and close scrutiny of operations revealed a heavier reliance on such assets in 1968 and subsequent years. The night operations from riverine craft that took place in the mid-1960s increased to include daylight heliborne raids, which occurred in the late sixties and early seventies.[6] Almost every SEAL post-tour report praised the Seawolves above all other air assets. Countless examples of their aggressiveness and skill were given in these reports. On many operations, the Seawolves would jettison their remaining ordnance when the SEALs' primary extraction helos were damaged by small-arms fire. Navy helicopters would then swoop in and extract a besieged team. It was also noted that the Seawolves inflicted heavy casualties on the enemy throughout the war.

The fixed wing OV-10 Black Ponies of VAL-4 (Light Attack Squadron) carried 5-inch Zuni rockets, a 2.75-inch rocket launcher, and a minigun pod. They also came into being in early 1967 and were a highly valued air asset, according to countless SEAL platoon post-tour reports. The Black Ponies were normally an asset that could be called upon when required; they were considered to be "on call". The increased armament allowed the light aircraft to not only act as a spotter, but to bridge the gap between its observation role and jet fighter-bomber support. Its slower speed and longer loiter time made the Black Ponies invaluable to the men on the ground.[7]

One other point about the close air support role of the Seawolves and Black Ponies bears mentioning. Whenever a small team of men on the ground required their assistance, the presence of the gunships helped draw the attention of the enemy forces toward the sky. Close air support and the distraction it created for the enemy often allowed the frogmen to escape or extract.

Navy Special Warfare patrols in Vietnam carried and employed a wide variety of equipment and weaponry, much of which was specially designed for them by supporting activities. Some of these items included simple uniforms. For camouflaged fatigues, the green leaf pattern was developed for all forces to use in Vietnam. Also worn by SEALs and UDT was the "tiger stripe" pattern, which gave the units an even more aggressive and offensive appearance. Combined with camouflaged face paint, the men struck a tremendous amount of fear into many Vietcong by their appearance alone.

Following an operation, such as an abduction or raid, intelligence would receive reports that word had quickly passed that the "green faces" had once again been in the enemy's rear areas, causing extreme psychological anxiety.

Many SEALs also preferred to wear blue jeans on missions. They felt that the material held up better when wet and could better withstand the assaults of Mekong mosquitos when soaked. To prevent having skin rubbed raw from lengthy soakings and from leeches attaching themselves, some wore women's large pantyhose. It must be remembered that UDTs and SEALs operated in water on every mission, and, if unchecked, such abrasions and leech bites over a six-month tour could take a heavy toll by passing disease and causing open wounds to become infected.[8]

A specific set of camouflaged fatigue jackets was developed especially for SEALs, three different variations of which were established. The first allowed a radioman to carry a patrol radio on his back with a cover to protect it. A second was designed for a 40mm grenadier, while the third was made for a basic rifleman. All had pockets to carry magazines and ordnance high on the body in order to keep them dry and out of mud. All had an internal bladder to provide twenty-nine pounds of flotation in water. The jackets were accepted favorably by the teams by the middle of the war.[9]

When trapped and about to be overwhelmed in the field, the frogmen were taught during training to put their backs to water for defense. To avoid capture, the men were trained to seek the safety of water and trust it as a natural avenue of evasion. With a full combat load, this was not always a natural act. The UDT life jacket was the main item used for normal flotation. The grey safety device was always worn by Naval Special Warfare forces to cross waterways and for insertions and extractions. Men with heavier loads, such as radiomen and machine gunners, oftentimes utilized two such devices. If they could no longer hold a position, frogmen were instructed to swim to safety off an enemy beach or down a river, moving with the current. UDT men wore the life jacket for safety while on beach reconnaissance. Heavy seas or an unusual ocean current or riptide could sweep the men from support boats during hydrographic recon operations. The life jacket could be inflated orally or by means of a CO_2 cartridge. It saved numerous lives in Vietnam and is still used regularly by SEALs today.

For footgear, SEALs and UDTs wore what fit their mission best. The jungle boot, developed during the Vietnam conflict, was a favorite. Tennis shoes and their UDT cousin, the coral bootie, were also worn. Finally, many SEALs often went barefoot to sneak quietly into an enemy camp and to leave no American-looking marks on a trail or in the mud.[10]

Berets were in vogue during the early years in response to the popularity of the army's Green Beret. Some early SEALs unofficially sported black and camouflaged berets. More commonly in the field, the floppy bush hat or olive drab medical cravat, worn like a pirate's bandana or as a sweatband, was utilized.[11]

The K-Bar was the common frogman knife. It had a plastic sheath that, unlike leather, would not fall apart after constant water soaking. Normally attached to the sheath was a Mark 13 day/night flare that would produce smoke at one end and a flare at the other for emergency signaling.[12]

Weaponry spanned a wide spectrum. The Ithaca Model 37 was a 12-gauge favorite. Combined with a magazine extension to carry shotgun ammunition and a "duckbill" attachment on the end of the barrel, the buckshot could be spread in a horizontal pattern.[13] The 7.62mm Heckler & Koch G-3 assault rifle saw limited testing by frogmen.[14] A maritime variation of the M16, dubbed the Mark 4, was produced for UDTs and SEALs. Almost identical to the normal service rifle, no storage space was provided in the stock of the weapon. Later in the war, a shortened version of the M16 (although there were different models, all were most commonly referred to as the CAR-15), was widely used by UDTs and SEALs.[15] Mud plugs were developed to protect the muzzle of the weapons from the thick Mekong Delta mud during insertions and movement. These small plugs would allow the frogmen to fire without fear of the barrel exploding from clogging with mud or water. The plug would be blown clear of the weapon when it was first fired. The .45 caliber M3A1 "Greasegun" was used in the early part of the war, having been kept in the inventory since World War II and Korea.[16]

Famous weapons designer Eugene Stoner produced the M63 weapons system widely popularized by the SEALs and commonly called the "Stoner." This weapon could be converted into several models to include an assault rifle and light machine gun with a long or short barrel. Its high cyclic rate of fire and ability to feed from either side for left- or right-handed carriers made it valuable. Additionally, it could carry a box or drum with a hundred or more protected rounds ready to fire. Though it was received with mixed opinions, it was used to great effect by the SEALs. The men who hated it, discarded it. Those who loved it, babied it because it required a great deal of maintenance.[17]

The 40mm grenade launcher also saw considerable use. For patrolling operations and ambushes, the single-shot M79 was later replaced by the XM-148 and M-203 launchers, which could be fitted beneath an M16 barrel.[18] Honeywell produced an automatic 40mm grenade launcher, dubbed the Mark 18, which was used from riverine craft and by the SEALs. The weapon was hand-cranked, much like the first Gatling guns of years past.

Also fired from riverine craft were 7.62mm miniguns. With an ultra-high cyclic rate of fire at 6,000 rounds per minute, they could provide a massive burst of fire support during extractions under pressure and on those occasions when riverboats ran into Vietcong ambushes. Later in the war, these weapons were also mounted for protection at several SEAL bases and the riverine post known as Seafloat.[19]

For close-quarters fighting, submachine guns and handguns were employed. Smith & Wesson produced the 9mm M-39, an automatic handgun. Several models were designed with threaded barrels to accommodate suppressors, commonly known as silencers. This series was dubbed the Mark 22 Hush Puppy.[20] Both it and a silenced version of Smith & Wesson's M76 submachine gun were used to eliminate barking dogs and other animals that would alert VC as SEALs quietly approached their encampments. They were also used against human sentries. Specially developed subsonic 9mm ammunition helped quiet the weapon's signature. The unsilenced version of the 9mm M76 was also widely used. Additionally, some SEALs carried the 9mm Carl Gustav Swedish K and Sterling submachine guns.[21]

A napalm grenade was tested in 1968 by men of SEAL Team One. The device weighed three quarters of a pound and had a bursting radius of ten feet.[22] The V-40 mini grenade, much smaller than conventional grenades commonly in use at the time, was employed in small numbers by SEALs starting in 1969.[23] Also tested was a prototype .50 caliber sniper rifle for long-range heavy punch.[24] Other equipment developed included a telescoping VHF antenna for easy use in the bush, a hand-held Doppler radar, and small-squad UHF radios.[25]

A waterproof tape recorder was specially designed for the SEALs in 1969 to be used during intelligence-gathering patrols. With the device, a recon patrol member could record information of value without having to write notes. Many of the patrols were conducted during the hours of darkness, and this device allowed the units to stop and take notes for only brief periods without using a light and notebook. The device saw only limited use and was only designed for short, shallow immersions, such as stream crossings.

The AN-PVS 2 Starlight scope allowed the men to see in the night like a cat. During riverine ambushes and on raids, this allowed frogmen to positively identify armed insurgents. A bullet-trapped grappling hook was invented to allow SEALs on riverine ambushes to recover targeted sampans more easily following contact. Fired directly from the muzzle of an M16, the hook would snag small boats before they could sink or be swept away by a river current.

With such a wide variety of weapons and equipment at their disposal, the successes of Special Warfare units is not surprising. Beyond this, other tactics and techniques were attempted. The utilization of specially trained scout dogs to hunt down enemy installations and booby-traps was popular in the late sixties.[26] An armed trimaran was modified by members of SEAL Team Two for small unit riverine operations in 1967. It later developed into the SEAL Team Assault Boat, or STAB.[27] A 50-round M16 magazine was tested, with only a fair appraisal.[28] An M16 front sight for use at night was developed using a beta emission element.[29] UDTs tested the Aqua Dart recon system, a one-man craft that could be driven up a waterway and provide 360-degree panoramic photography.[30]

Throughout the war, the teams utilized and tested a wide range of mission equipment. In the end, it was the equipment and other support that helped carry the frogmen of UDT and SEAL units to mission accomplishment. The specialized equipment and weaponry complemented the operational personality of the men who employed such devices.

Notes

1. Jim Mesko, *Riverine* (Carollton, Texas, 1985), pp. 26-29; *U.S. Naval Special Warfare Handbook* (Millington, Tennessee, 1974), pp. iv-29; unclassified command history for SEAL Team One for the year 1968, Enclosure 2, p. 2.

2. Mesko, *Riverine*, p. 50; *U.S. Naval Special Warfare Handbook*, pp. iv-29.

3. Unclassified command history for SEAL Team One for the year 1970, Enclosure 3(b).

4. For details of the development of a wide variety of small craft utilized by Special Warfare units in Vietnam, see Norman Friedman, *U.S. Small Combatants* (Annapolis, Maryland, 1987), pp. 365-377.

5. Unclassified command history for USS *Perch* (APSS 313) for the years 1964-1966; unclassified command history for USS *Tunny* (APSS 282) for the years 1966-1969; unclassified command history for USS *Grayback* (LPSS 574) for the years 1970-1973; John B. Dwyer, "Surface Action," *Soldier of Fortune* (May 1987), pp. 44-47, 111.

6. Mesko, *Riverine*, pp. 42-45.

7. Ibid., pp. 47-49.

8. *The Boston Herald*, 15 January 1987, p. 30.

9. *MIL-C-29105(SA)*, Dated 23 August 1971, Military Specifications For Coats, Ammunition Carrying, Buoyant, and Bladder, Flotation.

10. *U.S. Naval Special Warfare Handbook*, pp. iv-29; Al Santoli, *Everything We Had* (New York, 1981), p. 205.

11. *New York Times*, 28 December 1966; *Pacific Stars and Stripes*, 29 December 1966; Leroy Thompson, *U.S. Elite Forces—Vietnam* (Carrollton, Texas, 1985), cover page, introduction page, and pp. 36-43.

12. *U.S. Naval Special Warfare Handbook*, pp. iv-29.

13. Unclassified command history for SEAL Team Two for the year 1968, Enclosure 1, p. 8; *U.S. Naval Special Warfare Handbook*, pp. xii-4.

14. Thompson, *U.S. Elite Forces—Vietnam*, p. 41.

15. Unclassified command history for SEAL Team One for the year 1969, Enclosure 2, p. (c)6; unclassified command history for SEAL Team Two for the year 1969, Enclosure 1, p. 14.

16. *U.S. Naval Special Warfare Handbook*, pp. xii-8.

17. Unclassified command history for SEAL Team Two for the year 1967, Enclosure 1, p. 6.

18. Thompson, *U.S. Elite Forces—Vietnam*, p. 42; unclassified command history for SEAL Team One for the year 1969, Enclosure 2, p. (c)6.

19. Unclassified command history for SEAL Team One for the year 1970, Enclosure 3(b); unclassified command history for SEAL Team Two for the year 1967, Enclosure 1, p. 6.

20. Unclassified command history for SEAL Team Two for the year 1968, Enclosure 1, p. 8; unclassified command history for SEAL Team Two for the year 1969, Enclosure 1, p. 17.

21. John B. Dwyer, "Swamp Warrior," *Soldier of Fortune* (December 1986), p. 72; J. David Truby, *Silencers, Snipers, & Assassins* (Boulder, Colorado, 1972), p. 91.

22. Unclassified command history for SEAL Team One for the year 1968, Enclosure 2, p. (c)6.

23. Unclassified command history for SEAL Team One for the year 1969, Enclosure 2, p. (c)6.

24. Unclassified command history for SEAL Team One for the year 1968, Enclosure 2, p. (c)6.

25. Unclassified command history for SEAL Team One for the year 1969, Enclosure 2, p. (c)6.

26. Unclassified command history for SEAL Team Two for the year 1967, Enclosure 1, "SEAL Team Newsletter."

27. Ibid., Enclosure 1, p. 6.

28. Unclassified command history for SEAL Team Two for the year 1969, Enclosure 1, p. 17.

29. Ibid., Enclosure 1, p. 17.

30. Unclassified command history for UDT 12 for the year 1968, pp. 1, 18.

CHAPTER FOUR

Backwater War (1967)

By the beginning of 1967, nearly 400,000 U.S. servicemen were involved in Vietnam. The war continued to build on all fronts, and the United States continued to pressure the North Vietnamese and Vietcong to find an end to the conflict. Navy Special Warfare involvement also expanded during the year. To date, only one frogman had been killed in UDT/SEAL operations in-country. The success of SEAL Team One platoons led to a wider role in the conflict for both SEAL teams. The West-Coast-based SEAL Team One expanded in manpower, putting additional operational platoons into the Mekong Delta. Meanwhile, for the first time, SEAL Team Two began to deploy platoons into the war zone at the beginning of 1967. This year would mark a great increase in the Delta fighting. The war in the backwaters of the canals and rivers would no longer be limited to the Rung Sat Special Zone (RSSZ).

The Vietcong increased their attacks on Saigon shipping in the RSSZ during January 1967. Out of a dozen incidents, three involved minings, while the majority of the others involved ambushes. Two SEAL squads were inserted by Mike boat to patrol the RSSZ on 6 January. While conducting their reconnaissance mission along the Rach Muoi Creek, the SEALs discovered a small base camp and subsequently destroyed it[1] (see Map 6). Another patrol on the 9th was detected by enemy forces as it searched a small complex fourteen miles south of Nha Be. While at least four VC attempted to surround the SEALs, the frogmen slipped into the Rach Cat Lai Be Creek and swam quietly downriver (see Map 6). They silently passed a large enemy base camp, but escaped to their helicopter extraction point. Once out of the area, air strikes were called in on the communist forces with unknown results.[2]

Documents captured in December 1966 during Operation Charleston revealed that the VC were using several fresh-water wells in the RSSZ for resupply. Subsequent aerial photography confirmed that the VC were using numerous trails leading to the wells. SEALs were immediately ordered to destroy them. On 12 January 1967, two six-man teams were inserted by helo; using explosives, the teams demolished eight wells near Thanh Thoi Hamlet in the lower RSSZ.[3] Intelligence reports from a U.S. Army advisor in Can Gio two months later indicated that this action caused great hardship among the communist units in the vicinity, forcing them to carry water from a much greater distance[4] (see Map 6). Four days later, the SEALs destroyed a large rice cache they discovered in a camp twelve miles south of Nha Be.

While the SEALs were moving to insert for one of the demolition operations, another VC ambush of an LCM riverboat occurred on 20 January. Many of the SEALs and navy crewmen onboard were wounded and one Vietnamese officer was killed, but the U.S. forces fought back aggressively and ended their mission by killing four enemy soldiers and capturing nearly 360 VC suspects, along with numerous documents and a large quantity of supplies. Most of the detainees turned out to be active Vietcong. The SEALs had been operating in conjuction with a U.S. Army unit that was sweeping the area. The SEALs mission had been to patrol the river and prevent enemy forces from evading the army sweep.[5]

Other patrols reconned the mangroves for VC activity, many times finding their movement hampered by thick vegetation. On 9 January, one patrol was forced to extract by McQuire

Rig (see glossary) via a helicopter wench after it was unable to make its way to a riverine extraction site.[6] A small and deserted VC camp and rice cache were found and destroyed by men from SEAL Team One on the 16th. The cache, which held an estimated 17.5 tons of rice, was scattered by 160 pounds of explosives that the frogmen had requested via helicopter.[7]

Although missions were run almost daily, only a handful of enemy contacts resulted. On countless patrols, the SEALs heard the Vietcong use small-arms fire in patterns, as signaling and warning from one enemy unit to another. It was easy for the communists to hear the approach of the river vessels used for insertion and extraction by the SEALs. The VC sensed the presence of the new, deadly navy units and gave them a wide berth.[8]

Also during January, Operation Deckhouse V utilized men from UDT 12 to find and mark safe channels in the Co Chien and Ham Luong rivers (see Map 5). The success of the operation in the Than Phu Secret Zone was due in large part to the fact that the UDT missions included channel searches, surf observations (SUROBS), mine searches, and salvage work.[9]

On 2 and 3 February, four SEAL Team One squads conducted a series of patrolling sweeps in the RSSZ. Several VC bunkers and a concrete cistern were demolished, and four enemy sampans were fired upon. Additionally, a small quantity of ordnance and equipment was captured.[10] Patrols all throughout the spring consisted of intelligence recons, listening posts, and ambushes, and there was a marked improvement in the objectives of the missions compared to the earlier, freestyle ambushes of the year before. A few of the operations were designed to abduct Vietcong for the purpose of gaining intelligence through interrogation. Many team members saw fresh evidence of enemy forces in certain areas, but few actually made any contact.

Almost immediately after arriving in-country on 31 January, SEAL Team Two patrols commenced operations. Prior to leaving the continental United States (Conus), two SEAL Team Two platoons, consisting of two officers and ten enlisted each, stopped over for two weeks in San Diego to train and confer with SEAL Team One elements.[11] During their stop on the West Coast, the men trained in weapons and tactics in the desert located east of the city, received intelligence updates and briefs, and prepared their equipment for deployment. The group, which was to include a specially trained scout dog named Prince, arrived at Binh Thuy airfield outside Can Tho at the end of the month. From there, they moved to Nha Be, where some initial orientation missions were run with elements from Team One before the East Coast units struck out into their own designated areas of operation in the Mekong Delta along the Bassac River and its tributaries[12] (see Map 5).

On 7 February, one platoon advised the 32nd Vietnamese Ranger Battalion and called in air and artillery support for the unit.[13] Yet, this type of initial mission was of little consequence. It took a few weeks to iron out problems concerning exactly how the SEALs were to be employed in the Delta. Many of the same questions that had faced SEAL Team One elements in the RSSZ a year before were now echoed in the Delta regions where other platoons were hoping to work. By the second week in March, these issues had been resolved. The Team Two SEALs were to perform the majority of their missions within five kilometers of the major rivers in the Delta, but they could penetrate further inland with special approval.

At times, the elements became the gravest enemy of all. Well before dawn on 13 February, men from UDT 12's Det Charlie launched from the deck of the *Tunny* in motorized IBSs off Sa Huynh in II Corps. Large swells met the men as they anchored the command boat just outside the surf zone and sent two swimmer scouts ashore. In the darkness of the squall, the command boat capsized as it was hit by an estimated twenty-foot breaker. The three men onboard were unceremoniously dumped into the water. They struggled to the beach as the other boat was rocked by the high surf and fought to remain upright. UDT men in the second boat activated an emergency flare to notify the sub of the situation.

The *Tunny* began to respond to the call for assistance and launched a third IBS.

The frogmen from the command boat were barely able to make their way ashore and link up with the scout swimmers stranded on the beach. After burying their radio and the remains of their boat, they began several attempts to swim through the surf. Three of the men made it to the second boat just before 0600. Meanwhile, the *Tunny* had moved to within 1,300 yards of the beach and anchored. She called on a nearby LST (Landing Ship, Tank), the USS *Westchester County,* for additional help. The LST launched an amphibious landing craft to join in the search. Just after it had launched, another swimmer was reported recovered by the second IBS. The last swimmer was recovered by the landing craft about an hour later, and the vessel linked up with the sub to transfer all hands. Luckily, the frogmen were uninjured, although they were exhausted by the ordeal. The necessary hydrographic data was finally obtained, and Operation Deckhouse VI, designed as another marine assault to throw the communists in I Corps off balance, was launched on 16 February.[14]

New methods and tactics were developed by the frogmen, mostly as a result of trial and error. The SEALs were beginning to discover that wearing boots into enemy territory was a dead giveaway. Enemy forces went barefoot in most areas, and they would easily pick up the tracks of their enemy's footwear. Many SEAL platoons began to go barefoot themselves and carried a pair of lightweight coral booties or tennis shoes to be used only in certain terrain. In the mud and on the hard-packed trails, bare feet additionally proved more sensitive and made careful movement along booby-trapped trails more positive. A low-strung booby-trap tripwire was more easily sensed on bare skin. Stalking without boots also proved to be an absolutely silent method to penetrate an enemy camp.[15] Squad radios were used in the spring without impressive results. They seemed too noisy for the small units attempting to remain as ghosts in the brush.[16]

U.S. ground troop involvement in Vietnam continued to expand steadily. In the third week of February, Operation

Junction City was conducted in III Corps near the Cambodian border. The largest military operation to date, it involved 22 U.S. battalions in a sweep-and-destroy operation that targeted guerrilla base camps in the South. On 3 March, UDT 11 relieved UDT 12 as the forward-deployed Underwater Demolition Team in WESTPAC. UDT 12 later received the Navy Unit Commendation for its 1966-1967 WESTPAC cruise. The citation noted that the frogmen reconned over 120 miles of beaches, rivers, and harbors in the combat zone and provided other valuable services to the Seventh Fleet's amphibious forces. Also in March, UDT 11 received the same award for operations between January 1964 and September 1966. Its effort included the reconnaissance of over 110 miles of beaches and rivers and countless missions in support of the Pacific Fleet's operations.[17]

Six LDNN were assigned to conduct training operations with U.S. Navy SEALs out of Nha Be beginning on 9 March. In the initial after action reports, the Americans felt that the LDNN accompanying the units would be of greater value given a little more time and experience.[18] On the 11th, a 2nd Platoon ambush (its first real contact of the tour) interdicted an enemy resupply attempt fifteen miles southeast of Can Tho (see Map 4). Four VC were killed, while the SEALs were extracted by riverine craft under fire.[19] On 12 March, twenty sensors were emplanted by a SEAL Team One platoon in Vam Sat.[20] On 15 March, Admirals Sharp and Ward and General Westmoreland visited Seal Team One's Detachment Golf to express their personal admiration for the job the SEALs were tackling all over the Delta.[21] That same day, a small SEAL Team One ambush netted three VC killed and several weapons and a small amount of operational equipment from an enemy sampan.[22]

The mud, tidal flows, and nipa palms were not always the only environmental hazard. On a riverine abduction/ambush mission on 17 March, a SEAL Team One frogman encountered an obnoxious crocodile. The amphibian finally forced the frogman to flee his position and shoot in self-defense. "At the bank, in about three feet of water, I saw what looked like a stump. The stump started moving closer to me. I stopped. It came closer and closer, and when it was about six feet away, I saw that the stump had two eyes and was pointing its snout at me . . . I moved back about three or four feet, pointed my M16 at him and fired," he later related. The noise compromised the ambush location and caused the men to extract.[23]

Always with a markedly unique sense of humor, frogmen throughout Vietnam faced their physical adversities with directness. A sign composed and posted by the SEALs at Nha Be read:

Welcome to the Nha Be summer resort. For your pleasure we provide *Swimming Facilities*: Delightful frolics under the ships in the harbor. *Boating Excursions*: Try one of our famous moonlight cruises down the river. *Camping Trips*: Enjoy a night out in the open air as you sit comfortably and companionably beside a trail or a stream.[24]

On 19 March, a SEAL Team One patrol carried a sniper rifle on an ambush/abduction mission with poor results. It seemed to be more trouble than benefit to lug the precision weapon through the mud and thick vegetation, only to find fields of fire that could be covered easily by a weapon with regular iron sights. The biggest problem was that the sniper weapon was not an effective tool at night for SEAL operations at that stage in the war, as the SEALs reported.[25]

The SEALs also attempted to pioneer other new techniques in order to gain the upper hand against the sly and elusive enemy. While most squads inserted by riverine craft into their patrol areas, some swam from their boats to shore. A SEAL Team One group on 19 March jumped from the stern of its PBR as it continued to move up a river. In this way, the engine noise continued at the same pitch and would not indicate to VC close at hand that men had been placed ashore. The team inserted with minimal equipment. No radios were carried. Each man had his weapon, two magazines of ammunition, a flare, and a red lens flashlight.[26] Many platoons and squads used this method during the war to insert. It was found in the early years that the engine noise at about 1,500 to 1,800 RPM from a PBR created enough ambient noise to cover the technique. Another method was to coordinate an overflight of helicopters. Their noise and distraction would often cover the noise of a team inserting or closing on a target.

Other patrols utilized false insertions and extractions to try to catch the enemy. The riverine craft would feint putting men ashore at various points to make the VC nervous and force them to move, a process similar to hunters flushing a rabbit or quail from the bush. The SEALs would then try to catch the VC in an ambush. During "false extractions," half of the team would depart the patrol area as others remained in place to lure the enemy into a sense of security as they saw and heard the partial patrol depart. A variation of the false extraction, the double-back ambush had the entire patrol fake a withdrawal to the water as if they were extracting. They would then hook around onto their own trail and lay an ambush for anyone tailing or tracking them.[27] The men of SEAL Team Two were shifted slightly once again to take advantage of these unorthodox tactics that they and other SEALs were mastering. On 31 March, 2nd platoon was moved to the PBR base at My Tho to begin operations in that part of the Delta[28] (see Map 5).

In April, more emphasis was placed on intelligence collection to determine VC patterns, locations, and lines of communication and supply. SEALs were sent out to occupy observation and listening posts concealed in dense undergrowth for up to seven days at a time.[29] On one such operation, a SEAL officer who had won an Olympic Gold Medal in swimming in 1960 lay silently along a river with three of his men. The enemy force spotted them and surrounded the entire area. For the next nineteen hours, the numerically superior VC searched for the squad, which hid in dense vegetation and chest-deep mud. At one point, one particular Vietnamese nearly stepped on the SEAL officer. The frogmen remained undetected and slipped away.[30]

On 4 April, SEAL Team One's Kilo platoon arrived in-

country, followed three days later by Lima platoon.[31] On 7
April, the newly arrived Kilo platoon from Team One was
transiting to an operational area near the mouth of the Vam
Sat River within the RSSZ when its riverine craft entered a
Vietcong ambush (see Map 6). This time, the SEALs' luck
ran out. The vessel took heavy fire, and was only able to
limp out of the area to escape the hail of enemy ordnance.
In addition to small-arms fire, the boat was also struck by
several enemy rockets. It was one of these B-40 rockets that
killed three SEALs onboard: Lt. Daniel Mann, Interior
Communications Electrician Third Class Donald Boston, and
Radioman Third Class Robert Neal. After removing itself from
the area to the Soirap River, the riverine craft evacuated the
dead and wounded by helo[32] (see Map 6).

In the after-action report, the SEALs indicated that the
LCM had been used for a recon by fire on this operation.
As the craft traveled upriver, its organic weapons were fired
ashore into the brush to try to get an equal response from
the enemy. By doing so, the enemy would reveal his location,
and the SEALs, along with close air support, could overwhelm
them. On the 7 April operation, the recon by fire had created
an aggressive response from the Vietcong. The SEALs, who
did not agree with being a part of this technique, felt that
the craft should be used to quietly insert and extract them
and for communications relay and support. Another hard
lesson had been learned.[33]

On the 18th, a three-man SEAL listening post killed three
Vietcong communications-liaison personnel as they attempted
a route crossing near Giai Island.[34] At the end of the month,
two SEAL squads conducted a daylight raid twelve miles
southeast of Can Tho. Six VC were killed and one captured
in the action.[35]

On the evening of the first day of May, the USS *Tunny*
bottomed out off the coast of Phuoc Tien Province in the
southern part of I Corps. A team from UDT 11's Det Charlie
locked out of the sub with their equipment and boats. After
ascending to the surface, the boat was inflated and the men
climbed aboard with their gear. Using an underwater acoustic

pinger, the submarine vectored the frogmen toward the target beach. A large number of small indigenous craft were sighted, but the group slipped ashore undetected. Using a new communications device, the men remained in contact with the sub via a length of wire taken from an MK 37-1 wire-guided torpedo. Following the reconnaissance, the team paddled back to the *Tunny*, which snagged their towing line with its periscope. The *Tunny* then towed the boats into deeper waters and surfaced for recovery. Another beach recon had been successfully completed.[36]

Later in May, Det Bravo from UDT 11 came under heavy mortar attack while supporting Operation Hickory in the Demilitarized Zone (DMZ). Teamwork and organization in the face of enemy fire helped expedite the evacuation and recovery of the wounded.[37]

On several operations later in the spring, teams laid sensors deep in enemy-controlled territory.[38] The McQuire Rig was used further for extraction when patrols were unable to find a landing zone large enough for a helo to touch down.[39] Other teams found that U.S. Army artillery spotting rounds could be fired within hearing range of the patrols as an aid to navigation when their operational areas lacked noteworthy navigational terrain features in the swamps.[40]

When laying in ambush, the SEALs at times would use hand grenades rather than weapons fire for small contacts so as not to give away their exact position in case the small contact turned out to be part of a much larger enemy element.[41] On 17 May, one SEAL Team One platoon even tried to use a PBR as bait. As the craft lay beached along a riverbank, the team set ambush positions to its front in the hopes that a few VC would attempt to get close enough to take a shot at the naval craft. One enemy soldier was seen creeping through the bush and was engaged, but he slipped away cleanly.[42] The cat-and-mouse game continued.

The first two SEAL Team Two platoons were now nearing the end of their tours. They prepared to return to the States, where they could instruct other East Coast frogmen on the methods of this new backwater war. On May 30, 4th platoon from Team Two relieved 2nd platoon in-country.[43] The debriefings of 2nd platoon members helped prepare other SEALs for their first encounter with the Vietnam Delta war. (Appendix C provides an exerpt from 2nd platoon's debriefing concerning lessons learned regarding weapons and equipment as an example of the type of information made available by the combat-experienced SEALs during this time.) The West Coasters continued to rotate men into the war and became ever more experienced. Echo platoon from Team One arrived at Nha Be on 16 June and immediately began running operations.[44]

In May, SEAL Detachment Bravo was established to advise Vietnamese Provincial Reconnaissance Units (PRUs) in the Delta. Half of SEAL Team Two's 4th platoon was assigned advisory roles as well as men from SEAL Team One. The mission of the detachment was to lead and advise the PRUs in their operations against the cadre of the communist guerrillas within the various provinces. Field units would react to intelligence reports and attempt to capture or kill known guerrilla leaders.[45]

The indigenous PRUs were a hardened lot of warriors. Many were criminals who chose to fight for the South rather than waste away in a Vietnamese jail. Some were former Vietcong. In all, it took the strong leadership of the army's Green Berets and the navy's SEALs to control these fighters in combat. Contrary to the popular impression, the PRUs did not specialize in covert assassination, though they did target specific VC leaders for abduction and capture. By detaining and questioning the captives, the Allies were able to ferret out more of the enemy infrastructure. If the PRUs could not net their targets, they often killed them in open combat.

On 7 June, a five-man SEAL Team Two patrol was conducting a demolition strike against a Vietcong rest area near the northern tip of Tan Dinh Island. Several enemy soldiers were seen maneuvering to set an ambush against the Americans, and the patrol leader immediately engaged them, killing one VC. An estimated twelve to fifteen other

VC then opened fire on the frogmen, and the SEALs pulled back under fire. Two other Vietcong were subsequently killed in the engagement, while the Americans escaped unharmed.[46]

Two squads attacked an enemy hamlet in a daylight raid two miles southwest of My Tho on the 18th (see Map 5). Three VC were killed, three wounded, and four others captured.[47]

Naval planners met at the end of June under Admiral Veth in a SEAL symposium to decide the future employment of SEALs in order to increase their already substantial effectiveness.[48] At the same time, frogmen continued to rotate into the combat zone. On 26 June, 5th platoon from SEAL Team Two relieved 3rd platoon in-country.[49] UDT 11's Det Bravo conducted river surveys and assisted in reconnaissance operations in the Mekong Delta during June and July.[50]

Other operations continued. Three Vietcong leaders, two men and a woman, were kidnapped from their base in II Corps, twenty miles northeast of Phan Thiet in the Le Hong Phong Secret Zone, by Team One SEALs from Juliett and Kilo platoons. They launched their commando raid on 4 July 1967 from an offshore destroyer, the USS *Brush*. One other VC was killed as she attempted to flee the raiding party. Important documents concerning enemy political actions were also captured. The SEALs launched their mission in small rubber boats and used swimmer scouts to recon their beach landing site prior to coming ashore. The dark moon and clear weather allowed them to move quietly in the sand dunes and steep hills of the region. Naval gunfire support played only a small supporting role to ground units throughout the war, but 164 rounds of naval gunfire were expended by *Brush* in strong support of this SEAL raid.[51] *Brush* and other naval vessels proved to be much more than passive insertion craft for SEALs on many operations.

Several other contacts, involving numerous VC killed in action, were made by SEALs while patrolling throughout July, mostly as a result of a refinement of tactics and techniques.[52] On 9 July, one of the operations by a squad from Team Two's 4th platoon captured important documents concerning the

VC infrastructure in the Binh Dai Special Zone (see Map 5). The ambush patrol fired on several VC along the Bong Ca Creek on the final day of their mission, twenty-eight miles southeast of Ben Tre. Four enemy soldiers were killed in the raid. Included in the seized information were two map overlays and a list of VC personnel from six districts. The captured data resulted in a larger operation conducted by the ARVN Seventh Division on 17 July.[53]

Two SEAL squads were landed in Bien Hoa Province near the suspected headquarters of the Vietcong commander of the RSSZ on 20 July (see Map 3). Four VC were killed by the teams as they attempted to slip out of the area using two different sampans. Numerous supplies and weapons were captured, but the VC commander was not located.[54] A SEAL Team One group was compromised on a mission on 21 July after having to shoot an aggressive wild pig; the team was extracted shortly thereafter.[55] At the end of the month, a SEAL patrol contacted an enemy force of unknown size while conducting a daylight raid on a base camp on Ilo Ilo Island (see Map 5). After a brief fight, the enemy broke and ran. The SEALs destroyed fourteen structures in the camp.[56]

UDT 11's Det Delta was based at Danang, with smaller teams "farmed out" to locations at Chu Lai and Cua Viet (see Map 2). On 15 July, Det Delta was forced to move unexpectedly from Camp Tien Sha to the Tien Sha Annex. The men of the unit did all they could to improve their physical circumstance, building a center for all the UDT detachments to enjoy as they rotated off the ARG and other vessels for rest and recuperation. Other detachments from UDT 12 and 13 worked out of the Danang base in their rotations through Vietnam later in the war. The facility was affectionately dubbed "Frogsville" by men in the teams.[57]

Besides their explosives employment in the I Corps area, the men also took advantage of other opportunities that presented themselves. From 16 to 22 August, one officer and two enlisted men from the detachment attended U.S. Army Airborne School at Phan Rang in South Vietnam. The condensed course lasted eight days.[58] By this time in the late

1960s, it was becoming more common for all frogmen to be qualified parachutists. Dets Echo and Foxtrot from UDT 11 were located aboard two different amphibious ready groups. The teams participated in nine different amphibious operations in Vietnam during the cruise. During one operation, Beau Charger, the beach party came under heavy mortar attack near Cam Pao. The officer in charge received the Vietnamese Cross of Gallantry for his actions, which organized the force and evacuated wounded and nonessential personnel from the beach.[59]

Two SEAL squads landed in an area near the mouth of the My Tho River on the night of 1 August and conducted a three-hour patrol. Three VC were killed and one captured in the fighting, while numerous documents and weaponry were also discovered.[60] A number of intelligence documents, along with forty 82mm mortar rounds, were recovered from two sampans, which were ambushed by a SEAL Team Two squad on 2 August.[61] In early August, the Army's 199th Infantry Brigade requested recon assistance from Det Golf in the Delta.[62] A combined SEAL/LDNN ambush team from Nha Be killed five Vietcong nineteen miles south of Saigon on 7 August. Two sampans had entered their kill zone, but only one was successful in escaping.[63] Also in August, one SEAL ambush by Echo platoon led to the capture of ten pounds of valuable enemy documents carried by a VC courier in the RSSZ.[64] Five VC were killed by Team One ambushers on the 6th.

It seemed that the combined efforts of all the SEAL squads was beginning to gel for naval planners. The navy could never hope to stop the flow of men and arms into the Delta using riverine craft, but their defensive patrols had a great impact. With the addition of several SEAL platoons, the navy had a significant offensive reaction force. The enemy forces seemed unable to predict where the SEALs would strike next. One thing they could predict, however, was that when they met the SEALs, the VC almost always took casualties. Most were lucky to escape with a wound. Although the SEALs continued to run a variety of patrols, the riverine ambush remained the simplest and most effective operation for the frogmen. On the 11th, an ambush patrol from Team One was forced to extract when one member was bitten by a spider and had a severe reaction. Only a quick medevac saved his life. The man had been clearing a field of fire in preparation for occupying an ambush site.[65] The Delta environment alone was sometimes the worst enemy of all.

In a large operation on 16 August, twenty frogmen and six Vietnamese swept the island of Culaodung (see Map 5). Located in the mouth of the Bassac River, the island had long been a VC stronghold. A defector provided reports, placing the number of enemy troops on the island at about two hundred men. The assault run began after dawn, and at 0900, the river craft were turned toward the bank. Overhead, three Seawolf helos provided fire support. For five hours, the SEALs fought brief skirmishes and destroyed bunkers and hootches (native shacks or quonset huts used as barracks) used by the Vietcong. Fourteen tons of rice were destroyed, along with fifty-three huts, fourteen bunkers, and six sampans. Only three VC stood to face the frogmen. All three were killed in the fighting.[66] "The Vietcong are really shook when we go into their backyard and hit them," one SEAL officer said. "Well, we hit them today and they'll know they're no longer safe in the areas they control."[67]

A Vietcong defector led another group of SEALs from 5th platoon into a VC camp on 18 August. Three enemy leaders were killed, and an armory and printing facility were destroyed.[68] Alfa platoon from SEAL Team One arrived in-country in August and began operations.[69] It was during August that a third direct-action platoon from SEAL Team One was committed to operations in Vietnam, joining the four others already conducting missions (two from each coast). The expansion was further evidence that naval planners were now much more comfortable with the SEALs' operations and welcomed their proliferation throughout the IV Corps region.

One particular SEAL ambush in 1967 in Kien Giang Province provided a surprise to a frogman force (see Map 3). The SEALs had been watching a reported supply route used by enemy forces on a remote canal. Late in the afternoon of the second day of their surveillance, a VC sampan floated into the kill zone. Besides the two indigenous guerrillas onboard, a tall, heavy Caucasian with a beard rode in the bow. He was dressed in what looked like a khaki uniform and was holding a communist assault rifle. Just as the craft pulled into the area, the communists became leery, as if sensing the danger nearby. Although initially startled at seeing the white man, the SEALs immediately let the law of the barroom prevail—when a fight is unavoidable, strike first, and strike hard. The frogmen unleashed a hail of fire into the enemy force. The Caucasian was hit in the chest in the initial burst of fire and went overboard. The VC attempted to jump in and assist him. Just then, a superior Vietcong force appeared and counterattacked. Outnumbered and outgunned, the SEALs fought a running gun battle to an area where they could extract. Later, they were debriefed about the incident by an intelligence officer. They were told to remain silent about the action. South Vietnamese intelligence had reported that the white man had been a Russian. It would remain a little-known fact that the guerrillas and North Vietnamese were assisted in their Third World brushfire war by a host of foreign advisors and technicians, including Soviets, Chinese, Eastern Bloc, Cuban, Korean, and other communist nationals.[70]

Rotations for all the teams continued. On 25 August, Det Charlie from UDT 11 moved to Okinawa to conduct readiness training while the USS *Tunny* underwent maintenance in Yokosuka, Japan.[71] On 28 August, 6th platoon from the East Coast's SEAL Team Two relieved a West Coast platoon from SEAL Team One in-country.[72] While the war was of primary concern to the men in the field, the political front proved just as unstable. On 3 September, Nguyen Van Thieu was elected president of South Vietnam, ending a series of power struggles between top leaders of the South which had occurred since the assassination of Diem in 1963. Besides the communist insurgency, the South Vietnamese fought many internal struggles for control.

During September and October, small high-speed fiberglass boats, called "Boston Whalers," were first tested by riverine forces. One application used by the SEALs was to recover ambushed sampans before they had a chance to sink or slip further downriver. These craft accounted for a higher confirmation of enemy KIA and the capture of even more documents and equipment as a result of higher recovery rates.[73]

On 16 September, three SEAL platoons inserted and swept Tan Dinh Island as part of Operation Crimson Tide. Three VC were killed, a number captured, and a large VC staging area was destroyed.[74] On 21 September, a SEAL Team One Alfa platoon ambush decimated a VC sapper squad, which was enroute to mine the Long Tau River. Seven VC were killed in the action, and their equipment was captured.[75] Another ambush on the 28th along the Thi Vai River, seventeen miles east of Nha Be, killed four VC and wounded one. One sampan and numerous documents were recovered.[76] Combined SEAL/LDNN missions on 13 and 28 September resulted in eleven Vietcong killed.[77]

On 6 October, Signalman Third Class Leslie Funk, a member of SEAL Team One, drowned while training for operations in the RSSZ. He was initially pronounced as missing, but his status was changed when his body was found.[78] With the heavier operational commitment, the teams were beginning to sustain additional casualties. On occasion, the VC now chose to stand against the frogmen. During an operation on 13 October, one particular SEAL stopped a VC attempt to overrun his unit with a heavy and accurate volume of 40mm grenade fire. Six enemy soldiers were killed by his defense.[79]

At times, the SEALs scored heavily by capturing documents or a key VC leader. Additional Crimson Tide sweeps of Tan Dinh Island on 19, 21, and 23 October saw light action for the SEALs; seven enemy soldiers were killed and several captured. One of the captives was identified as the man who had murdered the national police chief in 1962. South Vietnamese soldiers working with the SEALs had to be restrained from killing the prisoner on the spot following the identification.[80] SEAL riverine ambushes on the 21st and 23rd killed four Vietcong.[81]

As the weather cleared toward the end of the year, more emphasis was placed on ambushes since this tactic yielded the largest volume of captured enemy documents. Enemy documents continued to be a tremendous intelligence resource. The East Coast SEAL platoons were now becoming manned by combat-experienced men, much the same as SEAL Team One platoons. On 24 October, 7th platoon from Virginia relieved 4th platoon.[82]

On 31 October, a SEAL ambush twenty-six miles southeast of My Tho killed two enemy soldiers. As the frogmen swept the area, they received weapons fire from a bunker complex and immediately went into the attack. Two more VC were killed, and the SEALs demolished fourteen bunkers and twenty structures, capturing several hundred rounds of ammunition.[83]

Eight ambushes during November and December were successful in making contact. An ambush team on 12 November along the Ba Gioi River, twelve miles east southeast of Nha Be, listened to a Vietcong unit training with weapons and grenades throughout the day. Before withdrawing by riverine craft, the SEALs finally killed three enemy soldiers in a sampan as the VC transited the area.[84] On 15 November, a SEAL Team Two squad killed a VC district security chief in a riverine ambush. The man had long eluded South Vietnamese forces and was notorious for atrocities he had participated in and supervised.[85]

The Vietcong continued to employ innovative munitions against the Allies. One SEAL received severe injuries to his left hand when he attempted to disarm a simple grenade booby-trap. It was then determined that the device was specially rigged to detonate when the grenade spoon was depressed toward the grenade body. The surprise caused a serious injury, but it resulted in the dissemination of the intelligence to other units which then began to watch out for similar devices around VC base camps.[86]

On 25 November, another SEAL Team Two platoon patrolled to several hootches and placed them under observation in the predawn hours. After light, two Vietnamese attempted to escape the area and were fired upon by the Americans. The shouting of fifteen to twenty men was then heard from three sides, and the SEALs called for a riverine craft to extract. During exfiltration, heavy fire was received from the three sides, and the SEALs fought their way to the river, at one time overrunning a bunker directly in the path of their escape route and occupied by four Vietcong. Six VC in all were killed in the action.[87]

Late in the year, one SEAL Team One squad found that using low-flying helos over its area covered the noise of a riverine craft used to insert the team. On three consecutive patrols, they were able to make contact by using this ruse.[88]

From 16 to 24 November, 7th platoon elements operated in Giao Duc District during Operation Cuu Long. They killed fifteen VC and captured eleven, along with one B-40 rocket, an AK-47, and sixteen Chicom rifles. The platoon also destroyed eighty bunkers and seven sampans.[89] The same platoon killed three enemy soldiers and captured one other in a sweep operation ten miles southwest of My Tho.[90] UDT 12 officially relieved UDT 11 of its WESTPAC duties as of 4 December.[91] On 9 December, SEAL Team One's Bravo Platoon relieved Echo platoon in-country; 8th platoon from the East Coast relieved 5th platoon.[92]

The 7th platoon killed six VC and captured one other while attempting to insert and move to a planned ambush site on 20 December.[93] On 23 December, the newly arrived Bravo platoon inserted six miles east of Nha Be for a thirty-six-hour recon/ambush patrol. The team began to patrol toward the southeast and east and had moved only a short distance before being contacted by heavy weapons fire. While acting as point man for the operation in the RSSZ, Seaman Frank Antone was hit by small-arms fire from the initial Vietcong burst and killed. The team had been patrolling deep inside enemy territory and had penetrated a VC regimental headquarters. The men fought their way to an extraction point and called for helo support. Antone, a Vietnamese LDNN also killed in the fight, and several other wounded men were extracted by McQuire Rig. The rest of the team was pulled out by army helos.[94]

At the end of 1967, nearly 500,000 U.S. servicemen were serving in Vietnam. The U.S. ground role continued to grow and had yet to peak. For the men of Naval Special Warfare, the war was now becoming an everyday reality, and 1967 became the first year that almost all the teams were deeply committed to the conflict. The beaches of every corps area were becoming quite familiar to UDT surveyors. By the end of the year, a majority of UDT and SEAL Team members were combat veterans, unlike the year before. As 1967 began, the SEALs were just gaining strong recognition for their abilities in the RSSZ. As the year ended, the frogmen were developing into an effective offensive naval instrument throughout the Mekong Delta. Their independent squad-size operations were netting significant results when appraised as a whole. Like the overall conventional capability, however, the men of Naval Special Warfare had yet to peak in number and effectiveness.

Notes

1. COMUSNAVFORV monthly summary, January 1967, p. 8.

2. Ibid., p. 8.

3. Unclassified command history for SEAL Team One for the year 1967.

4. Unclassified command history for SEAL Team One for the year 1968, Basic Narrative, p. 5.

5. Ibid., Basic Narrative, p. 4.

6. Unclassified command history for SEAL Team One for the year 1967.

7. Ibid.

8. Ibid., Combat Operations Report Summaries.

9. Unclassified command history for UDT 12 for the year 1967, Enclosure I, p. 1.

10. Unclassified command history for SEAL Team One for the year 1967, Combat Operations Report Summaries.

11. Ibid., Enclosure I, p. 1.

12. Ibid., Enclosure I, pp. 1, 2.

13. Recommendations for Presidential Unit Citation for SEAL Team Two, dated 15 August 1969, Enclosure 5, p. 1.

14. John B. Dwyer, "Surface Action," *Soldier of Fortune* (May 1987), p. 87.

15. Interview with Capt. Thomas E. Murphy by the author, NAB Little Creek, Virginia, 10 August 1987.

16. Unclassified command history for SEAL Team One for the year 1967, Combat Operations Report Summaries.

17. Unclassified command history for UDT 11 for the year 1967; unclassified command history for UDT 12 for the year 1967.

18. Unclassified command history for SEAL Team One for the year 1967, Combat Operations Report Summaries; COMUSNAVFORV monthly summary, March 1967, p. 66.

19. COMUSNAVFORV monthly summary, March 1967, pp. 7-8.

20. Unclassified command history for SEAL Team One for the year 1967, Combat Operations Report Summaries.

21. Ibid., Basic Narrative, p. 2.

22. Ibid., Combat Operations Report Summaries.

23. Ibid.; William Tuohy, "He Waits To Kill," *True* (May 1968), p. 70.

24. Tuohy, "He Waits To Kill," p. 36.

25. Unclassified command history for SEAL Team One for the year 1967, Combat Operations Report Summaries.

26. Unclassified command history for SEAL Team One for the year 1967, Combat Operations Report Summaries.

27. Ibid.; unclassified command history for SEAL Team Two for the year 1967; recommendation for presidential unit citation for SEAL Team Two, dated 15 August 1969, Enclosure 5.

28. Unclassified command history for SEAL Team Two for the year 1967, Enclosure I, p. 2.

29. *U.S. Naval Special Warfare Handbook* (Millington, Tennessee, 1974), p. xv.

30. Erick Berry, *Underwater Warriors* (New York, 1967), pp. 101-102.

31. Unclassified command history for SEAL Team One for the year 1967, Basic Narrative, p. 2.

32. Ibid.; COMUSNAVFORV monthly summary, April 1967, pp. 2-3.

33. Unclassified command history for SEAL Team One for the year 1967, Combat Operations Report Summaries.

34. COMUSNAVFORV monthly summary, April 1967, p. 9.

35. Ibid., p. 8.

36. Dwyer, "Surface Action," pp. 46-47.

37. *UDT 11 Cruisebook 1967,* Team History.

38. Unclassified command history for SEAL Team One for the year 1967, Combat Operations Report Summaries.

39. Ibid.

40. Ibid.

41. Ibid.

42. Ibid.

43. Unclassified command history for SEAL Team Two for the year 1967, Basic Narrative, p. 2.

44. Unclassified command history for SEAL Team One for the year 1967, Basic Narrative, p. 3.

45. Unclassified command history for SEAL Team Two for the year 1967, Basic Narrative, p. 2.

46. COMUSNAVFORV Monthly Summary, June 1967, p. 11.

47. Ibid., p. 6.

48. Unclassified command history for SEAL Team One for the year 1967, Basic Narrative, p. 3.

49. Ibid., p. 2.

50. *UDT 11 Cruisebook 1967,* Team History.

51. Unclassified command history for SEAL Team One for the year 1967, Basic Narrative, p. 3, and combat operations report summaries; COMUSNAVFORV Monthly Summary, July 1967, pp. 31-32.

52. Unclassified command history for SEAL Team One for the year 1967, Basic Narrative, pp. 3, 4.

53. Recommendation for Presidential Unit Citation for SEAL Team Two, dated 15 August 1969, Enclosure 5; COMUSNAVFORV Monthly Summary, July 1967, p. 32.

54. COMUSNAVFORV Monthly Summary, July 1967, p. 23.

55. Unclassified command history for SEAL Team One for the year 1967, Combat Operations Report Summaries.

56. COMUSNAVFORV Monthly Summary, July 1967, p. 2.

57. Unclassified command history for UDT 11 for the year 1967, p. 5; *UDT 11 Cruisebook 1967.*

58. Unclassified command history for UDT 11 for the year 1967, p. 6.

59. Ibid.

60. COMUSNAVFORV Monthly Summary, August 1967, p. 25.

61. Recommendation for Presidential Unit Citation for SEAL Team Two, dated 15 August 1969, Enclosure 5.

62. Unclassified command history for SEAL Team One for the year 1967, Basic Narrative, p. 4.

63. COMUSNAVFORV Monthly Summary, August 1967, p. 79.

64. Unclassified command history for SEAL Team One for the year 1967, Basic Narrative, p. 4.

65. Ibid., Combat Operations Report Summaries.

66. COMUSNAVFORV Monthly Summary, August 1967, p. 34.

67. *New York Times*, 18 August 1967, p. 10.

68. COMUSNAVFORV monthly summary, August 1967.

69. Unclassified command history for SEAL Team One for the year 1967, Basic Narrative, p. 4.

70. Roger F. Granger, "Uncle Ho's Foreign Legions," *Gung Ho* (August 1981), p. 48.

71. Unclassified command history for UDT 11 for the year 1967, p. 4.

72. Unclassified command history for SEAL Team Two for the year 1967, Basic Narrative, p. 2.

73. Unclassified command history for SEAL Team One for the year 1967, Basic Narrative, p. 4.

74. Recommendation for Presidential Unit Citation for SEAL Team Two, dated 15 August 1969, Enclosure 5, p. 2.

75. Ibid.

76. COMUSNAVFORV Monthly Summary, September 1967, p. 23.

77. Ibid., p. 101.

78. Unclassified command history for SEAL Team One for the year 1967, Enclosure 3, p. 4.

79. Recommendation for Presidential Unit Citation for SEAL Team Two, dated 15 August 1969, Enclosure I, p. 2.

80. COMUSNAVFORV monthly summary, October 1967, p. 54.

81. Ibid., p. 27.

82. Unclassified command history for SEAL Team Two for the year 1967.

83. COMUSNAVFORV Monthly Summary, October 1967, pp. 35-36.

84. COMUSNAVFORV Monthly Summary, November 1967, pp. 21-23.

85. Recommendation for Presidential Unit Citation for SEAL Team Two, dated 15 August 1969, Enclosure 5, p. 3.

86. COMUSNAVFORV Monthly Summary, November 1967, p. 27.

87. Recommendation for Presidential Unit Citation for SEAL Team Two, dated 15 August 1969, Enclosure 5, p. 3.

88. Unclassified command history for SEAL Team One for the year 1967, Combat Operations Report Summaries.

89. Unclassified command history for SEAL Team Two for the year 1967.

90. COMUSNAVFORV Monthly Summary, November 1967, p. 29.

91. Unclassified command history for UDT 11 for the year 1967, p. 8.

92. Unclassified command history for SEAL Team One for the year 1967, Basic Narrative, p. 4; unclassified command history for SEAL Team Two for the year 1967.

93. COMUSNAVFORV Monthly Summary, December 1967, p. 28.

94. Unclassified command history for SEAL Team One for the year 1967, Basic Narrative, p. 4, and combat operations report summaries; COMUSNAVFORV Monthly Summary, December 1967, pp. 24-25.

CHAPTER FIVE

Tet
(1968)

As 1968 began, U.S. involvement in Vietnam had escalated to an enormous degree since Navy Special Warfare units had first been introduced. U.S. military leadership was certain that victory was only a matter of time. The actual Vietcong guerrilla forces were being interdicted with greater success, and North Vietnam was finding it necessary to throw more and more of its own regular armed forces into the struggle against the South. It was an election year back in the United States, and although opposition to the prolonged war was increasing, the political leadership was equally certain that a win in Vietnam was in store in the not-too-distant future. But of the events of the year, those during the upcoming Tet celebration were to eclipse all others in 1968.

On 2 January, a group of SEALs, guided by a Vietcong defector, located a small enemy camp twelve miles southeast of Can Tho on May Island in the middle of the Bassac River (see Map 5). Six enemy soldiers were killed in a brief firefight, and two structures and eight hundred pounds of rice were destroyed. Later the same day, the same defector helped the SEALs capture a communications courier, but the enemy soldier was killed when he attempted to escape as the team moved for its extraction.[1] On 7 January, 7th platoon and two LDNN killed four VC traveling in three motorized sampans along a small river.[2] Bravo platoon from Team One discovered a deserted base camp on the same day. Moving through the area, Bravo platoon destroyed 21 hootches, 25 bunkers, a sampan with motor, 40 grenades, 5 booby traps, and 3,000 pounds of rice. Additionally, a kilo of documents was captured.[3]

The year 1968 was to be a costly one for SEAL Teams One and Two. Six men from Team One had already been killed in fighting during 1966 and 1967. For such a small community of men, the losses were a hard reality of war. On 11 January 1968, a SEAL Team One man became the first fatality of the new year. Seaman Roy Keith was killed by small-arms fire while operating in Ba Xuyen Province in South Vietnam. His Bravo platoon squad came upon a VC bunker that contained a five-man enemy rocket crew. One VC burst from the structure, firing an AK-47 and mortally wounding Keith. The rest of the SEALs attacked and killed four of the five men and captured the rocket launcher, three rockets, and three assault rifles. SN Keith would be the first of many SEALs killed in action in the heavy fighting of 1968.[4]

On 12 January, UDT 12's Det Golf was established in the Mekong Delta at Dong Tam outside My Tho (see Map 5). The group was originally assigned to test a new Aqua Dart river reconnaissance system under the operational control of CTF 117 (Mobile Riverine Force). The original detachment of frogmen was composed of three officers and eight enlisted men. One of four Aqua Dart systems came with the group, while the other three systems were to arrive in-country at a later date.[5]

Also on 12 January 1968, *Time* published a small article on SEALs and their exploits in Vietnam. The article followed a popular cartoon series carried in the Pacific *Stars and Stripes* daily, commonly read by U.S. forces throughout the theater. As part of the Buzz Sawyer comic strip series, the navy had suggested adding a segment on SEALs to help introduce the secret maritime units to the world. In the cartoon, Sawyer accompanied a SEAL raiding party on a commando strike into North Vietnam to capture a Soviet-made radar control van from a surface-to-air missile site. The navy made no comment on the fictitious mission, but *Time* did detail some of the statistics racked up by the teams up to that time. According to the *Time* account, "In some 600 missions, nearly all of them furtive forays into Communist-held areas, they have laid waste Communist installations (including 70 rivercraft, more than 200 bridges, factories and other structures, and at least 200 fortified positions), thrown the Communists off balance and killed more than 175 Communist soldiers and captured 60 while losing only six dead of their own and none at all to capture." *Time* reporter Glenn Troelstrup became the first newsman allowed to accompany a SEAL patrol on a combat operation. The riverine ambush saw a brief, violent firefight, accounting for two VC killed. Troelstrup noted that the frogmen were highly successful in turning the Vietcong from the hunters into the hunted.[6]

Another SEAL ambush occurred on 12 January along the Cat Co stream six miles southeast of Nha Be in the RSSZ. Warning and signaling shots between VC units were heard by the men for several hours, but the enemy did not escape the patrol. Their ambush netted four VC killed and two sampans with outboard motors destroyed. While withdrawing from the position, the SEALs came under fire from a position across the stream. The position was silenced by a return volley of 40mm grenade fire. The SEALs attempted to make further contact by reinserting upstream. No other enemy forces were encountered, however, and after patrolling for some time, the team withdrew.[7]

Gunner's Mate First Class Arthur Williams was mortally wounded on 18 January as his platoon was making an emergency extraction under fire. The SEAL Team Two 6th platoon member received a gunshot wound under his arm and the round lodged in his spine. He died shortly after, becoming the first SEAL Team Two fatality of the war.[8] On the same day, death dealt a tragic blow to UDT 12. The commanding officer of the Team, Lt. Commander Robert Condon, was killed when a B-40 rocket slammed into the LCM he had been embarked upon. He had been in-country observing the evaluation of recon gear Aqua Dart that his men were testing.[9]

Combined SEAL/LDNN actions accounted for a handful of enemy KIA and the capture of enemy munitions around the My Tho area during mid-month. Two LDNN detachments operated with SEAL units out of Binh Thuy and Nha Be at this point in the war.[10] In January, another SEAL Team Two member from 7th platoon was killed. Aviation Machinist's Mate Second Class Eugene Fraley had been preparing a booby-trapped demolition charge. The device was to be used on an upcoming patrol. As he removed it from the sandbag enclosure in which it had been assembled, the device detonated.[11] The teams were sustaining increased casualties as their employment grew. At the same time, the men became bolder as they gained confidence through their experience and familiarity with their specific operational areas.

On 22 January, two small SEAL squads lay in ambush along a canal on the Tien Giang River, seventy-seven miles southwest of Saigon. While patrolling along one side of the waterway, one SEAL squad opened up on a sampan that was moving without lights around 0200 on the 23rd, killing four Vietcong. As the squad moved to the southeast, they killed two more enemy soldiers in a second unlighted sampan. At that time, a small force of VC located on the canal bank, reacting to the American fire, opened up on the opposite bank in the general direction of the American fire. A larger enemy force situated on the receiving end of the Vietcong fire initiated a return volley on their comrades. The SEALs laid low and watched as the two communist forces battled each other. From its ambush position, the second SEAL squad opened up on the VC forces along the two banks and additionally caught a sampan with a lone enemy soldier embarked. During the movement to extraction, a final enemy soldier was killed by the SEAL force. After the free-for-all engagement, the frogmen found eight VC bodies. The squads then linked up and withdrew.[12]

On the same day, Bravo platoon worked with elements of SEAL Team Two to clear a portion of a canal blocked by a man-made dam. Three hundred pounds of explosives proved to be the standard frogmen solution. The canal was easily cleared for transit by rivercraft.[13] The frogmen were utilized at times for this type of administrative support, which enhanced civic action projects.

Also on the night of 22 January, a squad from Team One's Alfa platoon conducted an ambush with five members of the Australian Special Air Service (SAS). The elite SAS of both Australia and New Zealand conducted recon, abduction, and ambush operations throughout the war as the primary special operations forces of their respective countries. Like the SEALs, they characteristically patrolled in small teams of five men as the eyes and ears of the regular forces. SEALs teamed up with the Australians on several occasions and maintained an excellent working relationship with the Allied unit. On the January mission, the combined team inserted from a helo using a rope ladder and extracted by river craft. Several VC were fired upon in three sampans, and two were killed. Uniforms captured in one craft indicated North Vietnamese regulars were operating with the Vietcong in the area.[14] Although seen mostly in the other provinces, this intelligence indicator was an ominous warning of the upcoming Tet events.

The following day, on 23 January, the intelligence ship USS *Pueblo* was attacked and seized by the North Koreans. The vessel's highly classified electronic intelligence equipment was now in communist hands, much to the frustration of U.S. political and military leaders. The damage done to the U.S. intelligence community was significant. Plans were submitted to destroy the vessel before the equipment could be dismantled on the captured ship. Utilizing the USS *Tunny*, one such proposal called for a team of U.S. Navy frogmen to conduct a raid inside Wonson Harbor, where the North Koreans had secured the captured ship. The plan was disapproved. Consideration had to be given to the captive crew and how the action might effect their treatment and possible release.[15]

SOG forces also began operations in January in an area of South Vietnam long denied access by friendly forces. Similar to the over-the-beach raids in North Vietnam, these operations differed by allowing U.S. SEALs to accompany their Vietnamese counterparts into combat. The teams used a wide variety of tactics, including daylight raids and night patrols conducted while disguised as Vietcong. Results in a little over a year included 92 VC cadre captured and 90 others killed, while friendly forces suffered 7 killed.

Operation Wind Song I was conducted in Kien Hoa Province on 25 January against a Vietcong-controlled area along the Thom and Mo Cay canals (see Map 5). The 6th and 7th platoons were placed ashore by riverine forces and conducted a sweep. Five enemy soldiers were killed in the sporadic fighting and 51 VC suspects captured, one of whom turned out to be a local Vietcong tax collector. Additionally, 30 bunkers, 25 sampans, and 5 tons of rice were destroyed.[16] SEALs continued to rotate by platoon; on 28 January, Delta platoon relieved Foxtrot platoon at Nha Be.[17]

At this point in the war, the communists decided to risk an all-out offensive in hopes that the general South Vietnamese population would join them in open revolt. This miscalculation cost the communists dearly. Already, they had begun a seventy-seven-day siege of the northern marine base at Khe Sanh in I Corps near the Laotian border. The battle would not develop into a disastrous U.S. defeat (such as the French suffered at Dien Bien Phu), as some had predicted.[18]

The Vietnamese holiday of Tet was chosen as the target date for the national offensive. The idea was to catch the U.S. and ARVN troops in a relaxed state. On this account, the enemy was significantly successful.

Communist forces struck heavily beginning on 31 January. Their objectives lay in the large cities and province capitals around the country. The coordinated assaults caught many Allied forces at rest, but the ARVN and Americans bounced back for a hard fight. In most towns, ferocious fighting became house-to-house as the enemy refused to be easily routed. The North Vietnamese forces used the Vietcong guerrillas as their vanguard. After the initial shock, the Allies were almost relieved to finally have enemy forces surface en masse so they could be heavily engaged. The problem was that the battles of Tet were to be fought among the populated centers of the South.

The small SEAL detachments throughout the country swung into action to protect the bases and towns they staged from. In My Tho, SEALS and PBR crews helped defend U.S. billeting facilities[19] (see Map 5). Three enemy battalions attacked the urban area and attempted to seize all the bridges used to enter and leave the city. During one point in the fighting, the VC used an armored sampan cruising up and down the river to fire at government forces. Two SEALs counterattacked the vessel with 66mm Light Anti-Armor Weapons (LAAWs) and put the craft out of action. At the Vietnamese SEAL course (LDNN) at Vung Tau, school was temporarily suspended. The students and cadre were sent into action in Saigon to defend the naval headquarters[20] (see Map 4).

SEAL Team Two's 8th platoon was inserted by river patrol boat (PBR) outside Chau Doc before dawn on the 31st on a combined operation with a local PRU force (see Map 5). While on a recon patrol near the Cambodian border at about 0200, the platoon was startled to detect the massing of enemy forces near the city. Vastly outnumbered, the SEALs and PRUs withdrew to report their intelligence as quickly as possible. With an estimated 1,400 men, the initial Vietcong attack on Chau Doc began at about 0310. The enemy's aim was to systematically cut off the town and take it piece by piece. Resistance was split into small pockets that could be more easily overwhelmed.

The SEALs linked up with a few U.S. Army advisors and tried to determine what exactly they could do. Their element was too small to even consider stopping the large communist forces. The command post where the advisors were located had little in the way of armament, and the order of the day was to get some bigger weapons into action. The SEAL OIC was told that the U.S. CORDS compound (a U.S. AID program) about a mile downriver contained some larger ordnance. Half the SEAL platoon was sent back to the PBR to move to the location and attempt to retrieve the weapons. The small team of men found two jeeps and mounted a .50 caliber machine gun on one. They then drove at breakneck speed up the road to smash through to the command post once again. Enroute, they passed the hospital, which had been turned into a VC fortress. Heavy fire was exchanged and the jeeps received damage, but the SEALs made it to the command post unharmed.

The 2IC told the SEAL platoon OIC that ten U.S. civilians were missing from the CORDS compound. One of the U.S. Army advisors, Drew Dix, volunteered to lead a team to two likely locations where the civilians might be hiding, if they were still alive. No time could be lost. Six SEALs and the advisor raced through the streets, exchanging fire with the communists along the route. They screeched to a halt in front of the house of a twenty-four-year-old USAID nurse.

The VC had already penetrated the house and were tearing it apart looking for anything of value. The nurse remained hidden in a dresser bureau in the living room. As the VC descended from the top floor, she panicked and bolted for the back door. As she swung it open, she was met by startled VC in the backyard. Just then, two SEALs kicked in the front door. The nurse turned to run to the frogmen, but tripped and fell. With a clear field of fire, the SEALs opened up, and as the bullets hit the back door, it swung shut. The SEALs and the army advisor scooped up the nurse and sprinted for the jeep. As they sped away, the VC reached the front windows of the house and threw a volley of fire down the empty road behind them. The rest of the Americans were rescued in less dramatic fashion at a second location, but the SEALs were not through yet.

The Americans continued to fight the enemy forces for two more days. As South Vietnamese forces reentered the town from the north, they were slowed by heavy fighting. They had reached the marketplace, only to become bogged down. The 8th platoon split into two squads and attacked the VC from the rear. Before long, they had reached the vicinity of the market. The house-to-house fighting was fierce at times, but the SEALs used every weapon at their disposal, including a 57mm recoilless rifle. The VC had utilized a theater for a command post. The SEALs settled on a three-story building nearby for a better firing vantage point.

It was at this point that Petty Officer Third Class Ted Risher was hit by a single bullet. The VC were attempting to escape through the back of the square. A SEAL LDNN advisor returned suppressive fire. He stood in a door frame, waiting until Risher had been evacuated. A bullet splintered the frame and sent a fragment into his eyelid. He wiped the blood from his eyes and continued to return fire until all of the SEALs were safe.

The frogmen found an old station wagon and hurried Risher back to the PBR. The river craft had sustained twenty-eight bullet holes from its share of the fighting. While the SEALs fought from inside the town, the river force had been moving up and down the waterway, firing at every target of opportunity available. The SEALs, along with the nurse who was rescued earlier, tried to render emergency medical care, but Risher died.[21] The U.S. Army Special Forces advisor who had led the SEALs on the rescue of the U.S. civilians earlier had also been heavily involved in the street fighting. As an advisor to local PRU forces, he helped dislodge the enemy from the town. For his actions, he was later awarded the nation's highest medal for valor, the Medal of Honor.[22]

The Tet fighting was a military disaster for the communist forces. In a bloody counterattack, U.S. Marines dislodged the VC and NVA from the Citadel in Hue in savage house-to-house fighting[23] (see Map 2). The VC guerrilla forces were decimated and would never fully recover as a result. This caused the North Vietnamese to throw even more of its own conventional forces into the fighting, but at the same time, it removed the VC as a major obstacle to total Northern domination of the South if the communists were eventually victorious.

Politically, Tet proved to be a major disaster for the Americans. Although they defeated the communists in all fighting, the press reports made it appear as if the enemy were unchecked and could strike at will. The dramatic reports from the besieged U.S. embassy in Saigon only accentuated the problem. Just when the United States seemed to be making headway in the war, Tet exploded in the headlines of newspapers in the States. The final fact seemed to remain: the war was far from over, and 1968 was another presidential election year. When the entire impact of Tet had finally been felt in the States, President Johnson announced a de-escalation on the last day of March. He also announced he would not seek reelection.

As the final shots of Tet echoed across the battlefields, U.S. forces resumed their activities. For the SEALs, it was time to gain the offensive back and push the war into the communist base camps once again. Two men from the 8th platoon were part of a recon mission along the Cambodian border in the Seven Mountains region from 14 to 18 February (see Map 5). The SEALs dressed in black pajamas and carried sterile equipment and weapons, equipment that could not readily identify them as Americans. The SEALs passed themselves off to local inhabitants of the region as Russian advisors. During their mission, they verified the presence of over four hundred enemy soldiers in camps around the region.[24]

Beginning on 16 February, six SEALs from 8th platoon and two from the 7th platoon were utilized in a two-week experimental program in conjunction with PRU elements in Phong Dinh, Vinh Binh, Chau Doc, and Kien Giang provinces (see Map 3). The men operated in two-man groups in each of the provinces. The program was employed to exploit intelligence gathered by the units in a timely manner.[25] Also on the 16th, Bravo platoon from Team One failed to make contact on a night ambush and subsequently boarded a riverine craft for extraction. Having used a red lens flashlight to signal the boat to their position, the SEALs noted a similar signal from the far bank. The VC appeared to be attempting to lure the craft into an enemy ambush. The SEALs answered the signal with a volley of fire that extinguished the light for good. It was noted in the after-action report that the signals for extraction should be changed on each patrol to avoid setting up a potentially fatal pattern.[26]

A 60-man PRU force led by a U.S. SEAL officer captured 23 Vietcong in fighting during a mission in Ba Xuyen Province on 17 February (see Map 3). Twenty other VC were killed in the fighting, while the PRUs suffered one KIA.[27] Platoons again rotated and carried home the stories of the Tet fighting to those in the States. On 21 February, Mike platoon relieved Alfa platoon at Nha Be.[28] SEAL Team Two's 9th platoon relieved the 6th platoon in Vinh Long on 24 February[29] (see Map 5). Two SEAL platoons, along with a small riverine force and backed up by Seawolf helo gunships, swept both sides of the Thom canal in Kien Hoa Province on the 25th. Five VC were killed, and 51 suspects were captured. The combined force also destroyed 30 bunkers, 25 sampans, and 5 tons of rice.

On the morning of 6 March, Team Two's 7th platoon combined with a PRU element to engage a superior enemy force of at least company-size strength. The seven-hour encounter, which relied heavily on fire support from river craft and helo gunships, produced six VC killed, including the enemy company commander, and netted a small group of weapons. Intelligence later identified the enemy as the VC 531st Company and elements of the 509th Company.[30] On 9 March, a SEAL Team Two squad, operating with a large group of PRUs and regional forces, killed six Vietcong and captured one other. In their after-action report, the SEALs noted they felt most uncomfortable working with such a large force, and SEAL operations remained characteristically small throughout the war, normally no more than six- to seven-man squads. Such highly trained small teams that worked smoothly together due to almost daily patrols or training moved quietly and effectively throughout IV Corps.[31]

Led by a Vietnamese civilian whose father had been killed by the VC, a SEAL platoon killed a Vietcong hamlet security chief and two cadre on 10 March. They were then led to a hut containing a female VC communications officer. Assaulting the structure silently, the SEALs captured the enemy officer alive and then withdrew from the area.[32] The same night, a squad from Mike platoon initiated a riverine ambush on three sampans with an estimated six Vietcong passengers. Three of the enemy were confirmed killed, and two were captured with three hundred pounds of rice and a U.S.-made M3A1 submachine gun.³³

On 13 March 1968, 7th platoon from SEAL Team Two landed thirteen miles east of My Tho, deep in enemy territory off the Cua Tien River (see Map 5). After insertion, the group patrolled silently to the north for about a mile. They then split into two small squads, one moving off into the northeast, the other to the northwest. The first squad, Alfa, moving toward the northeast, engaged two VC and then suddenly heard an estimated fifty others off to their east. The squad evaded further to the north, calling helo support from gunships and troop carriers. The guerrillas pursued. Before the squad was picked up, it fought off twenty VC approaching from the east. The small group had been very fortunate while fighting the largely superior enemy forces. During the melee, the patrol leader himself had killed one VC with small-arms fire and another in hand-to-hand combat.

The other squad, Bravo, originally split off and patrolled to the northwest. Before long, it had infiltrated 5,000 meters, where it discovered an enemy battalion base camp. The team found a large barracks building and halted. The group was split, with three SEALs moving forward stealthily to investigate the structure. At about 0300, Interior Communications Electrician Senior Chief Bob Gallagher quietly led two others into the complex. Inside were approximately thirty Vietcong, who were asleep with all their personal weapons and equipment close at hand. A startled sentry discovered the group, and a vicious firefight at point-blank range broke out. Although half of the guerrillas were killed in the ferocious initial exchange, the SEALs suffered five men wounded. The officer in charge was hit so badly that he could no longer walk. The SEALs regrouped and began to evade as a large number of VC attempted to pursue. The less seriously wounded team members carried their more seriously wounded comrades. Gallagher, wounded in both legs, had downed five enemy soldiers himself in the initial fight. Now he led the squad on a desperate and treacherous retrograde action one thousand meters to the south. The VC combed the area with all available forces, passing at one time within thirty meters of the SEALs.

Helo support was called; as they neared, the SEALs marked their position with tracer fire by shooting into the air. The VC knew the group was in the area, but they could not distinguish the U.S. fire from their own. The helos pinpointed the frogmen and swooped in to recover them. As the helos were loaded, Gallagher assisted in holding off the attacking VC forces. He was again wounded, but managed to get himself and the rest of the squad out alive. Subsequent artillery fire and air strikes were called in to demolish the camp.[34] Speaking about Gallagher later, one SEAL commented: "They said he'd never walk again after his third tour in 'Nam. He walked and went back for a fourth tour."[35] For his actions on 13 March, ICCS Gallagher was awarded the nation's second highest medal for valor, the Navy Cross.

The following night, 8th platoon from Team Two established a riverine ambush three thousand meters out from an ARVN outpost. After about an hour, a lone VC in a sampan moved into the kill zone. Two SEALs hurled themselves from their ambush positions on the bank and landed on the craft, capturing the enemy soldier after a brief struggle. It was discovered through questioning that he was a member of a local VC battalion. The SEALs once again settled into their positions, and about half an hour later, six armed VC who entered the area were engaged and killed. The SEALs then used the previously captured sampan to recover the damaged craft. It was later discovered that the dead included the deputy battalion commander and three of his cadre, a company commander, and a reporter from Hanoi. A significant amount of communications equipment was also captured. As a result of the operation, the battalion was out of action temporarily, unable to launch an attack it had scheduled on Binh Thuy airfield.[36]

On 20 March, SEAL Team One's Delta platoon was teamed with armed navy helicopters in Operation Quick-Kill, seven miles southeast of Can Tho (see Map 5). After enemy forces fired on a riverine patrol, the reaction force was launched into the area and engaged the enemy in a three-hour firefight on May Island in the middle of the Bassac River. The riverboats, helo gunships, and SEALs accounted for 27 VC killed.[37] During the month, LDNN worked with SEALs on twenty-six different operations, accounting for 34 Vietcong killed, 2 captured, and 28 VC suspects detained. The combined actions of SEAL/LDNN units were beginning to reach a level of respectable results by spring 1968. Additionally, LDNN continued hull searches in the port of Saigon to thwart enemy sapper attacks.[38]

On 29 March, 7th platoon from Team Two combined with a squad from SEAL Team One's Delta platoon for a small raid ten miles south of Ben Tre (see Map 5). Guided by a former VC (Hoi Chanh), the group inserted and patrolled silently to a target area around four indigenous huts, surrounding the structures and preparing to sweep through the objective. Before they could begin, two armed VC walked into the security element of the unit. The enemy soldiers were engaged in hand-to-hand combat and killed before they could warn their comrades. The SEALs then attacked and held the site, killing two more Vietcong as they attempted to escape. The Hoi Chanh located a well-camouflaged arms cache hidden in one of the huts. This particular cache included a complete grenade factory. A villager then led the team to a second cache in another nearby hut. The captured equipment and weaponry was quickly loaded into a PBR, but a receding tide forced the SEALs to destroy most of the ordnance in place. It turned out that the cache was the largest to be captured to date in the entire Mekong Delta and included:

- 28 Claymore mines
- 30 water mines
- 2 German machine guns
- 2 M-1 carbines
- 2 75mm recoilless rifles
- 5 120mm homemade rockets and launchers

25 Chinese communist (CHICOM) grenades
19 C/S (combat teargas) grenades
50 electrical blasting caps
7 boxes Vietcong grenades
8 cases CHICOM ammunition
1 CHICOM carbine
1 box medical supplies
20 pounds ordnance documents

Additionally, numerous fuses, primers, and blasting caps were discovered as well. General Westmoreland sent a personal "well done" to the unit for the operation.[39]

The SEALs were now finding regular success in their patrols, and oftentimes teamed up with PRUs, LDNN, and other SEAL platoons on their missions. On 7 April, Team Two's 7th platoon and Team One's Delta platoon engaged an estimated VC platoon in a heavy firefight four miles northeast of Vinh Long (see Map 5). The two units had set up separate sites about a mile away from each other. After first light, the 7th fired on the forward element of the VC force and received heavy counterfire. The SEALs beat a hasty retreat to a landing zone, where helos picked them up. Delta platoon first moved to their assistance and then finally made it back to the river for extraction by boat. Five VC were killed before both units extracted.[40] The next day, LDNN Training Class III from Vung Tau captured five suspected VC members and returned them for questioning. Attrition rates for the Vietnamese trainees were comparable to those of the Americans in BUD/S training. LDNN Training Class III retained thirty-eight LDNN trainees by the end of April.[41]

Team Two's 10th platoon relieved the 7th on 22 April at My Tho.[42] In one of their first operations in-country, the 10th platoon was guided to a Vietcong meeting by a VC defector. After the SEALs secured the area, the defector pointed out six cadre, who were then detained and turned over to the National Police. Once interrogated, the VC gave information that led to the arrest of over one hundred other guerrillas in the My Tho area. These Vietcong had infiltrated every U.S. and Allied agency and military unit in My Tho.

Their arrests denied the enemy vital intelligence utilized in hit-and-run guerrilla attacks. It was also a frightening indicator of how deeply the VC and North Vietnamese had penetrated the government.[43] On 26 April, Bravo platoon listened to deceptive Vietcong radio calls during their extraction. Local enemy forces were attempting to lure the navy riverine craft into a trap by making the members on the boat believe that the SEALs needed an emergency pickup. The Boat Support Units (BSUs) were always ready to press into a firefight to extract a SEAL patrol in trouble. Such a deceptive call could easily have made an inexperienced crew fall into a VC trap. Once again, the Vietcong proved the depth of their resourcefulness.[44]

On 25 April, one of the three SEAL Team One platoons that had been working in the RSSZ was transferred into the IV Corps region to begin operations in the Mekong Delta. It was during the next three weeks that SEAL Team One detachments suffered five fatalities. On 29 April, Boatswain's Mate First Class Walter Pope was killed accidently by nonhostile machine-gun fire while enroute to an operational area.[45] On 6 May, Petty Officer Second Class David Devine was killed in action when he drowned during a beach insertion along the Ham Loung River.[46] Both deaths occurred in Kien Hoa Province (see Map 3). Storekeeper Second Class Donald Zillgitt was killed by small-arms fire on 12 May while leading a team of fifty-three PRUs in Vinh Binh Province. The team was sent to counterattack a Vietcong force that had overrun the hamlet of Giang Lon, three miles northwest of Phu Vinh (see Map 5). After landing by helicopter about mid-day just south of the hamlet, the PRUs came in heavy contact and were pinned down in a rice paddy. Before long, they were about to be overwhelmed. Zillgitt deployed the men, then led two fierce assaults against the communists. On the second attack, he fell mortally wounded. His PRUs continued the assault, driving the communists out of the hamlet and killing seventeen of their number.[47] Three days later, Petty Officer First Class Donnie Patrick from Mike platoon was killed by an explosion, believed to have been a mine, in Vinh Long

Province. The explosion occurred as the platoon was inserting from a riverine craft four miles southeast of Cho Loch (see Map 5). Mike platoon stood down until the end of the month due to the injuries sustained by seven other SEALs in the same incident.[48] Finally, on 19 May, Chief Electrician's Mate Gordon Brown was killed by a booby trap while leading a PRU patrol in Kien Giang Province (see Map 3). He was moving to investigate a wooden box discovered by his patrol when the device detonated. Six of his PRU force were seriously wounded.[49] The fatalities were a grim reminder of the hazardous daily missions the frogmen conducted, almost always deep within territory controlled by the communists.

In the early hours of the morning of 11 May, Team Two's 3rd platoon initiated an ambush on a large guerrilla force. The enemy soldiers countered and pinned the Americans down, wounding the SEAL patrol leader. Although wounded, the officer called in close air support on the superior VC unit and led a stiff attack on the communists. As a result, the frogmen were able to extract successfully. On 14 May, 8th platoon became engaged with an 82-man, well-trained and equipped enemy force near the Cambodian border, twelve miles south of Chau Doc (see Map 5). The SEALs had set an ambush along a reported VC infiltration route, soon discovering that their intelligence was quite accurate. The VC had the SEALs pinned down in a graveyard for four hours, while the frogmen moved from tombstone to tombstone returning a heavy volume of fire. The communist force had come from across the border, and each time they attempted to overwhelm the SEALs, they were beaten back. Just as it seemed the Americans were finished, Navy Seawolf helo gunships arrived overhead and, with artillery support to add punch, drove the enemy back across the border. The OIC of the SEALs, who led his team back to base without a single casualty, later declared he thought the fight was the end of the road for his platoon until support arrived. Twenty-four enemy soldiers were killed and an additional forty wounded.[50]

On 16 May, a combined SEAL/PRU element struck out into enemy territory to search for a Vietcong unit that had mortared Chau Doc. The team, which came under heavy attack from mortars, RPGs, and automatic weapons, utilized helo assets for fire support. They patrolled nearly 1,500 meters to a small pagoda, where a large firefight erupted. The unit moved to a clearing and extracted at about 2100. The next day, an ARVN sweep located thirty-six guerrillas killed by the fighting.[51] Before the end of the month, Delta platoon worked with several men of EOD to destroy a 750-pound bomb in a recently-vacated VC base camp.[52]

In the spring, 200,000 antiwar protestors had joined in New York to demonstrate against the war. Martin Luther King and Robert Kennedy were assassinated. The summer brought urban riots in black communities on a huge scale. Unrest at home seemed to be a hallmark for the year 1968, but in Vietnam, the war continued.

The larger successes enjoyed by the SEAL platoons during the spring of 1968 surpassed the previous gains of earlier years. Although SEAL casualties had occurred, especially in Team One units, the general attitude of the men was bold and aggressive. It was not uncommon for SEAL platoons to attack a much larger group of enemy troops. On one mission, while embarked on riverboats, a patrol struck a group that turned out to be the rear security element for two VC battalions. Rather than break contact, the SEALs initiated a heavy volume of fire and then struck ashore to press the attack. After a fierce, fifteen-minute firefight, the communist forces broke and ran.[53] On yet another operation, on a dark, rainy night, six SEALs discovered three huts in enemy territory. Sneaking into one and returning, a SEAL scout reported seeing six to eight weapons inside next to a number of sleeping men. The patrol leader multiplied this by three (for the number of hootches) to estimate a force of about eighteen to twenty-four men. Considering the SEALs still had the element of surprise, he felt the odds were about even. The team split up and set directional Claymore mines facing the huts. They were able to kill nineteen guerrillas without firing a gunshot.[54]

UDT, meanwhile, continued to survey hundreds of miles of coastline. In May, Det Bravo from UDT 12 surveyed the

Hon Heo Peninsula ten miles north of Nha Trang (see Map 2). Many of the surveys were routine. Many were not. On a large number of operations, the lightly armed frogmen came under frequent attack, particularly from sniper fire.[55] Mostly exposed and with little cover, they conducted their work in the open surf and on beaches, sustaining several casualties. When they were not fighting the enemy, they were braving the elements. They were also instrumental in many salvage, rescue, and body recovery operations.[56] On 25 May, UDT 12's Det Foxtrot, located onboard the USS *Thomaston* (LSD 28), assisted in the recovery of fourteen men who had been aboard a CH-46 helicopter that went into the ocean astern of the USS *Valley Forge*. All hands were saved without serious injury.[57]

Late the following month, Team Two's 9th platoon killed a communist propaganda team that traveled from hamlet to hamlet in attempts to coerce the populace into supporting the guerrilla struggle. Eight VC were captured and three other suspects who were detained turned out to be Cambodians brought into the region by the communists to assist the VC agricultural effort. They had been undergoing political indoctrination when captured.[58]

On 6 June, Juliett platoon relieved Bravo platoon at Nha Be.[59] On the 21st, Mike platoon killed nine VC on a patrol while searching for a reported arms factory during a seven-hour operation on the west bank of the Co Chien River four miles north northwest of Phu Vinh[60] (see Map 5). Delta platoon was called upon to dive to the wreckage of a helicopter that crashed into the Long Tau River just a few hundred meters from the Nha Be helo pad (see Map 6). Four bodies of U.S. servicemen were recovered.[61]

On 26 June, Juliett platoon killed eight Vietcong in two sampans in a riverine ambush, five miles north of Phu Vinh; three days later, a squad from Juliett ran down eight more enemy soldiers who attempted to evade their patrol. During the three-hour patrol, the enemy forces were encountered on an island in the Co Chien River, seven miles northwest of Phu Vinh. All the VC were dispatched in the fighting.[62] Mike platoon captured two enemy troops and killed four others in two separate ambushes on 29 and 30 June.[63]

Det Bravo from UDT 12 had been working from the USS *Diachenko* (APD 123). Around this time, it attempted a survey of a beach where VC activity had been reported. Two prior attempts to recon the beach had resulted in the frogmen coming under fire and being forced from the shore. This time, flank security was again established as the men worked with minimal weaponry. Again, the UDT men came under attack. Weapons fire erupted from the nearby jungle, and three VC soldiers charged the group. One of the young frogmen on security hit the middle guerrilla with a 40mm grenade. It exploded and dropped all three Vietcong. The rest of the frogmen retreated into the water, firing as they went. Offshore, supporting vessels added gunfire to help the team extract. This time, all the men were recovered safely. It had been another close call.[64]

Another Detachment of UDT 12, Det Delta, continued to assist the U.S. Naval Support Activity at Danang (see Map 2). When the communists blocked modes of transportation by demolishing bridges or sinking boats in narrow channels and rivers, Delta was often called upon to demolish the obstructions. At other times, they assisted the Danang Harbor security when suspicious underwater activity was detected in the vital harbor. The VC and NVA sappers were good at their work, and many were trained in surface swimmer attacks. A few were even trained in scuba attacks.[65]

UDT 11 was awarded the Navy Unit Commendation for similar operations, involving ordnance disposal and search and salvage operations, between August 1968 and March 1969. Especially noted was its assistance in two major amphibious assaults: Bold Mariner and Valiant Hunt.[66] During many of their clearance operations, their waterborne explosions produced a number of large sea bass and other fish. Dubbed "DuPont Fishing," their lures often supplied local Vietnamese with another meal following the blasts.[67]

In the Mekong Delta, UDT's Det Golf patrolled with the riverine forces. When Vietcong bunkers and complexes were discovered, the frogmen would be sent into enemy territory to demolish the facilities. Sometimes they were called upon to search for the bodies of Americans lost among the inland and coastal waterways. In one instance during July, UDT 12's Det Golf recovered the body of an important U.S. Army colonel. He was lost when the helicopter he was embarked upon crashed into a river. Authorities feared he had been captured when he could not be located. The recovery was conducted under enemy fire.[68]

The activities of the UDT men in the Mekong Delta region allowed SEALs to concentrate on only combat patrols. Earlier in the war, SEALs were often called upon to conduct demolition and recovery operations. By mid-1968, these duties were generally a UDT mission, although SEALs were still involved from time to time. The UDT men were engaged frequently by enemy forces with small arms and constantly ran the gauntlet of VC river ambushes. Their toughest assignment was to disable Vietcong booby traps by blowing them in place. Large air-dropped ordnance was oftentimes secured by the guerrillas after it would fail to detonate. The VC would utilize every item they could get their hands on to booby-trap their facilities against U.S. and ARVN patrols. In July, a second UDT Det in the Mekong Delta was established to support CTF 117, the Mobile Riverine Forces. Detachment Hotel operated originally from the USS *Windham County* (LST 1171).[69] The increased work load on the West Coast UDT Teams resulted in the formation of a third team out of San Diego, UDT 13. The command was recommissioned (after having served earlier in World War II) on 1 July 1968.[70]

The SEALs attached to PRU units continued to contribute against selected VC infrastructure targets. In July, Frank Bomar, who stood 6 feet 4 inches and weighed 240 pounds, led a Vietnamese raiding party on a mission to capture a known Vietcong village chief. The unit was ambushed and attacked from three sides. Bomar directed close air support and raced 250 yards through gunfire to carry a wounded South Vietnamese to safety. He then led the Vietnamese on a fierce attack on the village, leaving the VC chief and eight other communist soldiers dead. He later received the nation's third highest award for valor during the operation, the Silver Star. Up until December 1969, Bomar had spent five combat tours as a SEAL in Vietnam, more than most frogmen. He would return for more.[71]

In July, a new twenty-four-foot, aluminum hull Light SEAL Support Craft (LSSC) arrived in-country. Designed to insert and extract the maritime commandos, the boat had a "V" hull and was powered by two 427 cubic-inch gasoline engines that drove water-jet pumps.[72] Before long, the craft was used to launch SEAL squads on a variety of operations.

Luck still played a part in the interdiction of guerrillas. Squads of men, at the right place and time, scored significant successes against the communists. A SEAL ambush on 2 July killed three VC, with two other probable kills nine miles east of Saigon. One of the dead was identified as an enemy artillery battalion commander. Another was thought to be an artillery staff officer who had been involved in numerous 122mm rocket attacks on Saigon. Indications were that he was enroute for another such mission on the night the SEALs interdicted.[73] Another ambush on the 16th, six miles east of Saigon, killed two Vietcong. Divers the following day recovered several assault rifles and over four hundred rounds of ammunition from the ambush site.[74]

On the 20th, a SEAL patrol inserted twenty-eight miles west of My Tho to ambush a known VC tax extortionist operating in the area. The enemy cadre was spotted several hundred meters away from the ambush position in the early hours of the morning, along with three armed Vietcong. Across a canal and too far away to be reliably engaged with small-arms fire, the frogmen called in helo gunships on the enemy position, but were unable to confirm any casualties.[75] Another small action on the same day by five SEALs and seven PRUs netted one VC killed, twelve miles southeast of My Tho, in the hours before dawn.[76]

Vietnamese LDNN Replacement Class III (Vietnamese SEALs) was graduated 22 June from training. The class was composed of two officers and thirty-eight enlisted. Immediately following graduation, they were given four weeks of

Upon receipt of the first Presidential Unit Citation from Lyndon Johnson in January 1968, members of SEAL Team One pose for photographers.

Prior to deploying to Vietnam, SEAL weapons familiarization training included communist bloc weaponry like this AK-47 assault rifle used by a West Coast frogman at the SEAL desert training site in southern California (above). Trained to take prisoners for intelligence collection, these SEALs rehearse with as much realism as possible (left).

Riverine extraction at the completion of a SEAL operation in Vietnam (below).

Special Warfare units train never to leave men behind. Here a SEAL squad rehearses a wounded-man drill. In Vietnam, no frogman was left on the missing in action or prisoner of war rolls.

UDT men performed reconnaissance on thousands of miles of coastline along Vietnam using both overt and clandestine methods like the one shown.

In preparation for the many canal and river crossings during patrols in Vietnam, these SEALs train along the Alamo River in southern California (left). The grey UDT life jacket was always worn by personnel for swimming and patrolling. It literally saved many lives (top and left).

A quiet insertion up a Vietnamese canal (below).

Training for Vietnam. A crouching SEAL team member holds the M3A1 submachine gun, better known as the "Grease Gun." This .45-caliber weapon was a holdover from the World War II and Korean War UDT battlefronts. The K-Bar knife with an MK13 day/night flare taped to the sheath is another UDT/SEAL mainstay (below). Moving upriver for another mission in the Mekong Delta (bottom). The 9mm Smith & Wesson M76 submachine gun, used extensively by SEALs (right).

UDT frogmen being towed to sea for a recovery via submarine following a clandestine reconnaissance. Note the periscope forward of the lead rubber boat (top). Life jacket built into a camouflage vest, designed especially for UDT/SEAL teams in Vietnam (right).

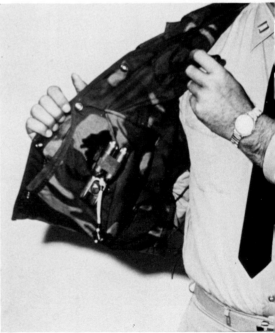

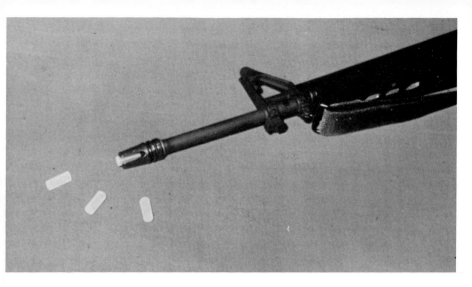

Mud plugs developed for frogman M16s to prevent barrels from becoming clogged with mud (top). CAR-15 with a Starlight scope for night vision. Such devices, used in riverine ambushes, allowed snipers to identify Vietcong guerrillas moving on waterways after dark (left). The 7.62mm mini-guns were used from riverine craft and helicopters to add firepower to SEAL support (bottom).

The 40mm, hand-cranked Honeywell MK18 grenade launcher was first used successfully from riverine craft in support of SEAL operations (left). The duckbill provided a horizontal dispersal pattern of shot from the Ithaca shotgun (below).

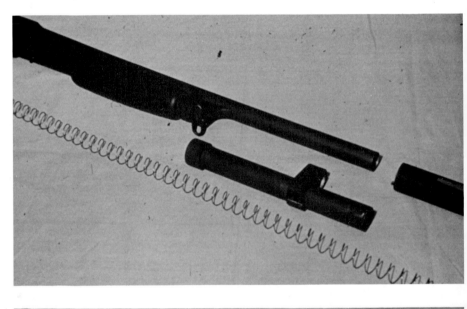

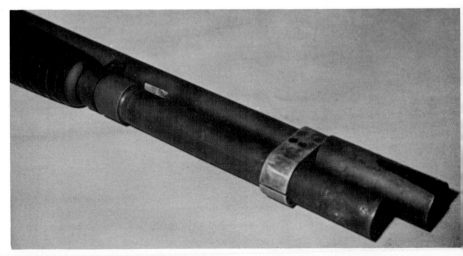

Seawolf helicopters provided transport, medevac, and vital fire support to operations in the Delta region (above). A SEAL squad carried a heavier array of weaponry to provide more firepower during its forays into Vietcong sanctuaries. This seven-man squad carries two 7.62mm M60 light machine guns, as well as the 5.56mm Stoner, M16, and 40mm M203 grenade launcher (top). Regular camouflage fatigues as well as tiger stripes were used extensively during operations (left).

South Vietnamese frogmen, named LDNN, worked daily with American SEALs during the war (top). A SEAL platoon loads a riverine craft prior to a mission in the Delta. Note the variety of weaponry, equipment, and uniform (including blue jeans). Such dress was common among SEAL and UDT units (above).

Frogmen cross one of numerous canals during a SEAL patrol in the Mekong Delta. The man in the center of the waterway holds a Stoner light machine gun (left). An experimental three-barrel grenade launcher tested by SEALs (below). Similar to an M79, this experimental pump-action 40mm grenade launcher was also tested by SEALs (bottom).

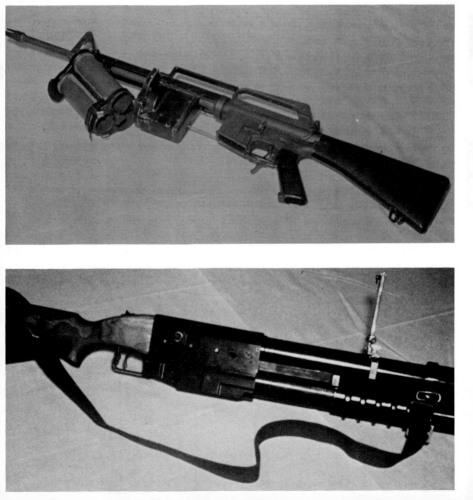

Receiving an operations order prior to a mission in Vietnam. Note the blue jeans, mixed uniforms, and Stoner 63, all trademarks of SEAL operations (top). Into the hinterland — Vietcong territory in the Mekong Delta (right). The M3A1 .45-caliber Grease Gun was an old submachine gun that saw wide service with the teams in earlier years. The M3A1 fired reliably right out of the water (below).

As advisers, SEALs saw extensive action in Vietnam (top). The M1911 .45-caliber automatic and the 9mm Smith & Wesson M39, the main sidearms of frogmen in Vietnam (left).

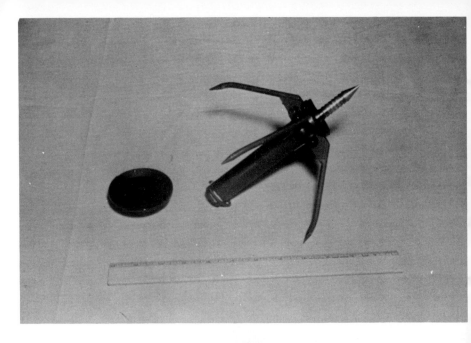

This grappling hook was developed especially for retrieving sampans after a SEAL ambush. This device was fired from the end of an M16, utilizing a bullet trap arrangement to prevent loss of Vietcong craft that sprang SEAL ambushes. In the early years of the war, many VC bodies, along with equipment and weaponry, could not be recovered due to the lack of such equipment (top). The Stoner 63 weapons system, used with great success by SEALs in Vietnam. These SEALs fire both the long- and short-barreled versions at the desert camp in southern California (right).

The 9mm Carl Gustav "Swedish K" submachine gun, also utilized by UDT and SEAL platoons in Vietnam.

Launch and recovery operations from the USS *Grayback*, designed specifically for clandestine UDT/SEAL operations (above and left).

The 40mm M79 grenade launcher was another weapon frequently utilized by UDT and SEALs. This weapon could be used straight out of the water with little preparation (top). Camp Kerrey SEAL training area in the desert near Alton Sea, California, as it appeared in the 1970s. The camp was utilized extensively by West Coast frogmen to prepare for operations in WESTPAC, including Vietnam. The camp was renamed in the mid-eighties for Billy Machen, the first SEAL Team One fatality of the Vietnam War (above).

advanced training at Vung Tau. Already combat veterans from their actions during the Tet Offensive, the class was put out on a large ambush as their first official combat operation.

The mission took place in Phuoc Tuy Province, thirty miles southeast of Saigon, on 19 and 20 July. U.S. SEAL advisors accompanied the force as it lay on a river. Just after midnight, one of the three LDNN squads fired on four unlighted sampans as they traveled into their ambush. Two of the craft were sunk and two VC killed. In short order, two more sampans entered the kill zone and were destroyed, with three more Vietcong killed. Two more sampans entered another LDNN squad's area and were fired upon, killing three more VC and capturing two others. Two more enemy soldiers were seen wading in water near the original LDNN squad position and were killed. The third LDNN squad used two Claymore mines to destroy yet two other sampans and kill an additional five Vietcong. The unit extracted at 0345 after a very successful night of hit-and-run against the communist insurgents.[77]

Hotel platoon relieved Delta platoon as part of Det Golf on 30 July.[78] SEAL patrols continued to sting the enemy in the Delta, but paid the price in return. On 2 August, Machinist's Mate First Class Joseph Albrecht from Team Two's 9th platoon was killed by a booby-trapped grenade while on a three-day operation with a PRU force in the Seven Mountains region near the Cambodian border (see Map 5). The platoon was on its last mission of the deployment; it withdrew after it became obvious that the mission could not be completed against the well-entrenched enemy forces. Booby traps were spiked throughout the entire area. One other SEAL was wounded in the incident.[79]

A SEAL Team Two squad laid an ambush along a known communications route on 11 August. Just before midnight, an estimated fifteen VC approached from the west and entered the kill zone. The SEALs immediately initiated an assault, killing five of the enemy, but were then taken under fire from four different positions. The frogmen called in mortar fire from a riverine boat and proceeded to evade south, where they were extracted about an hour later.[80]

On 15 August, a combined SEAL Team Two platoon and PRU force hit a VC political school seven miles southeast of Go Cong (see Map 5). In a brief firefight, six enemy soldiers were killed and one captured. An agent later confirmed that seventeen enemy troops had been killed.[81]

On the same day, Storekeeper First Class Robert Wagner of SEAL Team One was killed twelve miles southeast of Ben Tre in Vinh Binh Province (see Map 5). He, too, had been killed by a booby trap during a recon patrol as a PRU advisor when a scout element attempted to pursue two fleeing Vietnamese. He had sustained fatal shrapnel wounds to the head and body from the incident and had been taken by medevac to Dong Tam.[82]

Five days later, Warrant Officer Eugene Tinnin of Juliett platoon was killed in a tragic accident on a patrol in Vinh Long Province, nine miles northwest of Mo Cay. After inserting by PBR, the unit patrolled to investigate a reported Vietcong squad base. Encountering a pagoda, four SEALs were left in ambush to keep the area secured and under observation in the early morning hours before dawn. Tinnin and five others patrolled further to try to locate a second reported structure. In the darkness, the men mistakenly circled back into the ambushing element's kill zone. Just prior to firing, both units were in radio contact with each other and believed they were some distance apart. Believing that a VC unit had entered their ambush, the first SEAL squad initiated fire. Tinnin was killed, and four other SEALs were injured in the affair (see Map 5). One of two LDNN accompanying the patrol was also wounded.[83] Tinnin was later buried at sea.

On another raid on the 17th, a SEAL Team Two patrol made contact with a local VC company. Although the frogmen managed to kill only one of the enemy, the man turned out to be the company commander.[84] On the 24th, an East Coast patrol combined with a PRU element to destroy a hospital complex and capture another grenade factory eight miles southeast of Go Cong near the mouth of the My Tho River (see Map 5). While moving toward their initial objective, they ran head-long into a forty-man Vietcong force that broke from the contact. Forty hootches were destroyed at the hospital site. Twenty-five VC were engaged at the factory, but they, too, chose to break and run. Also captured were the following:

6 82mm mortar rounds

9 61mm mortar rounds

25 105mm recoilless rifle rounds

21 grenades

3 kilos of documents

Additionally, numerous grenade molds and tools were captured, and thirty-two Vietcong were killed in the operation. During their extraction, the team came under indirect enemy weapons fire and had to call in support of their own from helo gunships and an LCM on a nearby river.[85]

On 28 August, the Joint Personnel Recovery Center (JPRC) received word from Can Tho in the Delta that two Vietnamese had escaped a VC POW camp the night before (see Map 5). Responsible for the coordination of prisoner recovery efforts, the JPRC sent a representative to the town to debrief the escapees. The former prisoners stated that the camp contained about thirty-five Vietnamese and eight American prisoners. A raiding party was immediately called for and a local PRU force, led by an American SEAL, was assigned the mission.

It was reported that the camp was guarded by only eight Vietcong. JPRC provided the raiders with special equipment, including radios, infrared strobe lights, a life raft, explosive bolt cutters, and Starlight night-vision scopes, which allowed a man to see in the night. The American frogman led a team of nine PRUs on an infiltration of the area on the night of 30 August. The group launched the operation after staging at an ARVN outpost. A 60-man PRU force stood ready to assault the camp in helos once called by the small ground force. The infiltration group was guided across a river by an orbiting aircraft and began a stealthy target approach under darkness. At dawn, the raiders were prematurely discovered while penetrating the target, but immediately pressed the attack. The sixty-man PRU force landed around the area from the helos and attempted to seal off the camp. Two of the guards were killed while the others fled the site. Forty-nine Vietnamese were freed, but the eight U.S. POWs reported to be at the complex had been previously moved on 28 August.[86] This was the type of operation that SEALs were designed to execute. Although this operation was conducted skillfully, U.S. planners were to find that precise and especially timely intelligence was an absolute key to full mission success. Throughout the Vietnam War and into the following decades, the United States would find that it would consistently fail to react quickly enough to employ special operations forces effectively.

The following night, a SEAL Team One platoon combined with an eighteen-man PRU force led by a U.S. SEAL to hit a reported meeting of district-level VC cadre and three village chiefs. The SEALs set up security as the PRU force began to close for the attack. Suddenly, a VC squad initiated fire on the SEAL rear security element, which in turn opened fire. The PRU force struck the objective immediately, having lost the element of surprise. Four enemy soldiers were killed in the encounter.[87] In the last week of August, 4th platoon from Team Two traveled to the Delta to relieve 9th platoon.[88] By this time in 1968, it was rare to find a SEAL who did not have a tour in Vietnam.

Another Team Two squad made contact during an ambush on 9 September and killed two enemy soldiers.[89] SEAL Team Two's Lt. Fredrick Trani was killed on the 14th by a booby trap while leading an LDNN patrol.[90] The 3rd platoon received word that a PRU agent, who had been captured by the communists but later escaped, was hiding out in a VC-controlled hamlet disguised as a Vietcong. The agent was awaiting rescue. The SEALs penetrated the area on 15 September and successfully rescued the agent, killing three enemy soldiers and capturing three VC cadre. The cadre led the frogmen and a PRU force to several arms caches in the next few days. The capture included the following:

    1 82mm mortar
    2 60mm mortars
    2 rocket launchers

3 machine guns
4 rifles
40 antiarmor grenades
5,800 small arms rounds [91]

Two nights later, one squad from 3rd platoon reacted to
a VC rocket attack on a merchant vessel that occurred the
same day in the Long Tau shipping channel. The SEALs
conducted a night ambush in the RSSZ and killed all six
of the VC rocket team, capturing their weapons.[92] A team
of SEALs also operated in the Qhi Nhon Peninsula in II
Corps for a profitable two-week period (see Map 2). On the
19th, a SEAL unit ambushed a VC mortar crew enroute to
Qui Nhon, where it had intended to mortar the city. The
ambush effectively thwarted the enemy operation.[93] Ten
pounds of valuable documents describing future VC plans
to attack the area and listing some of the local infrastructure
were captured. On 3 October, five SEALs and two LDNN
led a thirty-five-man PRU force against a small enemy complex
that had fired on their patrol six miles southwest of My Tho
(see Map 5). Seven VC were killed and one captured, along
with a small amount of weapons and documents.[94]

These various operations illustrate the continued
operational success of the SEAL squads. Much of their value
was just beginning to stem from intelligence nets the SEALs
themselves were establishing in their own areas of operation.
In most areas, the strength of the frogmen gained the
confidence of the local inhabitants, who sometimes provided
important and critical information.

In early October, a Vietnamese woman provided intelligence regarding a POW camp in which her husband was
being held. A combined SEAL/PRU force inserted on Con
Coc Island (77 miles southwest of Saigon at the mouth of
the Bassac River) from six PBRs before dawn on 6 October
to conduct a raid on the facility (see Map 5). They overran
the camp, capturing two VC guards and a large amount of
documents and money. The camp was destroyed, along with
a tax collection station. Also secured in the raid were twenty-
four Vietnamese prisoners, some of whom had been held

since the Tet Offensive earlier in the year.

Twelve miles north of My Tho on the same day, another squad of SEALs and a SEAL-led PRU force broke into yet another VC POW camp after being led to the facility by two wives of inmates (see Map 5). The rescue team traveled three hours up the Bassac River to insert by riverine craft. The SEAL squad led the final assault in order to quickly cut off the guards from the prisoners. In this manner, they could protect the POWs during the firefight by preventing the Vietcong from firing into the prisoner cages as they fled the camp. The SEALs fired their weapons slightly high initially so as not to accidently hit the POWs. Seven VC were killed and two more guards were captured, as were numerous documents. Twenty-six Vietnamese prisoners were also liberated.[95] One SEAL who was on the operation later described a highly emotional scene as the frogmen secured the camp and helped the liberated prisoners back to the extraction boats.

During October and November, a series of maritime operations under the code name Bold Dragon was executed. This series marked the first coordinated operations of that size under the direct control of the Chief of Naval Operations, Vietnam. The force included two SEAL platoons operating from U.S. naval vessels off the coast and supported by army and navy helo gunships. Phase I was conducted off Long Tau and Ba Xuyen, while Phase II was off Phu Quc Island[96] (see Map 2). Also throughout October and November, numerous small ambushes made contact, stinging the VC forces and keeping them off balance. SEAL Det Bravo, the PRU advisors, was expanded from one officer and twelve enlisted to include thirteen officers and twenty-one enlisted on 4 October.[97]

During an operation on 10 and 11 October, Yeoman Third Class Gary Gallagher was serving as one of those PRU advisors in the Mekong Delta. The mission of his unit was to capture prisoners for intelligence purposes. As the unit patrolled, several enemy troops were captured and detained. The force split into two different groups and advanced along two different banks of a canal. Vietcong were believed to be in the immediate vicinity, and it was at this point that one of the prisoners let out a loud warning to his comrades in the field. The half of the patrol on the opposite bank from Gallagher immediately began to receive a heavy volume of small-arms fire from a numerically superior force. Gallagher realized that he had to link up the entire unit to extract safely from the area. He took control of the prisoners and led his half of the team across the canal. On the other side, he rallied his men and directed their fire. Their heavy and accurate return volley temporarily suppressed the enemy, and Gallagher was able to immediately lead his men in a hasty but controlled withdrawal. Before completing the extraction, he revived a seriously wounded companion and physically carried the man over eight kilometers to safety. For his actions, he was later awarded the Navy Cross.[98]

Three separate actions on 21 October netted four VC killed and four sampans destroyed ten miles south of Saigon.[99] The month ended on a fatal note as Petty Officer Second Class Roberto Ramos from SEAL Team Two's 4th platoon was killed on the 29th during a combined SEAL/PRU operation. Ramos was one of three U.S. SEALs leading a one hundred-man PRU force when it contacted a Vietcong battalion. He was hit by small-arms fire twenty-nine miles south of Long Xuyen. Fixed-wing and Cobra gunships were called to help the unit break contact[100] (see Map 3).

SEAL Team Two's 5th platoon relieved the 10th at My Tho in late October. In the six months to come, the 5th platoon would find that squad-size operations would still yield the greatest results for the average SEAL unit. It also would find that the use of indigenous sampans for insertions and movements would be very helpful, as well as more clandestine for patrols, so long as the external appearances were changed regularly. Like other platoons, the 5th would find that the use of indigenous personnel dressed similarly to enemy forces, such as in black pajamas and carrying Soviet weaponry, would almost always be readily taken in by villagers and provided with information on enemy activity in the area.

A SEAL ambush on 15 November four miles southwest of My Tho engaged ten Vietcong as they moved about the area. A sharp firefight followed, killing five of the enemy. As the SEALs moved to extract by helo, mortar fire was placed into the area.[101]

A combined SOG team consisting of six Vietnamese and several U.S. SEALs penetrated fourteen kilometers into the Le Hong Phong Forest on 21 November in search of a reported Vietcong hamlet. A prisoner captured by a SOG team on another operation had revealed the existence of the previously unknown hamlet. The area was well beyond the reach of artillery, and thus no friendly unit had ventured into the forest. After an all-night penetration, the team found the hamlet and killed several guerrillas, as well as capturing the complete files of the assistant VC village chief.

On 22 November, Electronics Technician Third Class James Sanders from SEAL Team One died while in Saigon, though not as a result of hostilities. Two days later, Alfa squad from SEAL Team Two's 4th platoon made a night insertion close to the Cambodian border. Its mission was to locate an enemy base camp and place it under observation to gather intelligence. While moving to their planned recon point, a lone VC soldier was sighted in an open field just after first light. Two of the SEALs were sent to stalk the soldier and attempt to capture him. The VC soldier detected their approach, and a brief firefight ensued, resulting in the enemy's death. Immediately after, the nearby base camp on Da Dung Mountain, now fully alerted, used its firepower against the SEALs. The incoming fire included .50 caliber machine guns, mortars, 40mm grenades, and a heavy volume of small arms. The main body of SEALs returned fire to cover the stalking pair, allowing them to seek cover. The patrol fell back, and a large VC force began pursuit. Helos were called in for support. While they provided covering fire, the SEAL patrol leader and one other member broke from the main group, located the two separated stalkers, and returned all hands to the security perimeter of men. The team then extracted.[102]

The heavy contact only convinced the SEALs that the camp

was a lucrative target. On 7 December, the frogmen returned once again to the base camp and set up their observation post undetected. Helo gunships were called in to engage the camp. About an hour later, the helos were called in once more, while the SEALs assisted with automatic weapons and mortar fire. The enemy returned a heavy volume of fire, and the SEALs fell back to avoid encirclement. Shortly after, they extracted. Fifteen VC were confirmed killed and twenty-nine wounded.[103]

From 16 to 23 December, UDT 11's DETs Bravo, Golf, and India combined to assist riverine forces on operation Silver Mace. The forces conducted the first UDT inland waterborne demolition raid of the war and cleared over fourteen miles of enemy-dominated waterways.[104] Det Delta, from the same team, recovered the first Det 10 reconnaissance drone on 11 December.[105] At the end of the year, Team Two's 6th platoon relieved 3rd platoon at Binh Thuy.[106]

Throughout 1968, Naval Special Warfare Units had been at the peak of their operating proficiency. The random hit-and-miss contact patrols and ambushes from the early years now gave way to operations that reacted on intelligence. Much of the intelligence was gleaned from networks being developed by the SEAL platoons in their respective areas. Although the ambush was still used heavily, more raids were now conducted to strike specific point targets. The VC lost numerous important arms and ordnance caches, as well as medical supplies and facilities during the year. Other operations teamed SEAL-advised PRU and LDNN units with SEAL platoons in more sophisticated combined missions. Their small-unit actions carried the war deep into the enemies' denied areas and extracted a heavy price from them. The increase in the combat experience level within the SEAL squads by the end of 1968 produced highly effective small units. After the heavy VC losses during Tet, the communists could ill-afford to tangle with the frogmen. When they did, they oftentimes lost heavily. But, the frogmen paid a heavy price in return. Nine men from Team One were killed and six from Team Two, as well as the commanding officer of

UDT 12. Countless others from both UDT and SEALs were wounded. Sacrifices were counted in many ways.

Notes

1. COMUSNAVFORV Monthly Summary, January 1968, p. 43.

2. Unclassified command history for SEAL Team One for the year 1968, Enclosure 4(b).

3. SEAL Team One Barndance Card 384B (Post-Operation Report).

4. Unclassified command history for SEAL Team One for the year 1968, Enclosure 2, p. 1.

5. Unclassified command history for UDT 12 for the year 1968, p. 1.

6. *Time* (12 January 1968), pp. 18-19.

7. SEAL Team One Barndance Card 383 (Post-Operation Report).

8. Unclassified command history for SEAL Team Two for the year 1968, Enclosure 1, p. 2.

9. Unclassified command history for UDT 12 for the year 1968, pp. 1, 20; Bernard Waddell, *I Am Somebody* (Boston, Massachusetts, 1986), pp. 231-232.

10. COMUSNAVFORV Monthly Summary, January 1968, pp. 109-110.

11. Unclassified command history for SEAL Team Two for the year 1968, Enclosure 1, p. 2.

12. COMUSNAVFORV Monthly Summary, January 1968, pp. 33-34.

13. SEAL Team One Barndance Card 386C (Post-Operation Report).

14. SEAL Team One Barndance Card 390 (Post-Operation Report). The bond between SEAL Team One and the Australian SAS continued to grow throughout the war. By the early 1970s, both units agreed to begin a personnel exchange program (PEP). One officer and one enlisted from SEAL Team One were posted to Perth, the home of the Australian Special Air Service, for a two-year period. Likewise, the SAS sent a similar contingent to San Diego. The program continued until 1984, when the Australian Army determined that one of their PEP billets should by all rights be involved in an exchange with the U.S. Army's Special Forces at Ft. Bragg, North Carolina. A PEP exchange between the Australians and SEALs continues today in the form of one enlisted.

15. John B. Dwyer, "Surface Action," *Soldier of Fortune* (May 1987), p. 47.

16. SEAL Team One Barndance Card 217 (Post-Operation Report).

17. Unclassified command history for SEAL Team One for the year 1968, Enclosure 2, p. 1.

18. For details of the Battle of Khe Sahn, see Robert Pisor, *The End of The Line* (New York, 1982).

19. COMUSNAVFORV Monthly Summary, January 1968, p. 23.

20. COMUSNAVFORV Monthly Summary, February 1968, p. 139; *Pacific Stars and Stripes*, 22 September 1968, p. 9.

21. Unclassified command history for SEAL Team Two for the year 1968, Enclosure 1, p. 2; *Pacific Stars and Stripes*, 22 September 1968, p. 9; COMUSNAVFORV Monthly Summary, January 1968, pp. 23-24; John B. Dwyer, "Swamp Warrior," *Soldier of Fortune* (December 1986), pp. 71-72.

22. Alexander Jason, *Heroes* (Pinole, California, 1979), p. 54.

23. For details of the battle for Hue, see Keith William Nolan, *The Battle For Hue Tet 1968* (Novato, California, 1983).

24. SEAL Team Two Barndance Card 228 (Post-Operation Report).

25. COMUSNAVFORV Monthly Summary, February 1968, p. 55.

26. SEAL Team One Barndance Card 402 (Post-Operation Report).

27. COMUSNAVFORV Monthly Summary, February 1968, p. 54.

28. Unclassified command history for SEAL Team One for the year 1968, Enclosure 2, p. 1.

29. Unclassified command history for SEAL Team Two for the year 1968, Enclosure 1, p. 2.

30. COMUSNAVFORV Monthly Summary, March 1968, pp. 39-41.

31. SEAL Team Two Barndance Card 241 (Post-Operation Report).

32. COMUSNAVFORV Monthly Summary, March 1968, pp. 30-31.

33. SEAL Team One Barndance Card 433 (Post-Operation Report).

34. COMUSNAVFORV Monthly Summary, March 1968, pp. 31-32; *The Navy Cross, Vietnam* (Forest Ranch, California, 1987), pp. 124-125.

35. Richard Hill, "Mean Mothers With Dirty Faces," *Esquire* (May 1974), p. 150.

36. SEAL Team Two Barndance Card 243 (Post-Operation Report).

37. COMUSNAVFORV Monthly Summary, March 1968, pp. 46-47.

38. Ibid., p. 121.

39. Ibid., pp. 35-37; unclassified command history for SEAL Team One for the year 1968, Enclosure 2, p. 2; SEAL Team One Barndance Card 442E (Post-Operation Report); unclassified command history for SEAL Team Two for the year 1968, Enclosure 1, p. 3.

40. COMUSNAVFORV Monthly Summary, April 1968, pp. 29-31.

41. Ibid., p. 105.

42. Unclassified command history for SEAL Team Two for the year 1968, Enclosure 1, p. 3.

43. Recommendation for Presidential Unit Citation for SEAL Team Two, dated 15 August 1969, Enclosure 5, p. 5.

44. SEAL Team One Barndance Card 495 (Post-Operation Report).

45. Unclassified command history for SEAL Team One for the year 1968, Enclosure 2, p. 2.

46. Ibid., pp. 2-3.

47. Ibid., p. 3; COMUSNAVFORV Monthly Summary, May 1968, pp. 38-39.

48. Unclassified command history for SEAL Team One for the year 1968, Enclosure 2, p. 3; COMUSNAVFORV Monthly Summary, May 1968, pp. 39-41.

49. Unclassified command history for SEAL Team One for the year 1968, Enclosure 2, p. 3.

50. COMUSNAVFORV Monthly Summary, May 1968, pp. 25-26.

51. Recommendation for Presidential Unit Citation for SEAL Team Two, dated 15 August 1969, Enclosure 5, p. 5.

52. SEAL Team One Barndance Card 480 (Post-Operation Report).

53. John G. Hubbell, "Supercommandos of The Wetlands," *Reader's Digest* (June 1967), pp. 53-54.

54. Dana Drenkowski, "America's Underwater Elite: The U.S. Navy SEALs," *Soldier of Fortune* (April 1979), pp. 49-50.

55. *Pacific Stars and Stripes*, June 1968.

56. Unclassified command history for UDT 12 for the year 1968, Chronology of Events.

57. Ibid., p. 15.

58. Recommendation for Presidential Unit Citation for SEAL Team Two, dated 15 August 1969, Enclosure 5, p. 6.

59. Unclassified command history for SEAL Team One for the year 1968, Enclosure 2, p. 3.

60. Ibid.; COMUSNAVFORV Monthly Summary, June 1968, pp. 35-37.

61. Unclassified command history for SEAL Team One for the year 1968, Enclosure 2, p. 3.

62. Ibid., p. 4; COMUSNAVFORV Monthly Summary, June 1968, pp. 37-39.

63. Unclassified command history for SEAL Team One for the year 1968, Enclosure 2, p. 3.

64. *Pacific Stars and Stripes*, 1 August 1968, p. 7.

65. Ibid., 29 August 1968.

66. Navy unit commendation for UDT 11, 28 August 1968 to 4 March 1969.

67. *UDT 11 Cruisebook 1968-1969*, "Delta's View of Danang."

68. Unclassified command history for UDT 12 for the year 1968, p. 21.

69. Ibid., p. 18.

70. *UDT 13 Cruisebook 1969*, Recommissioning Page.

71. *Pacific Stars and Stripes*, 2 December 1969, p. 7.

72. COMUSNAVFORV Monthly Summary, July 1968, p. 27.

73. Ibid., p. 31.

74. Ibid., pp. 33-34.

75. Ibid., pp. 39-40.

76. Ibid., p. 40.

77. Ibid., p. 134; *Pacific Stars and Stripes*, 3 August 1968; COMUSNAVFORV Monthly Summary, June 1968, p. 105.

78. COMUSNAVFORV Monthly Summary, July 1968, p. 57.

79. COMUSNAVFORV Monthly Summary, August 1968, p. 2; unclassified command history for SEAL Team Two for the year 1968, Enclosure 1, p. 4.

80. Recommendation for Presidential Unit Citation for SEAL Team Two, dated 15 August 1969, Enclosure 5, p. 7.

81. Ibid.

82. COMNAVSUPPACT Saigon 161500Z Aug 68; COMNAVSUPPACT

Saigon 180341Z Aug 68.

83. CTU 116.6.2 201150Z Aug 1968; COMUSNAVFORV Monthly Summary, August 1968, p. 3.

84. Recommendation for Presidential Unit Citation for SEAL Team Two, dated 15 August 1969, Enclosure 5, p. 7.

85. Ibid., pp. 7, 8.

86. CINCPAC 052130Z Sep 68.

87. CTU 116.6.6 310400Z Aug 68.

88. Unclassified command history for SEAL Team Two for the year 1968, Enclosure 2, p. 1.

89. Recommendation for Presidential Unit Citation for SEAL Team Two, dated 15 August 1969, Enclosure 5, p. 8.

90. Unclassified command history for SEAL Team Two for the year 1968, Enclosure 1, p. 5.

91. Recommendation for Presidential Unit Citation for SEAL Team Two, dated 15 August 1969, Enclosure 5, p. 8.

92. Ibid.

93. COMUSNAVFORV Monthly Summary, September 1968, Enclosure 2, p. 2.

94. COMUSNAVFORV Monthly Summary, October 1968, Enclosure 2, p. 1; Recommendation for presidential unit citation for SEAL Team Two, dated 15 August 1969, Enclosure 5, p. 9.

95. COMUSNAVFORV Monthly Summary, October 1968, Enclosure 2, pp. 2-3; *Pacific Stars and Stripes*, 8 October 1968; Matthew Fleck, "Don't Run a Perfect Op," *Gung Ho* (May 1984), pp. 20-25.

96. Interview with Capt. Robert Gormly by author, 23 August 1987, Virginia Beach, Virginia.

97. Unclassified command history for SEAL Team One for the year 1968, Enclosure 2(b), p. 1.

98. *The Navy Cross, Vietnam*, pp. 123-124.

99. COMUSNAVFORV Monthly Summary, October 1968, Enclosure 2, p. 4.

100. Ibid., 1968, Enclosure 2, p. 4; unclassified command history for SEAL Team Two for the year 1968, Enclosure 1, p. 5.

101. COMUSNAVFORV Monthly Summary, November 1968, Enclosure 2, p. 3.

102. Recommendation for Presidential Unit Citation for SEAL Team Two, dated 15 August 1969, Enclosure 5, p. 9.

103. Ibid.

104. Unclassified command history for UDT 11 for the year 1968, Enclosure 1, p. 8.

105. Ibid., p. 7.

106. Unclassified command history for SEAL Team Two for the year 1968, Enclosure 1, p. 5.

CHAPTER SIX

Unending War
(1969)

The inauguration year of 1969 began with the Nixon administration assuming the political reins in the White House. At the end of October 1968, President Johnson had ordered a bombing halt of North Vietnam in a political effort to support Hubert Humphrey's Democratic bid for the presidency and in hopes that the North Vietnamese would enter into serious peace negotiations. In return, the communists utilized every stall and political tactic to prolong the discussions. The more time the peace talks consumed, the more time was bought for the goals of the revolution. The escalation of the Vietnam conflict, and especially the Tet Offensive of 1968, had created a very vocal sector of U.S. opinion against the war, and especially against the Democratic administration. In Vietnam, the battlefield held the same face. For the men in the war, it was becoming a conflict with no end in sight. As 1969 began, the SEAL and UDT platoons and detachments continued to carry the war into enemy-controlled territory.

On 10 January, a seven-man squad from Team Two's 6th platoon made an early-morning insertion along the Vam Co River (see Map 6). As part of Operation Giant Slingshot, the group patrolled inland for about a kilometer. At that point, they discovered a huge arms cache. It took them the next three hours to carry out the entire net. Included were the following:

320 mortar, rocket, and recoilless rifle rounds

25 hand grenades

27,000 rounds of small arms ammunition[1]

On the 11th, a SEAL Team Two patrol was moving to a night insertion in the RSSZ. Moving in the Long Tau shipping channel, the LCM was towing a smaller Light SEAL Support Craft (LSSC) alongside. The LSSC suddenly capsized, throwing the now-unconscious navy coxswain, who was wearing a heavy flak jacket, under the Mike boat. One SEAL immediately dove into the eight-knot current and went underneath the vessel. With no visibility, the SEAL located the crewman and brought him to the surface.[2]

Three days later, on 14 January, Signalman First Class David Wilson from Team One's Charlie platoon activated a booby-trapped 105mm howitzer round and was killed five miles southeast of Vinh Long during a river insertion from a LSSC (see Map 5). Wilson was the fourth man to exit the riverine craft when he stepped on the pressure-activated device. Another wounded SEAL was also evacuated to the hospital at Binh Thuy.[3] That same day President Johnson awarded SEAL Team One its first Presidential Unit Citation as one of his final acts in office. The commanding officer and seventeen men of the unit attended the ceremony at the White House. All had served in the team in Vietnam during the period between 16 July 1966 and 31 August 1967.[4] Also on the 14th, a SOG team consisting of both U.S. and Vietnamese SEALs attacked a North Vietnamese squad in a VC hamlet. The NVA squad leader and two of his men were killed, as was the VC Hamlet Security Chief. On 16 January, Team Two's Gunner's Mate First Class Harry Mattingly was killed while leading a PRU operation in Vietnam.[5] This year began with success, recognition, and fatalities. The only clear difference from the previous year's end was a mark on a calender.

On the 19th, a squad from Team One's Alfa platoon set a hasty ambush along a river after discovering a bunker and hearing voices in the area. Three sampans were fired upon, killing five VC and causing a large secondary explosion in one of the craft. The team caught small-arms fire from both banks as it withdrew and extracted.[6]

On 21 January, Delta platoon from Team One was assigned to CTF 115 (Coastal Surveillance Group).[7] The headquarters for this group was at Cam Ranh Bay in II Corps, along the Vietnamese coast (see Map 2). CTF 115 was assigned the duty of stemming the flow of seaborne infiltration of arms and forces. Their assets included up to 84 Swift boats that assisted in interdiction missions. Also on the 21st, swimmer delivery vehicles (SDVs) were first successfully utilized from the USS *Tunny* to conduct hydrographic surveys. Some initial mechanical problems then occurred with the *Tunny*, and the detachment returned to Subic Bay for repairs.[8]

By the end of the month, the Four-Party Paris Peace Talks opened. It did not appear that meaningful discussions toward a peaceful resolution of the conflict were about to emerge. Between 2 and 25 February, senior SEAL officers and commanders toured their forces in the Pacific. The commanding officers of SEAL Teams One and Two accompanied the Commander of Naval Special Warfare Group, Pacific, in an inspection of deployed UDT and SEAL detachments and platoons in Vietnam and throughout the Western Pacific.[9] Also in mid-February, Team Two's 7th platoon relieved the 4th platoon in Vietnam.[10] UDT 11's Det Delta, working out of Frogsville in Danang, continued operations, including the recovery of numerous valuable Det 10 pilotless reconnaissance drones[11] (see Map 2).

On 5 February, a seven-man squad from Team Two conducted a patrol in reaction to information supplied by a friendly agent. Their early-morning foray led them to a hut along the My Tho River where several armed men were observed. The squad crept closer and contacted the small enemy force, killing five. It was discovered that the team had hit an enemy postal station, and its haul included fifteen pounds of valuable documents and VC mail.[12] Another Team Two squad from the 5th platoon operating out of My Tho conducted an ambush along the same river ten days later, killing five high-ranking VC officials, wounding two others, and capturing several small arms and two pounds of documents.[13] On 4 March, UDT 13, the newest West Coast Underwater Demolition Team, relieved UDT 11 in WESTPAC.[14] Included within its ranks was the 5th platoon from UDT 21, whose home station was Norfolk, Virginia. The East Coast frogmen (two officers and twenty enlisted) were assigned to supplement the four platoons of the undermanned UDT 13 for the deployment.

On 2 March, a 5th platoon squad struck once again along the My Tho River. After insertion, the unit patrolled for about an hour before discovering two huts. The squad's indigenous interpreter was sent into one hut to mingle with its occupants, acting as if he were a Vietcong guerrilla. He returned to report the presence of several VC in the second hut. While the SEALs moved to surround the structure, a VC guard took them under fire and alerted his comrades nearby. A number of enemy soldiers were seen fleeing the area and were engaged by the squad. Ten were killed, one wounded, and a number of small arms and rockets were captured.[15]

MACV-SOG commandos continued their forays into North Vietnamese waters. Between January 1968 and May 1969, 140 missions were run, and forty-one enemy craft were destroyed, including a trawler. An estimated eighty enemy crewmen were killed in the actions, and 185 were captured. SOG units suffered four men killed and four missing during the combat actions.

About this time, it was discovered from two enemy defectors that the communists had an important intelligence unit and a four-man sapper team operating from Ham Tam Island in Nha Trang Bay in II Corps (see Map 2). The communists had a large network of agents who had infiltrated important areas inside the city to gain important data critical to their operations. At the same time, these people were also used to disrupt U.S. and South Vietnamese operations. In such close proximity to this important central coastal city, the unit had operated under the noses of Allied forces for some time. Now, the location of their base of operations was known, though a large attack on the island would only result in the destruction of the unit. The agents had to be taken alive in order to ferret out the entire network of communist agents. It would take a special approach to try to capture them.

A seven-man SEAL squad under the command of Lt. (Junior Grade) Joseph Kerrey was tasked with the mission. On 14 March, Kerrey and six other SEALs clandestinely inserted on the island, along with one LDNN and two defectors who had provided the information. The men were racing against the clock. The defectors, who were from the communist unit on the island, had grown weary of the long struggle and separation from their homes and had thus surrendered. They told the SEALs to expect about five lightly armed enemy cadre at the locations to which they would guide them. Their comrades would soon discover their absence and would surely vacate the island. Time was of the utmost importance.

Kerrey and his men stealthily slipped ashore undetected from a small skimmer craft under a dark and moonless night. The SEAL lieutenant led his group about 350 feet up a rock cliff in order to get above the enemy force undetected. The free-climbing was done without the safety of ropes. After descending a short distance on the other side, the first group of communists was located. Still undetected, Kerrey split his men in order to keep the enemy covered. He moved out with the rest of the team to locate the remaining enemy cadre. For maximum stealth, Kerrey and his men removed their boots and continued their search while barefoot.

Their luck had run out, however. The communists had seen them first and engaged them with weapons fire. Kerrey himself was severely injured when a grenade exploded at his feet and hurled him into some rocks. The lower half of his right leg was destroyed, and he began bleeding profusely. The group that attacked the frogmen was much more heavily armed than the defector had indicated. The SEALs immediately countered under Kerrey's direction, and a sharp firefight ensued. The second element's fire was called in, catching the VC force off guard in a hail of crossfire. Four VC attempting to escape were killed, while three others were killed as they stood to fight. The SEALs suppressed the enemy force and secured the area. A tourniquet was applied to Kerrey's leg to stop the bleeding. The team moved to an area where evacuation could be conducted, and helicopters were called in for the prisoners and wounded.

The SEALs had captured several extremely important communist members who would later provide information critical to the Allied forces. Additionally, three large bags of material, including documents, weaponry, and personal equipment, were captured. Some of the documents contained lists of the communist subversives within the city. Kerrey himself sustained significant injuries from the encounter, but he remained in control until nearly unconscious during the evacuation. One other man on the patrol, the corpsman, lost an eye in the encounter. For his actions, Kerrey would become the first frogman in U.S. Navy history to receive the nation's highest award for gallantry, the Medal of Honor, in May 1970.[16]

This operation was a classic example of utilizing the full potential of highly trained SEALs in a true maritime special operation. Coupled with precise and timely intelligence, the probability of mission success was greatly enhanced.

The next day, North Korea shot down a U.S. reconnaissance plane, killing thirty-one aboard. Incidents such as this called for potential retaliatory strikes against the perpetrators. The Joint Chiefs of Staff normally would produce a large list of potential targets and actions that could be taken against the aggressors. With such vast territory adjacent to the sea, as in the case of North Korea, retaliatory options utilizing frogmen were always strongly considered. Although the *Pueblo* incident was fresh in the American conscience, the Nixon administration, deeply involved in Vietnam, only threatened action if another provocation occurred.

On 20 March, a PRU force led by a SEAL from Team Two made a helo assault into enemy territory in the Mekong Delta. The VC force they had targeted was well-entrenched and returned a heavy volume of small-arms fire. Two of the indigenous PRUs were wounded. The SEAL advisor moved through fire to provide first aid to the two. He then directed the assault team's fire and called for helo medical evacuation.

Braving enemy fire once more, he carried the more seriously wounded trooper to a helicopter. He returned to lead the group in an attack of the enemy positions, resulting in four VC killed and the capture of one VC and two rocket launchers.[17]

On the 23rd, 7th platoon was serving as part of Det Alfa from SEAL Team Two. Some of the platoon were flying aboard two navy Seawolf helicopters on a visual recon and strike mission in Kien Giang Province along the Cambodian border near Da Dung Mountain (see Map 5). The helos came under enemy fire and proceeded to make strafing runs on the VC positions. One helo was hit and damaged on its second pass, and it crashed in an open rice field. Radioman Second Class Robert J. Thomas (known as R.J.) was thrown from the aircraft on impact, receiving several injuries. Stunned by the crash, he struggled to his feet as the wreckage began to burn. He rushed to aid crewmen still trapped inside. Enemy forces began to fire at the downed helo from the mountain and a nearby tree line. Thomas succeeded in removing one crewman from the wreckage and putting him in a covered position.

Meanwhile, an accompanying helo, under intense fire, had dropped a second man into the site. He too became wounded as he and Thomas broke into the flaming wreckage and recovered the trapped pilot. Thomas continued to try to remove the other two crewmen trapped underneath the helo, but he was finally driven away by intense heat and exploding ordnance onboard. Thomas and the other navy man then removed the injured crewmen to a safer distance. The VC were now closing in on the four men. Thomas, renown among even the teams for his shooting skill, had lost both his rifle and personal handgun in the crash. He now began to engage the closing VC, while armed with only a helicopter crewman's handgun. As he shielded one of the injured and used the man's body as a benchrest to steady his aim, he picked off several approaching VC, killing at least one man. His accurate fire shook the enemy and helped thwart their advance as an army helo swooped into the site. Two army crewmen raced over to the men to assist, and all six men succeeded in getting aboard. The helo then flew the men to safety. As fighting continued in the area, two additional SEALs rappelled into the crash site from yet another helo and recovered the bodies of the two dead crewmen from the wreckage. For his actions, RM2 Thomas was later awarded the Navy Cross.[18]

Also during March, a PRU force, led by an American SEAL, hit a Vietcong provincial committee meeting after inserting directly onto the site by helo. The intense fighting resulted in forty VC killed, including two regional and one provincial level political cadre. No friendly forces received injuries.[19] On 25 March, another seven-man squad from the 5th platoon embarked on a sampan up the My Tho River. It was searching for a VC unit of unknown strength reported to be in the area. While nearing Thoi Son Island in the middle of the river, the squad observed a large number of armed men in an open area on the island. The SEALs immediately inserted onto the canal bank and began to engage the force. Their initial fire killed eight of the enemy, but it sent an alarm throughout the area. The SEALs began to receive a heavy volume of fire from three different locations from an enemy force estimated at over two hundred men. The SEALs called for helicopter gunship support and were able to extract under fire without casualties.[20]

On 3 April, two SEALs and an LDNN lifted off the helo pad at the MACV compound at Ha Tien near the Cambodian border (see Map 4). The U.S. Army UH-ID immediately experienced problems and crashed into the Gulf of Thailand directly offshore. One SEAL was thrown into the cockpit when the helicopter hit the water, while the other was knocked unconscious. Both recovered from the initial shock and went into action. After escaping the cockpit, one SEAL pushed the LDNN and a door gunner out the side of the aircraft, allowing them to escape. The other SEAL released the other door gunner from his safety harness, and swam him to the surface and then to a nearby sampan. He then returned to the sinking helicopter to assist his friend. Both dove down to help the trapped copilot. They located the copilot's door to the cockpit and pried it open. While one SEAL held the door, the other entered the cockpit and freed the flier. They swam him to the surface and to the safety of rescue craft.[21]

On 7 April, a combined U.S./Vietnamese SEAL SOG team rescued the family of a defector from VC custody against two-to-one odds. The lightning daylight raid was conducted with the benefit of artillery and air support outside normal SOG channels. Forty VC from two platoons were killed by the SEALs, who also destroyed a seven-ton rice cache in the action. SOG forays into North Vietnam continued. Support units, as well as the combat teams, functioned at a high tempo to get the job done. Four boats returned from missions with severe battle damage, only to be returned in operational condition by repair technicians within thirty-six hours. The SOG successes resulted in a recommendation for the award of the Presidential Unit Citation to the group during 1969.

With the establishment of better intelligence nets, SEAL squads and SEAL-led PRU elements continued to have greater success in abducting or killing communist cadre. A SEAL abduction patrol on 15 April ambushed two sampans at the tip of the Ca Mau Peninsula, killing five Vietcong.[22] SEAL Team Two's 8th platoon relieved the 5th platoon on 18 April.[23] Frogmen were now gaining multiple tour experience in the war, which increased their effectiveness. Another SEAL element conducted an operation near the Bay Hap River in An Xuyen Province on 11 May (see Map 3). The frogmen flushed out several VC while searching some structures they had found, engaging them with small-arms fire. Six VC were killed.[24]

Three SEALs from Team One's Charlie platoon were killed on 18 May in Kien Giang Province. Two of the men were attempting to remove explosives from a CHICOM 82mm mortar round in the MACV compound at Rach Gia when the ordnance exploded (see Map 5). Killed were Aviation Electronics Technician First Class Kenneth Van Hoy, Machinist's Mate Second Class Lowell Meyer, and Quartermaster Second Class Ronald Pace. A week later (on the 25th), Hospital Corpsman Lin Mahner from the same team died of wounds sustained during the incident.[25]

Throughout the spring, the underwater demolition detachments were by no means idle. At the beginning of April, Det Delta in Danang was dissolved. This made a few more UDT men available for assigment to SEAL Team One. Team One had a tremendous tasking for missions by this time and required additional manning to fill its platoon assignments. UDT Dets Echo and Foxtrot were moved into the Frogsville facility and spent a majority of their time thereafter ashore. On 12 April, UDT 13 suffered its first combat fatality of the war. Chief Hospital Corpsman Robert Worthington, a member of Det Golf working in the Mekong Delta, was part of a sweep-and-destroy operation on the Duong Keo River. His riverine craft entered a VC ambush and was hit by heavy small-arms and rocket fire. An entire convoy of PCFs had moved up the river, and Worthington's was at the end of the column. As the others succeeded in exiting the kill zone of the ambush, more and more VC gunners were able to concentrate their fire at the trail craft. The boat became disabled and turned into the bank and beached, isolating the crewmen. The UDT men manned all available weapons and kept the communists at bay for forty-five minutes. The intense fighting at one point came down to a close-quarters hand grenade battle within twenty meters of the two enemies. One strong-armed frogman hurled a grenade into a VC spider hole, knocking one enemy sniper out of the fight. Unable to overrun the position, the VC finally withdrew. In the end, the vessel was totally destroyed. It was determined that a B-40 rocket explosion had killed Worthington.[26] On 5 May, another ambush in the same spot by VC firing B-40 rockets from the north bank of the river destroyed another PCF, wounding four UDT men.[27]

A combined UDT/Vietnamese force moved up the Cua Lon River on 25 April (see Map 4). It had entered the river from the Gulf of Thailand aboard four navy Swifts and then turned into the Cai Ngay River, searching the banks in the area. A VC encampment was discovered, and one fleeing enemy soldier was shot while another was captured. The UDT men destroyed 104 communist structures, 21 bunkers, and 39 watercraft. This was but one of a number of raids into the Nam Can Forest at the southern tip of the country to fragment the long-term VC stronghold. The raids had begun in earnest in October 1968. By the end of May 1969, 126 VC soldiers had been killed and several thousand communist structures, bunkers, and watercraft destroyed. UDT men were at the heart of it all, applying their expertise in explosives and demolitions.[28] Six other Vietnamese from their elite frogman core had been working with men from UDT 11 earlier in the year south of Danang, learning how to clear riverine areas of mines and booby traps. The UDT detachment was teaching the Vietnamese how to conduct the demolition work without U.S. assistance. By this time, the United States was beginning to try to turn the conduct of the war over to the South Vietnamese.

UDT 13 had begun its first WESTPAC deployment in March. By the beginning of May, a new submarine asset was ready to join the Seventh Fleet in support of UDT and other combat swimmer operations. The USS *Grayback*, LPSS 574, was originally launched from Mare Island Shipyard in Vallejo, California, on 2 July 1957. By the spring of 1960, she joined the fleet as a Regulus II Missile launch platform. Up until about 1960, she had completed nine successful patrols. Soon after, the Pacific Fleet began receiving Polaris submarines. By the mid-1960s, her original role was no longer needed, and she was decommissioned on 25 May 1964. In late 1967, the *Grayback* went back into the Mare Island Shipyards to begin a complete overhaul of her systems. This time she was being refitted to serve in the role as a launch platform for combat swimmer operations. The two large Regulus missile hangars on her bow were now converted. Each bay was fitted with a pressure hull. Forward of the pressure hull would be berthing and equipment inside the sub for a large complement of frogmen. Aft of the hull, each bay could be flooded to lock out, launch, and recover swimmers while the sub lay submerged. The *Grayback* was also the only U.S. submarine at that time designed to be able to bottom out on the ocean floor while conducting operations.[29]

By now, the UDT teams had trained with and utilized small craft known as swimmer delivery vehicles, or SDVs. These small, free-flooding submersibles were first developed during World War II. The earliest models were nothing more than slow-moving, steerable craft that resembled torpedoes. The frogmen would sit astride the vessels and guide them underwater into enemy harbors to attack naval vessels moored or at anchor. Over the years, the craft had become much more sophisticated. The frogmen would now guide the craft from inside while breathing on scuba systems. This would extend the range of SEALs and UDTs on their missions and allow them to work against gentle currents that would not allow a swimmer penetration. On the *Grayback*, an SDV could launch, conduct its mission, and recover without the submarine ever surfacing.

The *Grayback* was recommissioned on 9 May 1969, and joined the Seventh Fleet. The conventional submarine, powered by diesel-electric propulsion, was the only sub in the navy home-ported outside the United States. From Subic Bay in the Philippines, she took UDT 12 men on-board to train as a crew for deployment to Vietnam. The sub could handle sixty frogmen, eight IBSs, and four SDVs in its compartments. Before long, the USS *Tunny* departed WESTPAC, and the *Grayback* prepared to take her place.[30] The normal UDT mission of hydrographic reconnaissance continued to be carried out by frogmen from surface vessels. While conducting a recon in I Corps, Det Bravo came under heavy fire on 27 June. Several UDT men were temporarily pinned down on the beach as others swam to safety. The enemy fire was finally suppressed and the mission continued. One frogman was wounded.[31]

In June, President Nixon announced the first troop withdrawals of the war. Twenty-five thousand soldiers were slated to return to the United States by the end of August. In a program labeled Vietnamization, the United States was now determined to prove to both North and South Vietnam that it was willing to turn over the conduct of the war to the South Vietnamese. This was the beginning of a policy change that would take considerable time to affect the direct-action SEAL platoons in IV Corps. For the time being, the SEALs continued their war. Golf platoon from SEAL Team One relieved Charlie platoon in-country on 20 May.[32] On 16 June, Team Two's 9th platoon relieved the 6th platoon in Vietnam.[33] On 8 June, the 8th platoon set a three-element ambush in Dinh Tuong Province. It inserted and patrolled 1,500 meters into the site in hopes of catching part of what was believed to be a fifty-man VC group. Just before dawn, a large firefight was initiated. Helos and OV-10 spotter planes had to be called in for fire support and extraction. Twenty-six enemy soldiers were killed. The SEALs got away clean.[34] On the 26th, three SEAL ambushes killed twelve communist soldiers.[35] On the 27th, three additional SEAL actions accounted for another dozen enemy soldiers killed.[36]

On 1 July, one squad from the 5th platoon of Team Two attempted to infiltrate a VC base camp in the Cai Lai District of Dinh Thoung Province. The group set up a trail guardpost and laid low. At about 0400 hours, voices were heard north of their position. The squad quietly patrolled about seventy-five meters to the north on the trail, where they discovered the camp. They took an undetermined number of Vietcong under fire, killing four. The SEALs then searched the camp and found several small arms with ammunition, grenades, clothing and equipment, and four kilos of documents. One of the enemy killed was an NVA engineer who had graduated from a Soviet engineering university in 1967. Another of the dead was the engineer's bodyguard, who had failed in his duties.[37]

The same day, a squad of the 8th platoon had set up a trail guardpost when they heard weapons firing to the north. The squad broke its position and moved to the area from which the gunshots had come. Questioning an old man, they were directed toward a small enemy unit. While approaching down a trail, one armed VC was taken under fire and killed. Four other communist soldiers fled the area.[38] Three days later, a squad of the 9th platoon captured one VC in the

Can Gio District. The enemy soldier was armed and provided a couple of bags of documents.[39]

Team One's Golf platoon killed four enemy soldiers and captured ten kilos of documents during a contact on 3 July. The river ambush utilized Boston Whalers in support. Initial reading of the documents revealed that the dead included two VC intelligence officers for Long An Province and a provincial-level communications liaison officer.[40] On the 10th of the same month, a squad from the 8th platoon from Team Two conducted a heliborne raid with a twenty-four-man PRU unit into a suspected VC POW camp. The team landed and swept north, killing three enemy soldiers in the encounter and capturing thirteen others. One additional VC was captured as he attempted to evade by swimming underwater. Since an army helicopter used for evacuation was badly damaged by ground fire, the SEALs called in navy gunships for support. Four additional enemy soldiers were killed by helo fire. No prisoners were found.[41]

Two days later, 8th platoon sent a squad on another heliborne attack with a PRU element. Local intelligence had identified another suspected POW camp holding ARVN troops in Kien Hoa Province (see Map 3). The SEALs and PRUs hit the ground and swept into the area, capturing thirteen VC after a brief firefight. As they waited for extraction, another Vietcong was captured, and two kilos of documents were found. As helicopters flew in to pull the team out, the unit received heavy fire from a nearby tree line, but escaped without injury. Five ARVN soldiers, captured during the 1968 Tet Offensive over a year before, were liberated.[42]

On the 14th, SEALs were inserted into an area to direct air strikes and naval gunfire on a concentration of Vietcong reported by a recently liberated Vietnamese POW. Several sampans and bunkers were destroyed, and a large secondary explosion was observed; two VC were killed.[43] The 9th platoon searched a small tunnel complex on 21 July after receiving intelligence from a PRU unit. One VC was captured and revealed the location of a small weapons cache as a result.[44] Golf platoon attacked a VC finance and propaganda center on 28 July in Long An Province. Ten VC and NVA soldiers were killed in the action.[45] Golf platoon from Team One struck on 26 July and 6 August on operations that netted fourteen VC killed, numerous weapons captured, and thirty kilos of documents seized. Four additional enemy soldiers were captured in the actions.[46] Kilo platoon from Team One relieved Delta platoon in-country on 20 July.[47]

A squad from the 9th platoon established a night guardpost on 2 August when a sampan with three armed Vietcong slipped quietly through the kill zone. The small craft was allowed to pass without incident; the SEALs were hoping to catch a bigger unit in the trap. After five hours at the site, the SEALs were rewarded. Three sampans with over a dozen enemy soldiers entered their area from the south a short time later. A sharp firefight was initiated, and the SEALs called helo fire into the enemy force. Ten communist troops were killed and several small arms captured, along with several kilos of documents.[48]

Nine days later, the 8th platoon again hit a suspected POW camp in reaction to intelligence provided by a surrendering enemy soldier. Inserting by helo, the camp was found recently deserted, but it had also contained a grenade workshop. The entire facility was burned to mark it as a target for helo gunships. In addition to the factory tooling, a large number of hand grenades were destroyed. After extracting, the USS *Pritchett* was called upon to place gunfire on the camp.[49]

On 19 August, seven VC were killed by a SEAL patrol when it conducted a raid on an enemy stronghold fifteen miles south of Saigon (see Map 5). The SEALs from the 9th platoon and several PRUs had inserted quietly into a target area to cover a small cluster of hootches. An hour later, the six PRUs extracted as a ruse while the SEALs remained hidden. At about 1800 hours, several armed Vietcong entered one of the huts. At the same time, several more were approaching in a sampan. The platoon took both targets under fire, and one squad was sent to search the river craft. Besides killing several enemy soldiers, one VC was captured, as were several small arms.[50]

Team Two's 10th platoon relieved the 7th platoon on 17 August.[51] Mike platoon from Team One relieved Echo platoon in-country on 20 August.[52] The continued six-month tours allowed SEALs to rotate into the war to gain experience more quickly. The idea behind the six-month tours originated with the navy concept of a ship's cruise, which was normally about half a year. It also allowed the men to remain relatively fresh. They operated in the worst possible swamp environments, and were nearly always wet on every patrol, with leech bites covering their bodies. The rotations kept the frogmen from becoming too debilitated.

A SEAL Team Two patrol on the 20th captured an NVA battalion commander.[53] On the 24th, a 9th platoon guardpost in Bien Hoa Province killed a single VC after ambushing a sampan and capturing two assault rifles.[54] Finally, on 30 August, a combined 9th and 10th platoon patrol initiated an ambush that killed three VC and captured one weapon.[55]

At the end of August and through the first part of September, UDT 12 relieved UDT 13 as the WESTPAC unit. By this time, a few more changes had been made in the UDT detachments. Det Bravo was deactivated because the need for its services no longer existed. Dets Echo and Foxtrot remained with the ARG but were staged from Frogsville in Danang. Golf staged from Seafloat, a cluster of barges anchored in the middle of a river at the tip of the Ca Mau Peninsula in the South, and Hotel staged out of Danang in the north. In July, half of Det Hotel had been moved to Danang, while the other half conducted special Research, Development, Training, and Evaluation (RDT&E) in Saigon. The entire detachment was finally reunited at the Frogsville base in I Corps. The *Tunny* was not available for submarine operations, and its replacement, the *Grayback*, would not be ready for WESTPAC operations until February 1970. As a result, Det Charlie was temporarily dissolved. Although amphibious operations were deemphasized due to the Vietnamization program, the detachments remained active in other areas. Canal blasting in the Plain of Reeds was one long-term project that received UDT attention (see Map 5), another being the Medical Civic

Action Program (MEDCAP). In this program, UDT men would carry and administer medical support to local Vietnamese villagers, oftentimes in enemy-controlled territory. For these and other inland operations, the patrols were assigned LDNN as point men, interpreters, and guides.[56]

A combined SEAL/PRU operation on 12 September hit Tan Tap Village in Long An Province (see Map 3). The group captured a small arms cache that included:

>   2 60mm mortars
>   2 M-60 light machine guns
>   1 RPD light machine gun
>   1 AR-15 assault rifle
>   1 carbine
>   11 SKS carbines
>   30 B-40 rockets
>   Numerous pieces of enemy equipment

On the 14th, Golf platoon set an ambush four miles south-southeast of Ben Luc. A large sampan containing twelve VC entered the site and was taken under fire, killing six enemy soldiers.[57] A squad of the 9th platoon acted on information provided by a friendly agent on 21 September. It patrolled to the vicinity of a small VC camp, where they heard voices and identified armed guerrillas. Helo gunships were called in as the SEALs attacked the camp, resulting in five VC killed and a number of weapons captured. The next day, the other squad of the 9th platoon returned fire from a cluster of hootches it found while patrolling. No enemy killed could be confirmed, but one enemy soldier was captured, as were two weapons.[58]

An ambush by a squad from 10th platoon netted one VC killed on 4 October after a sampan wandered into the site at about 2030 hours. The team had inserted by PBR in mid-afternoon to set up the guardpost. Following their initiation, they came under fire and extracted by helo with weapons and documents.[59] The same day, two SEALs from the 9th platoon led a PRU operation that resulted in additional captured documents, as well as two VC killed and one captured.[60]

SEAL Team One sent Alfa platoon in-country as an augmentation platoon on 6 October.[61] On the 9th, a squad from 10th platoon operating with a platoon of PRUs inserted by helo and set up a guardpost on a trail in mid-afternoon in an area where VC activity had been previously reported. An hour later, a helo returned to extract some of the PRUs in a false extraction and was taken under fire. Helo gunships were called in on the suspected enemy location. Just before dark, two VC were shot as they entered the guardpost area. The unit moved to extract and was fired on as helos picked them up.[62] The next day, one squad from 9th platoon chased three VC suspects who avoided the guardpost they had established. The SEALs were suddenly taken under fire from a nearby tree line and called in helo gunships on the position. A search of the area found one VC body and several weapons.[63] Also on the 11th, a SEAL-led PRU operation abducted the commanding officer of four VC batallions from his headquarters in Long An Province. The men fought a small guerrilla security team as they extracted by helicopter with their prize.

A small ambush on 13 October by 9th platoon SEALs killed two Vietcong in a sampan and captured several small arms, including two RPG-2 launchers and four B-40 rockets.[64] A combined unit of PRUs and a SEAL Team Two squad swept a target area on the 15th with negative results. The PRUs extracted, leaving the SEALs in a stay-behind ambush. Later, the SEALs initiated fire on four VC moving across a rice field and then called in helo support. Before extracting, they found one VC body.[65]

The teams continued to field squads that were effective in their small-unit combat patrols, but fatalities were still sustained. On 17 October, Lt. (Junior Grade) David Nicholas from SEAL Team One was killed by friendly fire from a blocking force during an operation three miles southeast of Old Nam Can (see Map 4). As Nicholas led a sweep of the area, a second element in a blocking position took the sweeping unit under fire. The SEAL officer was hit in the upper left side of the chest and died within minutes.[66]

The next day, 3rd platoon relieved 8th platoon in-country.[67] Another Team Two platoon inserted before midnight on the 26th in search of several VC and infrastructure cadre on the south bank of Dong Cung Lake. Guided by a defector, the SEALs found several abandoned huts. After questioning an old woman, the unit patrolled further and captured two VC in the area, one of whom later turned out to be a hamlet and propaganda chief.[68] The next night, a SEAL unit inserted by boat at a point eight miles east of Nha Be. The SEALs observed a VC sampan pass through their ambush site and took the craft under fire. After conducting a false extraction, the team became engaged an hour later from the far bank. They returned fire and searched the area, finding five dead VC. On 31 October, the commander of Naval Special Warfare Group One and the commanding officer of SEAL Team One toured units of Group One and Two, as well as UDT Dets deployed in Vietnam on 31 October.[69]

In November, the U.S. Army announced the beginning of an investigation into an alleged massacre of Vietnamese civilians by U.S. Army soldiers in the hamlet of My Lai the previous year. The investigation and conviction of First Lieutenant William Calley, the officer in charge of the platoon who conducted the operation, gained worldwide attention and added yet another ugly scar to an increasingly unpopular war. As the war became more unpopular by the month, the peace talks continued in their halting manner. Through it all, the White House continued to follow the policy of Vietnamization. For some, it seemed as if Vietnamization could not come soon enough.

On 2 November, a SEAL Team Two squad captured three VC and a number of weapons and ammunition after inserting from a PBR after dark.[70] On the 10th, a squad from the 9th platoon was forced to call in Air Force close air support on a bunker complex after receiving small-arms fire from the site. Four secondary explosions were seen and one VC body was found during the search that followed.[71]

Two actions occurred on 14 November. The first took place on the Ba Kher canal. Six SEALs from Team Two, along with two LDNN and their U.S. SEAL advisor and a Vietnamese agent, departed their base in an LCM. At about 0240 hours, the unit switched to smaller craft and proceeded up the canal in search of a large enemy force reported in the area. Around dawn, the agent hailed one VC on the trail. As the man attempted to flee, the SEALs killed him. Two others approached from the east and were also killed in a brief fight. Interrogation of local inhabitants revealed the two hundred-man force traversed the area regularly.[72]

The second action that day involved a squad from Team Two's 10th platoon. After inserting by helo, the team patrolled west and set up a guardpost on a trail. The uneventful overwatch position was broken at noon, and the unit patrolled north. Suddenly, voices and coughing were heard to the patrol's front. Helos were called in to overfly the area. Under cover of their noise and distraction, the SEALs penetrated the camp, discovered several VC, and engaged them in a firefight. Four enemy soldiers were killed and several small arms captured.[73] A squad from the 9th platoon ambushed three VC on a trail the following day as part of Operation Wolfpack II. One enemy was killed and one CHICOM submachine gun was captured.[74]

During a mission by SEAL Team Two members on 24 November in the RSSZ, a patrol spotted a camouflaged sampan in a canal and attempted to quietly approach the scene. Several VC were encountered, and a fierce firefight broke out. Although outnumbered, the unit continued to fight. The machine gunner had been moving directly behind the point man in the event that immediate fire suppression was needed. In this instance, the tactic, commonly used by SEALs, proved invaluable once again. A strong volume of fire was leveled at the VC almost instantly. Even after receiving a wound to his left leg, the machine gunner continued to fire until he was shot in both hands and his ammunition box destroyed. Despite his wounds, the SEAL continued to attempt to pull hand grenades from his web gear to use in the fight until he fell unconscious.[75] On the same day, Lt. (Junior Grade) John Brewton from Team Two was critically wounded in action. While leading his men against a numerically superior enemy force, he was wounded in the arm and back. He continued to call in helicopter gunship support and sustained another wound. Following the action, he was evacuated to a hospital in Saigon, where he died of his wounds in January.[76] Another small SEAL ambush from the 10th platoon on 26 November destroyed a lone Vietcong sampan, killing all its occupants.[77] Bravo platoon from Team One relieved Charlie platoon in-country on 28 November.[78]

Hospital Corpsman First Class Richard Wolfe from Team One Mike platoon was killed in action seven miles northeast of Seafloat on 30 November (see Map 4). While inserting on an operation to capture a reported VC finance chief, the helicopter Wolfe was embarked in landed on top of a Vietnamese hootch. The men began to jump out of the helo and slide off the roof of the hut when the roof gave way. The helo went out of control and crashed, injuring several men. The combined force pulled the crewmen and injured from the wreckage and moved to the extraction site. At that time, it was noted that Wolfe was missing, and the patrol leader returned to the crash with other SEALs to search for the missing man. He was found dead in the wreckage, along with two VC who had been in the hut. The team carried his body to the extraction site and was pulled out by helo.[79]

One squad from the 9th platoon conducted an operation on 3 December in Hai Yen District. After inserting by sampan, the unit heard voices in the area. Several VC were encountered, and the ensuing firefight resulted in four enemy troops killed and several small arms captured. The team then patrolled to the west and established a guardpost on a river. Two communist sampans entered the kill zone around dawn and were fired upon. One Vietcong was killed. While several members searched the area, another sampan was taken under fire, the result being that one more VC was killed and two weapons captured.[80]

The 10th platoon took eight VC under fire along a heavily traveled trail after dark on the same night. In return, they received heavy weapons fire from the area. Two SEALs were wounded, and the patrol had to extract by river craft under cover of helo gunships. Two VC were confirmed killed.[81] On the 6th, men from the 3rd platoon captured a hamlet-level propaganda member along a canal. The man was detained after being caught in violation of curfew.[82] Four VC were killed by a SEAL patrol 187 miles south of Saigon during the second week in December.[83] Immediately after inserting by sampan on a mission on 11 December, a SEAL patrol made contact with a sizable VC force. Nine enemy soldiers were killed in the fight and fifteen kilos of documents captured, along with a small supply of ordnance.[84]

On the 19th, Team Two's 4th platoon relieved the 9th platoon in-country.[85] In their post-tour report, the 9th platoon, which had worked out of Nha Be, felt that it was now necessary to employ their ambushes further up the small streams and tributaries of the large rivers in the RSSZ in order to meet regular success. The VC in the area had been effectively challenged by riverine patrols and ambushes that were on the larger rivers and had moved their base camps further into the swamp.

It was apparent that the SEALs were continuing to bring the war to the enemy. Seal Team One's Charlie platoon deployed as an augmentation force in-country on 27 December.[86] Aviation Electrician's Mate First Class Curtis Ashton from SEAL Team Two was killed while leading a PRU patrol on the 27th in Long An Province, eight miles southeast of Nha Be (see Map 6). Ashton's PRU team had been laying in a riverine ambush, along with some members of 4th platoon. While occupying a position, one of Ashton's concussion grenades accidentally detonated, killing him instantly.[87]

The year ended in death, as it had begun. The SEALs in IV Corps were operating in high gear throughout 1969 and reacting well to intelligence provided by indigenous sources. The almost exclusive night combat actions of the early war years now gave way to both day and night operations. SEALs increased in effectiveness with their now mutiple-tour experience. Their operations covered a wider spectrum than in the early years. Helicopters were utilized for more of the insertion and extraction profiles, giving the frogmen more range and speed for reaction. The UDT detachments continued to branch out into the land warfare role of bunker-destruction, combat salvage, and mine neutralization missions. Their use as only a hydrographic recon element was changing by the year. With the addition of the *Grayback* and SDVs, the UDT men became an important clandestine force. As for the United States, the policy of Vietnamization had been initiated. It was now a time of disengagement, but not yet so for the men of Special Warfare.

Notes

1. Recommendation for Presidential Unit Citation for SEAL Team Two, dated 15 August 1969, Enclosure 5, p. 10.

2. Navy and Marine Corps Medal Citation for SF1 Joseph M. Silva, SEAL Team Two.

3. COMNAVSUPPACT Saigon 141738Z Jan 69.

4. Unclassified command history for SEAL Team One for the year 1969, Enclosure I, p. 1.

5. Unclassified command history for SEAL Team Two for the year 1969, Enclosure I, p. 7 and Enclosure 2, p. 1.

6. COMNAVSPECWARGRUPAC 230540Z Jan 69.

7. Unclassified command history for SEAL Team One for the year 1969, Enclosure I, p. 1.

8. Unclassified command history for UDT 11 for the year 1969, Enclosure I, p. 2.

9. Unclassified command history for SEAL Team One for the year 1969, Enclosure I, p. 1.

10. Unclassified command history for SEAL Team Two for the year 1969, Enclosure I, p. 7.

11. Unclassified command history for UDT 11 for the year 1969, Enclosure I, p. 2.

12. CTE 116.3 050630Z Feb 69.

13. CTE 116.3 150215Z Feb 69.

14. *UDT 13 Cruisebook 1969*, "A Word from the Skipper."

15. CTE 116.3 020635Z Mar 69.

16. Alexander Jason, *Heroes* (Pinole, California, 1979), p. 125; *The Omaha World Herald*, "The Medal of Honor" (Midlands Magazine), 9 November 1980, p. 20.

17. Silver Star Medal Citation for EM1 John S. Fallon, SEAL Team Two.

18. *The Navy Cross, Vietnam* (Forest Ranch, California, 1987), p. 320; *Pacific Stars and Stripes*, 26 March 1969, p. 6.

19. Unclassified command history for SEAL Team One for the year 1969, Enclosure 3(a), p. 10.

20. CTE 116.3 251430Z Mar 69.

21. Navy and Marine Corps Medal Citation for BM1 Alfred J. Ashton, SEAL Team Two.

22. COMUSNAVFORV Monthly Summary, April 1969, Enclosure 3, p. 5.

23. Unclassified command history for SEAL Team Two for the year 1969, Enclosure 1, p. 7.

24. *Pacific Stars and Stripes*, 14 May 1969.

25. COMNAVSUPPACT Saigon 171536Z May 69; COMNAVSUPPACT Saigon 171538Z May 69; COMNAVSUPPACT Saigon 171540Z May 69; COMNAVSUPPACT Saigon 250638Z May 69.

26. Unclassified command history for UDT 13 for the year 1969, Enclosure 1, p. 5; *UDT 13 Cruisebook 1969*, "Death of the 43."

27. Ibid., "Death of the 43."

28. *Pacific Stars and Stripes*, 29 April 1969 and 29 May 1969.

29. Ibid., 23 April 1969 and 11 May 1969; *Navy Times*, 31 October 1973 and 15 June 1981.

30. John B. Dwyer, "Surface Action," *Soldier of Fortune* (May 1987), pp. 47, 111.

31. *UDT 13 Cruisebook 1969*, "Ambushed Near Danang."

32. Unclassified command history for SEAL Team One for the year 1969, Enclosure 2(b), p. 1.

33. Unclassified command history for SEAL Team Two for the year 1969, Enclosure 1, p. 7.

34. CTU 116.6.3 080155Z Jun 69.

35. COMUSNAVFORV Monthly Summary, June 1969, Enclosure 4, pp. 10-11.

36. *Pacific Stars and Stripes*, 1 July 1969.

37. Recommendation for Presidential Unit Citation for SEAL Team Two, dated 14 November 1972, Enclosure 1, pp. 3-4.

38. CTU 116.6.3 020310Z Jul 69.

39. CTU 116.9.6 060758Z Jul 69.

40. CTG 194.0 051307Z Jul 69.

41. Recommendation for Presidential Unit Citation for SEAL Team Two, dated 14 November 1972, Enclosure 1, pp. 3-4.

42. Ibid., p. 4.

43. CTU 116.6.3 150615Z Jul 69.

44. CTU 116.9.6 220740Z Jul 69.

45. COMUSNAVFORV Monthly Summary, July 1969, p. 69.

46. CTF 116 081116Z Aug 69.

47. Unclassified command history for SEAL Team One for the year 1969, Enclosure 2(b), p. 1.

48. Recommendation for Presidential Unit Citation for SEAL Team Two, dated 14 November 1972, Enclosure 1, p. 4.

49. Ibid.

50. *Pacific Stars and Stripes*, 22 August 1969; Recommendation for Presidential Unit Citation for SEAL Team Two, dated 14 November 1972, Enclosure 1, pp. 4-5.

51. Unclassified command history for SEAL Team One for the year 1969, Enclosure 1, p. 7.

52. Ibid., Enclosure 2(b), p. 1.

53. CTU 116.9.6 270934Z Aug 69.

54. CTU 116.9.6 250332Z Aug 69.

55. CTU 116.9.6 310204Z Aug 69.

56. Unclassified command history for UDT 12 for the year 1969.

57. COMUSNAVFORV Monthly Summary, September 1969, p. 8.

58. CTU 116.9.6 220304Z Sep 69.

59. CTU 116.9.5 052340Z Oct 69.

60. CTU 116.9.6 050758Z Oct 69.

61. Unclassified command history for SEAL Team One for the year 1969, Enclosure 2(b), p. 1.

62. CTU 116.9.6 101510Z Oct 69.

63. CTU 116.9.6 111325Z Oct 69.

64. Recommendation for Presidential Unit Citation for SEAL Team Two, dated 14 November 1972, Enclosure 1, p. 5.

65. CTU 116.9.6 161308Z Oct 69.

66. NAVSUPPFAC Cam Ranh Bay 180230Z Oct 69.

67. Unclassified command history for SEAL Team Two for the year 1969, Enclosure 1, p. 7.

68. CTU 194.2.6 271551Z Oct 69.

69. Unclassified command history for SEAL Team One for the year 1969, Enclosure 1, p. 1.

70. CTU 194.2.6 021720Z Nov 69.

71. CTU 116.9.6 101740Z Nov 69.

72. Recommendation for Presidential Unit Citation for SEAL Team Two, dated 14 November 1972, Enclosure 1, p. 5.

73. Ibid.

74. CTU 116.9.6 151606Z Nov 69.

75. Bronze Star Medal Citation for EN2 Robert D. Christopher, SEAL Team Two.

76. Unclassified command history for SEAL Team Two for the year 1969, Enclosure 1, p. 10.

77. CTU 116.9.6 270148Z Nov 69.

78. Unclassified command history for SEAL Team One for the year 1969, Enclosure 1, p. 1.

79. NAVSUPPACT Det Binh Thuy 010950Z Dec 69; COMUSNAVFORV Monthly Summary, December 1969, pp. 63-64.

80. Recommendation for Presidential Unit Citation for SEAL Team Two, dated 14 November 1972, Enclosure 1, p. 6.

81. CTU 116.9.5 040231Z Dec 69.

82. CTU 194.2.6 070600Z Dec 69.

83. *Pacific Stars and Stripes*, December 1969.

84. COMUSNAVFORV Monthly Summary, December 1969, p. 65.

85. Unclassified command history for SEAL Team Two for the year 1969, Enclosure 1, p. 7.

86. Unclassified command history for SEAL Team One for the year 1969, Enclosure 2(b), p. 1.

87. COMUSNAVFORV Monthly Summary, December 1969, p. 96.

CHAPTER SEVEN

Vietnamization (1970)

By the beginning of 1970, the United States was determined to disengage its forces in Vietnam. The U.S. pullout was to be complemented by the gradual move to turn the course of the fighting over to the South Vietnamese. In February, Henry Kissinger entered into secret peace negotiations with the communist Vietnamese. The stalled Paris Peace Talks were obviously only a world-stage for the communists. The serious work would have to be enacted in private. In Cambodia, where the VC and NVA kept their staging bases politically outside the range of conventional U.S. military forces, Prince Norodom Sihanouk was overthrown in a coup by pro-U.S. Lon Nol.

The spring again brought huge antiwar protests in the eastern United States, including Washington, D.C. As U.S. conventional forces began to withdraw from South Vietnam under Vietnamization, the special force units continued their activities to help the Allies maintain security. It was to be a very busy year in the mangrove swamps and along the rivers and canals as Navy Special Warfare Units throughout the South continued heavy operations.

Three VC soldiers were captured by a combined SEAL/LDNN ambush squad on 2 January, three miles northeast of Song Ong Doc.[1] Eight other Vietcong were killed in a SEAL sweep operation sixteen miles west of Seafloat on 8 January[2] (see Map 4). On 11 January, Lt. (Junior Grade) John Brewton died from wounds sustained in November during a SEAL operation.[3] Three enemy sampans were ambushed by frogmen on the morning of 15 January about eight miles southwest of Seafloat, resulting in seven VC killed.[4] A SEAL Team One squad killed six communist soldiers in a riverine ambush twenty kilometers northeast of Old Nam Can on the 21st, capturing a small quantity of weapons and ordnance and numerous documents, including twenty-five enemy maps.[5]

January was also an active month for UDT frogmen. Chief Hospital Corpsman Donel C. Kinnard was serving with UDT 12's Detachment Golf in the Mekong Delta during the first of the year. The detachment was utilized during a sweep-and-clear operation supporting the 2nd Battalion, Fifth Mobile Forces Command, on 20 and 21 January. Kinnard became the central target of VC gunners as he tried to beach a damaged sampan previously occupied by three enemy soldiers. With great effort, he was able to capture the craft and several small arms. Another time, his team was subjected to intense small-arms and rocket fire. Kinnard himself was wounded in the arms and legs by shrapnel. He then hurled a few grenades of his own across a canal toward the enemy gunners. As the battle progressed, a lone North Vietnamese officer crept up behind the frogman and attacked him. Kinnard engaged him in fierce hand-to-hand combat and succeeded in overpowering the communist officer after several minutes of fighting at close quarters. For his actions, he was later awarded the Navy Cross.[6]

A week later (27 January), Chief Shipfitter Guy E. Stone, another UDT 12 frogman, was accompanying a UDT element on a bunker destruction mission. The sweep had taken the team to a graveyard along the Vinh Dien River. While probing the area, Stone encountered eight VC waiting in ambush for his teammates. Stone screamed a warning, and the enemy opened up with automatic weapons and grenades. Stone sought cover and then helped direct the fire from his men. He charged to within fifteen feet of the enemy position and hurled three grenades. He spotted two Vietcong who were attempting to escape, and he grabbed a teammate's weapon to shoot them. Six VC were killed in the action, and two were captured. Stone's early warning had saved the lives of four Allied personnel. For his actions, he was later awarded with the Navy Cross.[7]

By this time in the war, UDT and SEAL elements found their own way to operate deep in VC territory at the tip of the Ca Mau Peninsula. Surrounded by swamps and mud flats and aware of the need for security of their own bases, the frogmen developed their own answer to the isolated Green Beret camps that lay deep in the jungles along the Laotian and Cambodian borders. Earlier in the fighting, detachments would sometimes stage from large naval support ships, such as the USS *Benewah* (APB 35), the flagship for the riverine assault force CTF 117, which could anchor out from shore and move when necessary. Both riverine craft and helicopters could operate from alongside and from the decks. Now the navy used a little different approach. A series of fourteen barges were welded together and anchored up the mouth of the Song Cua Lon River near Old Nam Can (see Map 4). Large support vessels could reach the base for resupply, and riverine craft could launch and recover for their operations. A helicopter landing pad also allowed the freedom of Seawolves and army helos to be utilized. The base was given the code name Seafloat, and that became the name most often used. The frogmen had other affectionate names for the anchorage, including the Pontoon Palace.

Moored in the middle of the river, it was difficult for communist forces to attack the complex. Local South Vietnamese forces provided security ashore on either side. Biet Hai Rangers occupied one bank, while Kit Carson Scouts, or KCS (former VC who had defected and worked on missions against their former comrades), lived on the other bank. There were occasional attacks, however. In 1970 alone, four VC sappers were caught as they attempted to attach explosives to the barges.[8]

River patrols continued throughout IV Corps. On the Kinh LaGrange and Kinh Gay Canal in the Plain of Reeds, small riverine boats were unable to turn around on their patrols due to the narrow straights of the waterway. Eight large clearings were blown in the canal by UDT men, enabling the craft to negotiate the area.[9] Det Delta from UDT 11, which had previously staged from Frogsville in Danang, now became a wandering band in the Mekong Delta. There the teams conducted whatever missions needed to be accomplished, including the Kinh LaGrange and Kinh Gay Canal project. Det Golf and Hotel personnel were also involved with emplanting certain riverine and inland areas with sensors to detect enemy movements under Project Dufflebag. At the end of February, UDT 11 relieved UDT 12 in WESTPAC as the deployed underwater demolition team.[10] During this month, the USS *Grayback* (LPSS 574) first deployed to support UDT WESTPAC operations, including Vietnam.[11]

SEAL squads continued to invent newer tactics and techniques and refine the ones passed down by others. On 12 February, 5th platoon relieved 10th platoon at Nha Be. In its post-tour report, the 10th stated that it felt its best results were achieved on riverine ambushes during the hours just before dawn and at high tide. To take full advantage of that pattern, the 10th remained in ambush positions for only three- to four-hour periods on the average, rather than all night or longer. The short ambushes kept all hands fresh and alert. Additionally, the platoon used the LSSC as its ambush platform, pulling it next to riverbanks under foliage. This technique also kept the SEALs fresher and provided a solid base from which to attack and recover a target sampan.

A SEAL advisor led seven LDNN on a raid on Dung Island at the mouth of the Bassac River on the night of 17 March. After stealthily approaching a reported VC camp, the men moved to enter a specific hootch. A firefight at point-blank range immediately broke out, wounding one LDNN. Under a steady stream of enemy fire, the American carried the LDNN to a nearby canal and paddled him in a small sampan to riverine craft standing by. He then returned through the firefight to rejoin his team and complete their operation.[12]

On 20 March, a SEAL Team One raiding party struck a Vietcong camp twenty miles southwest of Tra Vinh. Four enemy soldiers were killed and the facility destroyed.[13] The next day, one LDNN was killed by small-arms fire while on an operation with SEAL Team One's Delta platoon northeast of Rach Gia.[14] On the 27th, ten SEALs and a guide inserted seventeen miles northeast of Seafloat on a mission to capture a district security chief. Light contact was made with a small enemy force; four VC were killed and two others captured, although the target subject escaped the patrol.[15] Detachment Bravo, consisting of SEALs who trained, advised, and led PRUs on combat forays into the enemy's hinterland for many years, was disestablished during March 1970 as part of the Vietnamization process.[16]

On 2 April, Echo platoon from SEAL Team One was inserted on a raid operation twelve miles northeast of Seafloat. Before it could move in on its target, the platoon received a report that a helicopter had crashed nearby. The patrol immediately moved to the location and secured the area. The uninjured crewmen were rescued and, before long, the downed aircraft was lifted out by a larger helo. Five Vietcong were killed as they attempted to move in on the crash site.[17] On the 6th, two SEALs and two Vietnamese discovered and destroyed a thirty-five-ton Vietcong rice cache eight miles northwest of Seafloat. The team saved 1500 pounds of rice, which was airlifted to the Pontoon Palace for use by the frogmen.[18]

Chief Gunner's Mate Barry W. Enoch from SEAL Team One was serving as the senior advisor to a combined U.S./ Vietnamese SEAL patrol in the Mekong Delta on 9 April. The Americans were from SEAL Team One's Charlie platoon, while the Vietnamese included a platoon of LDNN. The unit was targeting VC infrastructure cadre in Long Phu District, An Xuyen Province, about twenty miles southwest of Tra Vihn (see Map 3). The team inserted by riverine craft and patrolled toward the target area. Enoch, who was carrying a radio and a grenade launcher, observed six VC attempting to evade the Allied force. He immediately charged forward and engaged them, hitting three of the six. Two others were wounded, one of whom bumped into the team shortly after and was killed.

The unit then came under intense small-arms and rocket fire from all quarters. Enoch realized the group was surrounded and deployed the men in a defensive perimeter. He continually shifted his position to encourage and direct his team and employ his own weaponry. His radio was damaged in the attack, but he continued to direct close air support to within twenty meters of his position. Under heavy fire, a wounded LDNN was removed by medevac, but the rest of the team could not be pulled out by helo. Low on ammunition, Enoch finally utilized the aircraft ordnance to cut a hole in the encirclement. Immediately, he led a charge through the path in the enemy encirclement and to a nearby river, where the team was extracted by boat. Intelligence later revealed eighteen VC killed by the frogmen and gunships. One LDNN was killed in the engagement. For his leadership and decisive action, Enoch was later awarded the Navy Cross.[19]

At the end of April, President Nixon authorized a large-scale penetration into Cambodia of up to nineteen miles. The operation was designed to clear out the communist sanctuaries long utilized by the North Vietnamese, as well as the headquarters for the Vietcong high command. The Cambodian incursion succeeded in throwing the enemy off balance for months, and they seemed unable to mount any major offensive the remainder of the year. At the same time, however, the operation also caused a tremendous uproar in the United States from those who believed the administration was trying to spread the war to surrounding nations. The death of four students at Kent State University in Ohio on 4 May, in a clash with National Guardsmen, only added to the antiwar cry.

Most of the SEAL operations during the month of April made little contact with the enemy, but several small caches of rice, demolitions, and equipment were discovered and captured.[20] Photographic Intelligenceman Second Class Douglas Hobbs was attached to SEAL Detachment Golf during May 1970. He had been assigned to the detachment on temporary duty from the Naval Special Warfare Group, Pacific. On 16 May, while transiting in a riverine craft on a combined

SEAL/KCS operation deep within enemy-controlled territory, the boat he was riding in encountered a communist ambush. Small-arms and rocket fire struck the boat, and he was killed while attempting to man a .50 caliber machine gun.[21]

During many of their operations, SEALs utilized scout dogs to assist in ferreting out enemy forces and bunkers. Silver, one of the several German shepherds used, even earned his jump qualification after completing five parachute jumps with his SEAL Team Two handler. The scout dog exited the aircraft while attached to his master's specially rigged harness. Another dog, Prince, departed Little Creek for his fourth tour of duty in Vietnam with 7th platoon on 12 June. Prince had earned two Purple Hearts up to that time for wounds sustained during combat operations.[22]

On 9 June, a SEAL Team Two patrol found and destroyed 3,600 kilos of rice in a facility along the Song Dong Dung River.[23] From time to time, the frogmen would try to apply their maritime raiding skills in drier territory. On the 17th, two SEAL advisors and nine LDNN occupied a road ambush. Utilizing the infamous "clothesline technique," a wire was strung across the trail in order to capture any suspect utilizing a bicycle. Although one startled subject was victimized by the device, he was found to have no weapon or documents and was released. Afterward, the unit decided to stick closer to water.[24] Delta platoon discovered and destroyed a large enemy weapons and ordnance cache on 18 June, just north of Soc Son.[25]

The teams, especially SEAL Team One, continued to be plagued by fatal incidents, both on and off the battlefield. June 23 brought the largest and most tragic loss of SEALs in a single incident. Five SEALs from two different SEAL Team One platoons (two from Golf and three from Echo) died near Can Tho when the helicopter in which they were embarked crashed for unknown reasons while on an administrative move (see Map 5). The Army Huey, call sign Vulture 27, had taken off from Seafloat enroute to Can Tho. Killed were Machinist's Mate Second Class Richard Solano, Boatswain's Mate Third Class James Gore, Signalman Third

Class John Durlin, Seaman Radioman John Donnelly, and Fireman Toby Thomas.[26]

Hotel platoon captured seven Vietcong after inserting by MSSC into an area on 25 June. Their intelligence had indicated the presence of the enemy soldiers, who chose to surrender to the frogmen when they were challenged at a riverine ambush site.[27]

On 9 July, a SEAL advisor led fifteen Kit Carson Scouts (KCS) into a base camp twelve miles southwest of Seafloat. A large cache of supplies and foodstuffs was found and captured.[28] Kilo platoon relieved Delta platoon in-country on 13 July.[29]

Vietnamization had not slowed the tempo of SEAL operations, nor the pace of platoon tour rotations. On the 15th, Juliett platoon inserted in the early morning on a mission to raid a VC POW camp in the Can Tho area. As *USCG WPB Point Cypress* and several riverine craft stood by, the team penetrated the target area. Intelligence reports indicated the POWs included two Americans and about thirty ARVN soldiers. As the team approached the target, a booby-trapped grenade was tripped, and the explosion alerted the enemy guards, who escaped into the swamp with the prisoners. As the SEALs hit the camp, three of the VC were killed in the fighting. While one ARVN prisoner was reportedly saved, the SEALs were unable to find the enemy trail, and the rest of the prisoners remained in Vietcong hands.[30]

A Seal Team Two squad inserted off a riverine craft the morning of 21 July on a mission to raid a VC base camp and way station in Cai Lai District of Dihn Tuong Province (see Map 18). Not long after inserting, the squad was silently patrolling up a small trail when it surprised an armed Vietcong guerrilla, who was picking up a booby trap. After firing at the guerrilla, the SEALs received a heavy volume of fire from their left flank. The SEALs suppressed the fire and then followed the trail into the base. Supplies and documents were located and secured. As the men prepared to depart the location, they came under heavy VC counterattack. Pinned down, the SEALs were unable to shift their formation to properly engage the enemy. The platoon commander signaled the last man in the group, the rear security, to lead the team out of the area to an extraction point. Under a running firefight, the rear security SEAL led the frogmen skillfully through a mine field to safety. There were no friendly casualties.[31]

A unique discovery was made by 6th platoon at a VC supply point eight miles southwest of Ca Mau on 24 July. Hidden under heavy camouflage was a French tractor with a wheel diameter of 4.5 feet. Nearby was a weapons factory, which held a portion of a downed aircraft being used to make rocket motors and parts. The entire area was subsequently destroyed by an air strike.[32] Hotel platoon from Team One conducted a POW camp raid on 30 and 31 July, with negative results.[33] A twenty-four-man LDNN team, led by four U.S. SEAL advisors, was used as a blocking force in the operation. Up until this point in the war, five LDNN training classes had been graduated. The LDNN fielded one fourteen-man platoon with two advisors out of Ben Luc and one twelve-man platoon with two advisors out of Danang.[34]

On the 4th of August, SEAL Team Two was awarded its first Presidential Unit Citation for combat operations in Vietnam. The citation noted the team's tremendous operational performance from 1 July 1967 to 30 June 1969. Several of the team's more successful operations were noted in the award, and the unit shared in the distinguished combat record of their combined efforts.

During this period, the plight of U.S. prisoners of war came into greater focus around the world. Known at that time was the fact that many of the Americans in captivity endured tremendous hardships. Many were tortured, beaten, and starved. Men like Army Green Beret First Lieutenant Nick Rowe had been held under savage conditions in the U Minh Forest, the Forest of Darkness, a longtime VC stronghold in IV Corps. Rowe managed to survive five years in captivity before escaping his captors in December 1968. Some of the prisoners' conditions had improved following the death of Ho Chi Minh the previous year and as a result of the public awareness campaign launched by the United States about the same time. However, the conditions of the men in captivity remained primitive and cruel, especially for those held in the jungle camps in Laos, Cambodia, and South Vietnam. In addition to the POWs, hundreds of other U.S. servicemen remained unaccounted for, and the fear was that many of them were also languishing in communist hands. U.S. forces placed a high priority on the attempts to locate and secure the release of POWs.

Many of the SEAL units in the South remained active in the early 1970s largely due to possible POW camp raids to locate and free men like Rowe from the swamps of IV Corps. Intelligence reports pertaining to POWs received by Allied forces were code-named Brightlight, and SEALs often launched operations in reaction to these reports. At times the naval commandos were specifically requested by local commanders. As an example, in the Ben Tre region, two unsuccessful POW camp raids were launched into the Thanh Phu mangrove in June and July (see Map 5). As a result, the local Navy Intelligence Liaison Officer (NILO) requested and received a SEAL platoon presence in his area beginning in July. SEAL Team One's Hotel platoon from Det Golf fulfilled the role.[35]

When 6th platoon departed Vietnam in October 1970, it voiced a proposal that had been considered at various times by the men in the field. The platoon proposed the establishment of three four-man SEAL Brightlight teams, each to cover one of the three southernmost provinces of South Vietnam. Each unit, containing one officer and three enlisted SEALs, would be located within the province capital. Most SEALs realized that it was the timely use of good intelligence that bolstered many successful special operations. In the major cities, they would have the latest and best intelligence and react immediately to Brightlight reports. They would plan and lead any available local forces in attempts to free captive Americans and Vietnamese. The men would serve a six-month tour and devote their full energies to nothing but prisoner recoveries. With Vietnamization and the troop withdrawal, the program was never adapted.

An escaped POW provided information about a prison camp to planners in late August 1970. At 0910 on the 22nd, Lt. Louis H. Boink of SEAL Team Two led 6th platoon of Det Alfa and a regional Vietnamese company on an insertion into VC territory. The team inserted six kilometers north of the suspected POW camp by air, while Australian B-57s began pounding the canal near the facility to cut off the enemy. The SEALs shot one VC as he attempted to enter a bunker. Army helo gunships then rocketed the areas north and west of the camp as a further blocking force. The escaped POW led the unit into the recently vacated camp, but the SEALs immediately picked up the trail of the communists heading south and began to pursue. The SEALs called in more close air support, including Seawolf gunships and naval gunfire support from the USS *Sutherland* (DD 743), five hundred meters south of the camp. For two hours, the SEALs remained in hot pursuit through the swamp, following a trail of clothing and abandoned equipment. At 1245, they discovered twenty-eight Vietnamese prisoners whose guards had just fled for their lives. Army helos evacuated the POWs, seven of whom were former VC caught while trying to defect to the government forces. No Americans were discovered in the camp.[36]

After almost a year of Vietnamization, the Special Warfare units had still not felt a significant slowdown in operational deployments. On 1 September, UDT 13 relieved UDT 11 in WESTPAC.[37] SEAL Team One Zulu platoon relieved Echo platoon in-country on 28 August.[38] In 1964, the Vietcong had built three dams across the Tong Doc Luc Canal in the area around My Tho (see Map 5). The Vietnamese were unable to utilize the waterway for trafficking. A detachment of UDT 13 men was called into action to assist the local villagers. While the Vietnamization of the fighting was in its initial stages, civic projects such as this were always considered important. The navy men blew the structures on 20 August, 9 October, and 20 October, using large amounts of explosives. The success of the operation opened the waterway once again.[39]

On 13 September, a SEAL Team One patrol killed five enemy soldiers and was shortly thereafter attacked by a forty-man force. The team was able to escape and reported six VC killed in the action.[40] The next day, another raid by SEALs was conducted on a VC POW camp in the Delta with negative results.[41] On 23 September, a squad from Zulu platoon from SEAL Team One, along with two Australian Special Air Service (SAS) advisors and a five-man UDT element, uncovered a large enemy arms factory, complete with operational machinery, in the Nam Can Forest (see Map 4). A defector gave the information about the location of the installation to the SEALs, who assaulted the complex. A large cache was located, as well as a complete assembly line for rockets and rocket launchers. Over 350 assault rifles were discovered, along with numerous machine guns, mines, grenades, and mortar rounds. Three VC were killed in the attack.[42] The close relationship between the Australian SAS and SEALs continued to flourish.

During September, two members of 7th platoon were assigned to conduct missions with the SAS in Phuoc Tuy Province. On 25 September, Kilo platoon captured a Vietcong tax extortionist ten miles south of Rach Gia.[43]

Nearly every member of both the 6th and Juliett platoons was wounded in two separate incidents at the end of the month. While on patrol, each team had directional VC Claymore mines initiated on them. The entire 6th platoon had been on a mission to destroy a Vietcong munitions facility. During its target penetration, the command-detonated mine had wounded the last seven members of the group. A firefight ensued during which the enemy munitions hootch exploded. During the chaos, the patrol leader sprinted to the rear of the team to assist in the recovery of his men. He then led the unit to a helo landing zone. Rapid response by air assets lifted the patrol to safety.[44]

SEAL Team One was awarded a Navy Unit Commendation on the 11th of September for actions between 1 September 1967 and 21 January 1968. While only a small mention of its operations was given in the citation, it was noted that the team's detachments had worked a number of missions in I, II, and IV Corps.

UDT 13 suffered the only combat fatalities of their 1970 WESTPAC cruise in September. While on a bunker demolition operation near Hoi An, about twenty miles south of Danang in I Corps, several Det Hotel members were injured in a blast that killed Seaman Luco W. Palma and Hospital Corpsman Third Class L. C. Williams[45] (see Map 2).

Yankee platoon from Team One relieved Foxtrot platoon in-country on 28 September.[46] On 12 October, SEAL Team One's Xray platoon relieved Hotel platoon in Kien Hoa as part of Det Golf. Most of their operations were launched into the Thanh Phu mangrove region (see Map 5). Golf had run a total of thirty-two operations during its short tour, including one unsuccessful POW camp raid. Xray platoon conducted most of its forays into the Binh Dai mangrove during its tour. The platoon's numerous successes were marred by four deaths within the platoon (including its OIC) during its six months in-country.[47]

On 5 October, Team Two's 7th platoon was reassigned from Nha Be outside Saigon to Frogsville in I Corps near Danang (see Map 2). The platoon was called into the area due to the large number of mining incidents on the Cua Viet River. It was hoped that SEAL patrols could capture or kill the communist troops of the 126th NVA Sapper Regiment (known as the Q-80 Sappers), which was responsible for the minings. The group also staged out of Cua Viet and the MACV compound in Quang Tri for a time but, in the end, they were sent back south to Nha Be when the mining incidents in the north seemed to come to an end. The day after the platoon left I Corps, its former staging base was hit by a rocket attack.[48]

On 16 October, a series of Special Warfare insignia was authorized for wear on the uniforms of UDT/SEALs. The UDT design consisted of a naval anchor at the center that ran vertically, with a Neptune's trident behind the anchor running horizontally. A Revolutionary War era flintlock pistol stood before the anchor at an angle. These symbols stood for the ability of UDT to work and strike from sea or land in battle. Before Vietnam, not all UDT members attended the Army's Airborne School to become static line parachute qualified. By the end of the war, parachuting was added as a requirement for all frogmen completing BUD/S.

The SEAL insignia included all the elements of the UDT design, but it also included an American eagle set astride of the trident with its wings spread to symbolize the ability of SEALs to also strike from the sky. (See Appendix 1.) Officers wore gold insignia, while the enlisted wore silver. Before long, changes were made due to the controversy caused by the many different types. Since all frogmen were parachute qualified, the UDT and SEAL symbols were merged as one by the early 1970s. The design that remained was the original SEAL design. All insignia were gold.

The breast insignia could only be worn by those men who graduated from BUD/S and had also served a six-month minimum probationary period within an active SEAL or UDT unit. This insignia was to a SEAL or UDT what a green beret was to the army's Special Forces or a Ranger tab for graduates of Ranger School. To the regular navy, which held great pride in its Naval Aviators' Wings, the Surface Warfare Insignia, and the Dolphins of the submarine fleet, the UDT/SEAL breast insignia was too large and stood out too loudly—just like the men who wore it. Encountering such an attitude, frogmen wore it much more proudly. It was formally called a Trident, but since it closely resembled the symbol of a world-famous beer manufacturer, a commodity consumed frequently by Navy Special Warfare men, the insignia became known within the teams as "the Budweiser."[49]

During October, two Vietnamese civilians posing as LDNN in Rach Soi stole a sampan and motor from the local populace. Several SEALs and LDNN, determined to retain their reputation, tracked the pair down, captured them, and turned them over to local authorities.[50]

On 5 November, 9th platoon captured two VC four kilometers south of Ca Mau. After extracting to their base, they were able to persuade the captives to divulge the whereabouts of their cadre leader. Within three hours, the platoon had captured him.[51] On 10 November, Whiskey platoon from Team One relieved Golf platoon in-country.[52] Also on that date, a SEAL patrol fought an enemy platoon in a bunker complex fifteen miles east-southeast of Soc Trang and ninety-five miles southwest of Saigon (see Map 5). Six VC soldiers were killed and nearly a ton of rice destroyed.[53] A large ordnance cache was discovered and destroyed by a combined SEAL/KCS team in the Thanh Phu Secret Zone on 12 November (see Map 5). The ordnance dump included:

15,000 rounds of AK-47 ammunition

9 land mines

30 60mm mortar rounds

10 100mm rockets

10 Claymore mines

100 40mm grenades

200 cluster bombs

4,000 rounds of carbine ammunition[54]

A second cache found the same day by two SEALs and a team of KCS twenty-four miles southeast of Ben Tre included:

12 57mm recoilless rifle rounds

2 cases of cluster bombs

5 155mm rounds

10 105mm rounds

30 60mm rounds

4 cases of .30-caliber rounds

100 50-caliber rounds

100 20mm rounds

5 5-kilo land mines

2 10-kilo land mines[55]

On the 19th, an eight-man SEAL squad and one KCS struck the same general area fifteen miles east of Soc Trang and 120 miles southwest of Saigon. After engaging three fleeing Vietcong, the team came under heavy attack from a bunker complex. Seven VC were killed in the fight as the SEALs extracted. Fixed wing air support was called in, and the complex was destroyed. Eight other enemy soldiers were killed by the air strikes.[56]

Early on the morning of 21 November, a hand-picked team of Army Special Forces and Air Force Special Operations men struck deep into North Vietnam to raid a prisoner of war camp at Son Tay, twenty-three miles west of Hanoi. The Green Berets met and suppressed heavy resistance in the operation. Unfortunately, no prisoners were present in the camp at the time of the operation. No SEALs were present in the strike force since a sufficient number of highly qualified Green Berets was available; however, one SEAL officer had served on the feasibility study group in July when the concept of the raid was in its infancy. Although the raiders were able to withdraw with only minimal casualties, the raid sparked a strong controversy in the United States and focused more anxiety regarding the plight of the prisoners.[57] This operation marked the most publicized special operation undertaken by U.S. forces in modern times, but it was tainted in press reports as a huge failure. It had obviously not succeeded in its objective to free American POWs, but otherwise it displayed all the elements of a highly successful mission. Executed with precision, the raiders struck with the element of surprise deep into denied territory. Their fight was brief and fierce, and, in the end, they suffered only very minor casualties. The intelligence they utilized was detailed and exact, yet not timely enough. Finally, the one factor that could not be controlled went against them: their luck did not hold. As with the many SEAL POW camp raids in the Delta, reaction by U.S. planners was often fast enough to compose a comfortable plan, but not fast enough to take full advantage of timely intelligence.

The next day, SEAL Team One's Lieutenant Couch led ten SEALs from Whiskey platoon, Det Golf, along with nineteen Vietnamese troops, on a mission to raid a suspected POW camp in the Mekong Delta. The SEALs had launched on a riverine patrol and captured a VC sentry, who was quickly persuaded to reveal the location of the camp. About eight miles east-southeast of New Nam Can, the force went into the attack and conducted a running firefight with eighteen VC guards (see Map 4). The Vietcong fled the area, and the

SEALs located and freed nineteen Vietnamese POWs. Two VC were captured, as well as several small arms and thirty pounds of documents. This was the newly arrived Whiskey platoon's first operation in-country. It would not be the last, and although no Americans were ever found in the Delta, it would not be the last SEAL attempt to find and release Allied prisoners of war. Men from UDT 13's Det Golf assisted in the extraction of the rescued prisoners by clearing a landing zone for army helicopters.[58]

On 4 December, 9th platoon killed six VC and captured one other in a series of small ambushes twelve miles southwest of Hai Yen.[59] Two days later, a SEAL unit attempted to aid a KCS whose brother and mother had been abducted by the Vietcong. Although the unit swept the reported target area, it was only able to locate the man's son, who had hidden himself from the Vietcong.[60] During a raid on the 13th, a lone VC in a suicide attack attempted to detonate a grenade among a small group of SEALs in Binh Thuy District. The communist soldier was killed, but he had managed to wound four of the frogmen.[61]

Victor platoon from Team One relieved Juliett platoon in-country on 20 December.[62] On the same day, a squad from Team One's Zulu platoon inserted at the mouth of the Trai Cheo Canal. After seeing a lone VC soldier, they stalked the man until eleven more communist soldiers appeared. The SEALs hailed the group, but the men scrambled to draw their weapons. The frogmen engaged them in a brief firefight, killing eight of the VC while the others escaped.[63]

During a night patrol on 20 December, a five-man SEAL patrol from Team One's Xray platoon inserted sixteen kilometers east of Ben Tre to interdict a communications liaison route (see Map 5) and stepped directly into an enemy ambush. Heavy fire by an estimated fifteen-man enemy force mortally wounded the patrol leader and automatic weapons man. The radioman and Vietnamese guide were also hit. Radioman Second Class Harold Baker, the rear security man, was in charge of watching the patrol's back. He went into the river during the initial fire, barely able to swim with the heavy load of his equipment. He struggled ashore, dragging the body of a patrol member with him. On the bank, he began a fierce counter-barrage, keeping the enemy force from overrunning the position. He then administered first aid to his team and helped evacuate them. Six other SEALs scrambled to the area to provide security. Two Xray SEALs, Electrician's Mate Third Class James Ritter and Chief Electrician's Mate Frank Bomar, a former PRU advisor with half a dozen SEAL Vietnam tours to his credit, died in the attack. Baker was later awarded the Navy Cross for his actions.[64] On the 27th, 9th platoon raided a VC POW camp six miles southeast of Hai Yen. Six guards were killed in the fighting, but the Vietnamese prisoners of war had been recently moved.[65]

Vietnamization and disengagement were now beginning to affect the direct action SEAL platoons. Some SEALs remained as advisors, but 1970 was the last year of heavy Special Warfare involvement in Vietnam. Captures of large arms cache and POW rescues still indicated the success of the frogmen. Additionally, intelligence from Naval Intelligence Liaison Officers (NILOs) was more effective than in previous years. The heavy mission tempo again took a serious toll in Special Warfare lives. For the frogmen who remained, the lethal dangers of the battlefield would not diminish.

Notes

1. COMUSNAVFORV Monthly Summary, January 1970, p. 36.

2. Ibid., 1970, p. 71.

3. Unclassified command history for SEAL Team Two for the year 1969, Enclosure 1, p. 10.

4. COMUSNAVFORV Monthly Summary, January 1970, p. 72.

5. Ibid., 1970, p. 73.

6. *The Navy Cross, Vietnam* (Forest Ranch, California, 1987), p. 184.

7. Ibid., p. 314.

8. COMUSNAVFORV Monthly Summary, June 1969, Picture of Seafloat; *UDT 11 Cruisebook 1970*, "Det Golf; Seafloat."

9. *UDT 11 Cruisebook 1970*, "Wanderers of the Delta."

10. Unclassified command history for UDT 11 for the year 1970, Enclosure 1, p. 1.

11. Ibid.

12. Silver Star medal citation for BM1 Ronald J. Rodger, SEAL Team Two.

13. COMUSNAVFORV Monthly Summary, March 1970, p. 39.

14. Ibid., 1970, pp. 28-29.

15. Ibid., p. 82.

16. Unclassified command history for SEAL Team One for the year 1970, Enclosure 2(b), p. 2.

17. COMUSNAVFORV Monthly Summary, April 1970, pp. 51-52.

18. Ibid., 1970, p. 52.

19. *The Navy Cross, Vietnam*, pp. 108-109; COMUSNAVFORV Monthly Summary, April 1970, pp. 23-24.

20. COMUSNAVFORV Monthly Summary, May 1970.

21. SEAL Team One Operational Summary Report For the Period April 21, 1970 Through May 25, 1970.

22. Unclassified command history for SEAL Team Two for the year 1970, Enclosure 1, p. 8.

23. COMUSNAVFORV Monthly Summary, June 1970, pp. 20-21.

24. Ibid., p. 13.

25. Ibid., pp. 23-24.

26. NAVSUPPACT Det Binh Thuy 250713Z Jun 70; NAVSUPPACT Det Binh Thuy 250722Z Jun 70; NAVSUPPACT Det Binh Thuy 250724Z Jun 70; NAVSUPPACT Det Binh Thuy 270856Z Jun 70; CTE 115.7.6.7 241105Z Jun 70.

27. COMNAVSPECWARGRUPAC 260808Z Jun 70.

28. COMUSNAVFORV Monthly Summary, July 1970, p. 6.

29. Unclassified command history for SEAL Team One for the year 1970, Enclosure 2(b), p. 1.

30. COMNAVFORV 221543Z Sep 70; COMUSNAVFORV Monthly Summary, July 1970, p. 18.

31. Bronze Star Medal Citation for Eugenio D. Crescini, SEAL Team Two.

32. COMUSNAVFORV Monthly Summary, July 1970, p. 11.

33. NAVSPECWARGRUV 050210Z Aug 70.

34. COMUSNAVFORV Monthly Summary, July 1970, p. 58.

35. Naval Intelligence Liaison Officer (NILO) Ben Tre End of Tour Report, March 1970 to March 1971.

36. Recommendation for Presidential Unit Citation for SEAL Team Two, dated 14 November 1972, Enclosure 1, p. 6; COMUSNAVFORV Monthly Summary, August 1970, pp. 19-20.

37. Unclassified command history for UDT 13 for the year 1970, Enclosure 1.

38. Unclassified command history for SEAL Team One for the year 1970, Enclosure 2(b), p. 1.

39. *Pacific Stars and Stripes*, 3 December 1970.

40. COMUSNAVFORV Monthly Summary, September 1970, p. 8.

41. COMNAVFORV 221543Z Sep 70.

42. CTE 116.1.3.1 240624Z Sep 70.

43. COMUSNAVFORV Monthly Summary, September 1970, pp. 14-15.

44. Ibid., pp. 18-19.

45. *Pacific Stars and Stripes*, 8 November 1970. At the time, no one was certain if it had been a command-detonated mine or one that was activated when a patrol member stepped off the trail. Earlier in the year, Palma was a member of the team that helped recover the ill-fated Apollo 13 mission when the spacecraft encountered problems enroute to the moon and was forced to return to earth without a lunar landing. The diverse and adventurous life of UDT missions many times appealed to young sailors who volunteered for the teams. Leading such a career, Palma had been part of a rescue team for lunar astronauts and faced an enemy of a U.S. ally, all within a matter of months. Every single loss in the small SPECWAR community was strongly felt by the whole.

46. Unclassified command history for SEAL Team One for the year 1970, Enclosure 2(b), p. 1.

47. Naval Intelligence Liaison Officer (NILO) Ben Tre End of Tour Report, March 1970 to March 1971.

48. Interview with Intelligence Specialist Master Chief Dennis Johnson by author, 19 August 1987, Virginia Beach, Virginia.

49. Unclassified command history for SEAL Team One for the year 1970, Enclosure 1, p. 1; *All Hands*, March 1970, p. 57.

50. COMUSNAVFORV Monthly Summary, October 1970, pp. 23-24.

51. COMUSNAVFORV Monthly Summary, November 1970, p. 11.

52. Unclassified command history for SEAL Team One for the year 1970, Enclosure 2(b), p. 1.

53. *Pacific Stars and Stripes*, 16 November 1970.

54. COMUSNAVFORV Monthly Summary, November 1970, p. 15.

55. Ibid., p. 36.

56. *Pacific Stars and Stripes*, 23 November 1970; COMUSNAVFORV Monthly Summary, November 1970, pp. 36-37.

57. For details of the Son Tay Raid, see Benjamin Schemmer, *The Raid* (New York, 1976).

58. *Pacific Stars and Stripes*, 2 December 1970; COMUSNAVFORV Monthly Summary, November 1970, p. 3.

59. COMUSNAVFORV Monthly Summary, December 1970, p. 13.

60. Ibid., pp. 13-14.

61. Ibid., pp. 38-39.

62. Unclassified command history for SEAL Team One for the year 1970, Enclosure 2(b), p. 1.

63. COMUSNAVFORV Monthly Summary, December 1970, p. 9.

64. *The Navy Cross, Vietnam*, pp. 21-22; COMNAVSUPPACT Saigon 220318Z Dec 70; COMNAVSUPPACT Saigon 220546Z Dec 70.

65. COMUSNAVFORV Monthly Summary, December 1970, p. 14.

CHAPTER EIGHT

The United States Pulls Out (1971)

As the United States turned more of the actual fighting over to the Vietnamese, conventional forces packed up and returned to the States. Special forces units were still very active, but during 1971 they would wind down considerably. Navy Special Warfare elements were spread throughout South Vietnam advising, assisting, and continuing some of their hit-and-run tactics. A new detachment, SEAL Det Sierra, consisting of LDNN advisors, was broken into five small units throughout the Delta. Alpha was located at Rach Soi on the Gulf of Thailand. Charlie was at Long Phu, while Delta was at Nam Can at the replacement base for Seafloat. Located ashore, this new facility was code-named Solid Anchor. Hotel platoon was in the north at Hoi An in I Corps. The final group was utilized as training cadre for the LDNN course at Cam Ranh Bay. The few remaining SEAL direct-action platoons served as a ready reaction force in the event that a Vietcong POW camp could be located.

At the beginning of the year, efforts were also underway closer to home to prepare the South Vietnamese to take over the conduct of the war. A SEAL Team Two platoon deployed to Puerto Rico for four months to train Vietnamese naval officers in Special Warfare techniques and tactics.[1] In Vietnam, Victor platoon killed three VC in a small ambush on 9 January.[2] On 12 January, Whiskey platoon killed two VC as the communist soldiers attempted to ambush the frogmen. The SEALs had been assisting in the demolition of log and mud barricades in a canal seven miles northeast of Nam Can.[3] On the 17th, another team captured nine VC cadre and thirty-five VC sympathizers in a small camp east of Nam Cam. UDT personnel were called in to demolish the facility after helo gunships raked the area.

Lieutenant J.F. Thames from SEAL Team One became the first SEAL fatality in 1971 during an operation on 19 January in the deep south near Nam Can (see Map 4). The combined twelve-man SEAL/LDNN team came under heavy fire from small arms during extraction following an operation thirty-three miles south-southeast of Ca Mau. The Light SEAL Support Craft (LSSC) in which Thames was embarked was hit by two B-40 rockets. The explosion damaged the craft badly, knocked several personnel overboard, and killed both Thames and two LDNN. A second SEAL advisor and another LDNN were wounded. One other LDNN was lost and could not be located after the action. The uninjured LDNNs returned a heavy volume of fire, keeping the Vietcong at bay.

Hearing of the fight while monitoring radio traffic from its base at Nam Can, Team One's Zulu platoon boarded helos and raced to the site to assist in rescuing the unit. Under enemy fire, several SEALs jumped thirty feet from their helicopter to link up with the shaken SEAL/LDNN force and push the VC back from the besieged team. As Zulu platoon swept the area and drove the enemy forces from cover, helicopter gunships added firepower. Medevac helos then lifted the wounded from the site.[4]

Fireman Harold Birky from the same team was killed four miles north of Ben Tre on the 30th (see Map 5). His platoon was engaged in a sweep-and-destroy operation when it encountered a Vietcong band patrolling west of a hootch complex. A firefight ensued, killing Birky and wounding two other SEALs. The young SEAL was shot in the hip and evacuated, but he died enroute to a medical facility. The rest of his team extracted under heavy fire and called in air strikes once out of the area.[5] Six Vietcong were killed when a SEAL patrol hit a bunker complex in An Xuyen Province on the 31st.[6]

In the beginning of February, Operation Lam Son 719 was launched by South Vietnamese forces into the panhandle of Laos. This massive undertaking, supported heavily by U.S. air assets, was designed to cut the Ho Chi Minh Trail around the town of Tchepone. The initial phases of the operation caught the communist forces by surprise, and the ARVN faired well. Before long, though, the North Vietnamese countered with massive troop attacks supported by communist artillery and armor. Overwhelmed, the South Vietnamese withdrew after a short and very costly occupation. Casualties were very heavy on both sides. Lam Son 719 was watched closely by those who designed Vietnamization. The operation was a bold thrust by the South to take the initiative in the war. In the end, questions arose in political arenas as to just how ready the South was to assume the sole responsibility for its own defense.[7] Lam Son 719 could not be termed a victory in that respect.

During February, UDT 12 relieved UDT 13 as the WESTPAC deployed underwater demolition team.[8] Ninth platoon raided a VC financial meeting on 9 February, killing four guerrillas and capturing four others.[9] On 13 February, Romeo platoon conducted a daylight helo raid on a suspected fourteen-man VC mortar team eight miles south of Rach Sio. Following air strikes in the vicinity, the SEALs engaged and killed three Vietcong; they then discovered and destroyed a twenty-man rest area.[10] Another group of SEALs attacked a reported NVA encampment on 20 February with fire support from Cobra helicopters and *USCGC Rush* (WHEC 733). An agent report later stated that one Chinese propaganda cadre was killed and two NVA and three Chinese proselytizing cadre were wounded.[11]

On 24 February, 10th platoon from Team Two inserted by helo into an enemy area, where it targeted a hootch complex based on intelligence from an informant. As soon as the platoon hit the ground, it came under fire but pressed the attack and suppressed the enemy force. Eight Vietcong were killed, and numerous weapons and ammunition were captured. Two kilos of important documents were also captured. Information received later revealed that the SEALs had killed a communist hamlet leader and enemy hamlet chief. Three other VC were captured, including a district leader.[12]

While transiting the Ham Luong Canal on 28 February, a SEAL squad received heavy injuries when a B-40 rocket slammed into its river craft. Although no one was killed, all hands were wounded, but they returned fire long enough to exit the area.[13]

It was also in February that the final three SEAL Team Two direct action platoons, 8th, 9th, and 10th, began their pullout. Located at the navy base at Dong Tam, 8th platoon had conducted most of its missions in Dinh Tuong Province. It left the country without relief in February, and its operational area was turned over to SEAL Team One's Det Golf, Victor platoon, which began operations from the navy base at Dong Tam.[14]

On 4 March, Xray platoon from Team One's Det Golf concluded its operational tour and departed Kien Hoa without relief. Although it sustained a higher than normal percentage of personnel casualties, the platoon's operational results were fairly typical of many platoons about this time. After 56 combat missions, the unit accounted for 36 VC KIA, 12 captured, and numerous small arms and ammunition captured, including 340 mines slated for use against U.S. forces, and 46 kilos of communist documents. Four men from the platoon were killed, and all the other men were wounded, three so seriously that they required evacuation to the States.[15] It was on the 4th of March that Lieutenant Michael Collins was killed in Kien Hoa Province after suffering multiple fragmentation wounds from a VC riverine ambush[16] (see Map 3).

In a sweep with local forces on 7 March, 9th platoon killed five VC and captured five others with weaponry.[17] Another SEAL Team Two squad was silently inserting into a canal bank on the 13th when a Vietcong ambush erupted. The sampan immediately turned into the bank, and the SEALs counterattacked, repelling the enemy fire and setting up a defensive posture to extract. Helo gunfire was called in on the suspected enemy position, and the squad made a safe extraction via riverine craft.[18]

On the 15th, a 9th platoon squad conducted a heliborne raid into the midst of a Vietcong wedding. The helo landed just outside the ceremonial hootch, and the fight was brief. Two enemy soldiers were killed and three others captured in the operation. The team spirited the captives away, along with a kilo of documents and a Vietcong flag.[19]

Five days later, the same 9th platoon squad inserted by helo into an area to find a small weapons cache. A guide led the team to discover ten German Mausers, a CHICOM carbine, and a French 7.5mm automatic rifle.[20] It was clear that the SEAL platoons remaining in-country did not intend to decrease their small unit actions during the spring, although the groups were being phased out of the action slowly. Until the last one left, the SEALs continued to sting the enemy at will.

Torpedoman's Mate First Class Lester Moe from SEAL Team One died during an operation in Kien Giang Province on 29 March. While serving as the point man for his patrol, he reportedly activated a "Bouncing Betty" mine and was killed.[21]

A 10th platoon mission on the 30th killed four VC, including a proselytizing section chief, a postal communications chief, and a commo-liaison messenger. Four kilos of documents were also captured.[22]

SEAL Team One's Whiskey platoon hit a VC camp southwest of Nam Can on 5 April and became heavily engaged with a superior force. Under cover of helo gunships, it was able to extract without serious injury.[23] Four SEALs from Team One, along with two Australian SAS and four South Vietnamese, captured a Vietcong leader in An Xuyen Province on the 7th.[24] Whiskey platoon killed three and wounded two Vietcong on 11 April, twelve kilometers north of Nam Can. After searching the hootch where the enemy soldiers were located, two radio receivers were discovered, as were a pistol and a grenade.[25] The 10th platoon made another helo assault into a VC area on 30 April, capturing six VC, killing one, and discovering seven kilos of documents.[26]

SEAL Team One was presented its second Presidential Unit Citation for combat operations in Vietnam on 26 April. The award was presented for missions completed between 22 January 1968 and 20 May 1969. The combined detachments carried out more than 350 patrols during that time, always in a harsh environment and almost as often in small groups deep within enemy-controlled territory.[27]

It was also in April that Team Two's 9th platoon was relieved by Team One's Papa platoon and returned to the States. Up until the end of its tour, the 9th platoon had split its two squads to double its efforts. One squad had operated out of the MACV District Compound in Ca Mau, running missions into An Xuyen at the southern tip of the country (see Map 3). The other squad operated in the same southernmost province from the MACV District Compound in Hai Yen. The SEAL Team Two Det Alfa OIC billet was dissolved on 8 April, and the final platoon in-country, the 10th, was assigned to the control of Team One's Det Golf OIC.[28]

These changes in platoon tours were not the only mark of Vietnamization that could be seen in SPECWAR. It was clear by this time that the remaining squads were still successful in small-unit tactics, but the impressive results of years past were now seldom seen. The pace of the patrols had also slowed to a degree. On 12 May, a small SEAL ambush team, based out of Ca Mau, killed three VC in a riverine ambush of four sampans.[29] The following day, a SEAL squad raided a Vietcong training site, killing two enemy soldiers, capturing two thousand pounds of rice, and leveling the camp.[30] On the 17th, a squad from Victor platoon, in conjunction with South Vietnamese ground troops, discovered a huge enemy arms cache buried in fifty-five gallon drums.[31] While inserting for an ambush patrol on the 29th, a SEAL squad came under fire from a sampan and immediately returned fire. Four armed VC were killed in the brief action.[32]

A SEAL patrol located an ordnance cache containing fifty-three B-40 rockets five miles northwest of Ben Luc on 4 June.[33] Two days later, a combined SEAL/Australian SAS team destroyed a VC supply cache using air strikes. The cache included twenty thousand pounds of rice.[34] Quebec platoon interdicted a VC meeting twelve miles southeast of Ben Luc on 21 June, killing five Vietcong.[35] In mid-June, the final SEAL Team Two operational platoon left the war zone without relief. The 10th had operated out of Vi Thanh since mid-January, after the construction of two sea huts there. Most of their operations had been conducted in Choung Thien Province[36] (see Map 3).

In the beginning of July, Team One's Romeo platoon stood down and returned to the States without relief.[37] On 7 July, a SEAL squad and four Australian SAS inserted six miles northwest of Dong Tam to conduct an ambush. Discovering hootches in the area, the unit moved to search them when it flushed out five VC who fled the area. Helo gunship strikes were called in, and the SEALs conducted a false extraction by having only a few men lifted out of the site. Shortly after, two armed Vietcong returned to the area and were engaged and killed.[38]

On 2 August, four men from SEAL Team Two departed Conus to replace four SEALs serving as the LDNN advisory group. These men were the last SEALs from Team Two to serve in-country as part of Det Sierra.[39] On 23 August, a six-man group from Team One's Oscar platoon, along with three Australian SAS, conducted an intelligence-collection mission. After inserting from riverine craft, the group quietly patrolled to a hootch near Binh Thuy. Two SEALs and the interpreter entered the hut and came face-to-face with ten Vietcong soldiers. Hand-to-hand combat immediately broke out as both sides fought to disengage. The Allied unit broke contact and moved to extract as other enemy forces in the vicinity combed the area in search of the combined team. Covered by air strikes, the group escaped by helo after having killed eight enemy troops.[40] On the 28th, two SEAL squads uncovered a small ordnance cache in a graveyard twelve miles northwest of Dong Tam. Two Vietcong soldiers guarding the site were killed.[41]

A detachment of one officer and three enlisted men from the SEAL Team One SDV department spent 8 August to 22 September with UDT 12 aboard the USS *Grayback* to assist in training. In a more bitter event, four men, two of whom were active members of SEAL Team One, were arrested in August when they attempted to smuggle heroin into the United States inside a night-vision scope.[42] This was to be one of the very few distasteful events that marred the strong combat record of the special warfare teams.

Twenty-seven LDNN and two U.S. SEAL advisors came under heavy attack from B-40 rockets and small arms in the Delta on 15 October. Casualties were slight, and the unit was able to suppress fire and move to clear a bunker complex.[43] The Vietnamese government awarded SEAL Team One the Vietnamese Cross of Gallantry on 21 October for its years of operations in Vietnam.[44] In mid-November, President Nixon announced that U.S. ground forces were now in a strictly defensive role. The few men who remained in-country now felt the full weight of rules of engagement.

Vietnamization also had come to the forces of MACV-SOG. The majority of the operational responsibility for the conduct of SOG missions was in the process of being turned over to the South Vietnamese by fall 1971. Commando raiding units were now called Sea Commando Teams, or SCTs for short. During October and November, fifteen newly assigned members were given additional tactical training by U.S. SEALs to prepare them for commando raids. Termed Dodge Mark operations, this training brought the total number of SCTs to five.

A SEAL Team Two man helped capture two VC on a patrol deep in enemy-held territory on 13 November. The unit then split into two elements to try to capture three other soldiers still at large. As they moved into position, the teams came under enemy fire. Realizing the two small groups were in a bad position, the SEAL climbed a tree to effect radio communications. Helos were called and directed fire into the enemy forces. The team broke contact and extracted with its prisoners.[45] Six LDNN operations were run in November, advised by U.S. Navy SEALs.[46]

On 29 November, the *New York Times* ran an article on the role of the remaining SEALs in Vietnam. It noted that while the majority of the platoons were now being pulled out of the country in accordance with U.S. political policy, a handful remained for possible prisoner recovery efforts. It also noted that the majority of SEAL combat operations had ended in October, and most of the thirty or so SEALs left in-country would depart in December. A few of the men who spoke to the reporter complained about the evolution of "rules of engagement" over the years. By the end of 1971, one man pointed out, the units had to announce they were coming into an operational area and then only fire when fired upon. To complete their missions under such conditions was virtually impossible. Many of the detachments decreased their operations for fear of being accused of atrocities. My Lai was fresh in the minds of the U.S. conscience.[47]

SEAL Team One's Mike platoon from Det Golf, the last Team One direct-action platoon in Vietnam, departed the country on 7 December without relief.[48] The large-scale direct SEAL involvement had now ended, just as many conventional forces had departed. Although scoring no overwhelming results, the platoons that patrolled during the year continued to hurt the communists throughout IV Corps. UDT operations were also effectively cut, although UDT men were still available on fleet assets. What remained at the end of the year were a handful of advisors, including frogmen, to help the South hold its government. As communist forces took advantage of the lull in fighting and the withdrawal of U.S. forces, the South waited for the storm to come. In December, the bombing resumed as the communists continued to stall at the peace talks. Deep in Laos and Cambodia, the communists were preparing for yet another large offensive. They continued to buy time.

Notes

1. Unclassified command history for SEAL Team Two for the year 1971, Enclosure 1, p. 13.

2. COMUSNAVFORV Monthly Summary, January 1971, p. 70.

3. Ibid., p. 6.

4. *Pacific Stars and Stripes*, 23 January 1971; COMUSNAVFORV Monthly Summary, January 1971, pp. 8-10.

5. *Pacific Stars and Stripes*, 1 February 1971; COMUSNAVFORV Monthly Summary, January 1971, pp. 37-38.

6. *Pacific Stars and Stripes*, 2 February 1971.

7. For details of Lam Son 719, see Keith William Nolan, *Into Laos* (Novato, California, 1986).

8. Unclassified command history for UDT 12 for the year 1971.

9. COMUSNAVFORV Monthly Summary, February 1971, pp. 29-30.

10. Ibid., p. 21.

11. Ibid., p. 31.

12. Recommendation for Presidential Unit Citation for SEAL Team Two, dated 14 November 1972, Enclosure 1, pp. 7-8.

13. COMUSNAVFORV Monthly Summary, February 1971, p. 49.

14. Unclassified command history for SEAL Team Two for the year 1971, Enclosure 1, p. 18.

15. Naval Intelligence Liaison Officer (NILO) Ben Tre End of Tour Report, March 1970 to March 1971.

16. COMUSNAVFORV Monthly Summary, March 1971.

17. CTU 116.2.3 071610Z Mar 71.

18. COMUSNAVFORV Monthly Summary, March 1971.

19. Recommendation for Presidential Unit Citation for SEAL Team Two, dated 14 November 1972, Enclosure 1, p. 8.

20. Ibid.

21. COMUSNAVFORV Monthly Summary, March 1971.

22. Recommendation for Presidential Unit Citation for SEAL Team Two, dated 14 November 1972, Enclosure 1, p. 8.

23. COMUSNAVFORV Monthly Summary, April 1971, p. 15.

24. Ibid., pp. 15-16.

25. Ibid., p. 16.

26. Recommendation for Presidential Unit Citation for SEAL Team Two, dated 14 November 1972, Enclosure 1, pp. 8-9.

27. Presidential Unit Citation for SEAL Team One, second award.

28. Unclassified command history for SEAL Team Two for the year 1971, Enclosure 1, p. 21.

29. COMUSNAVFORV Monthly Summary, May 1971, pp. 18-19.

30. Ibid., p. 19.

31. Ibid., p. 36.

32. Ibid., p. 20.

33. COMUSNAVFORV Monthly Summary, June 1971, p. 4.

34. Ibid., p. 13.

35. Ibid., p. 8.

36. Unclassified command history for SEAL Team Two for the year 1971, Enclosure 1, p. 25.

37. COMUSNAVFORV Monthly Summary, July 1971, p. 30.

38. Ibid., pp. 37-38.

39. Unclassified command history for SEAL Team Two for the year 1971, Enclosure 1, p. 3.

40. COMUSNAVFORV Monthly Summary, August 1971, pp. 8-9.

41. Ibid., p. 19.

42. *Pacific Stars and Stripes*, 21 August 1971.

43. COMUSNAVFORV Monthly Summary, October 1971, p. 6.

44. Unclassified command history for SEAL Team One for the year 1971, Enclosure 1(b)1.

45. Bronze Star Medal Citation for HM3 John K. Myers, SEAL Team Two.

46. COMUSNAVFORV Monthly Summary, November 1971, p. 38.

47. *New York Times*, 29 November 1971, p. 2.

48. Unclassified command history for SEAL Team One for the year 1971, Enclosure 1(b)1.

CHAPTER NINE

End of a War (1972)

Though the United States was attempting to finally disengage from the war in 1972, a presidential election year, the fighting was far from over. Vietnamization was in full swing, and U.S. conventional forces were either home or on their way. The United States had traversed a full circle. The largest presence by Americans seemed to be, as it was at the beginning of the conflict, in the advisory and support roles.

No direct-action SEAL platoons remained in Vietnam, but a number of individual SEALs remained as advisors or were attached for special operations purposes to MACV-SOG. Nasty boat operations against North Vietnamese targets continued until 1972. Of the twenty-six PTFs utilized in the operations, six boats became combat losses (PTFs 4, 8, 9, 14, 15, and 16), while many others were damaged. The last SEAL Team Two members in-country were four men comprising an LDNN advisory group. One of these U.S. advisors was critically wounded when he was shot in the abdomen during an LDNN combat operation on 15 January.[1] SEAL Team One continued to keep a regular SEAL platoon on deployed status in WESTPAC for possible contingencies. On 10 January, Alfa platoon with Lieutenant Melvin Dry as the OIC, departed for that duty, staging on the island of Okinawa.[2] On 5 February, the last SEAL Team Two advisors departed Vietnam without relief. The two officers and two enlisted men had been part of the LDNN advisory group under Detachment Sierra. This action completed SEAL Team Two's in-country participation in the war, although some Team Two members worked throughout the country while attached technically to SEAL Team One elements.[3]

Within SOG, the South Vietnamese ran most of the field operations by spring 1972. Between 16 and 18 March, South Vietnamese SOG divers recovered a UH-1C helicopter and three bodies from the bay at Danang, including a Vietnamese general and a U.S. colonel. The missing helicopter had crashed into the bay two weeks earlier.

The Vietnamization process culminated in Operation Bach Dang between 13 and 27 March. During the mission, three Sea Commando Teams were launched in over-the-beach reconnaissance operations in An Xuyen Province in support of the Vietnamese 21st Division. The men were launched from the South Vietnamese navy ship My Tho. On the 29th, SOG SCT divers searched a canal in the Thuan Hoa District of Ba Xuyen Province for the body of a U.S. POW allegedly dumped there during 1971. The search produced negative results.

With the U.S. combat troop level at an all-time low and a presidential election around the corner in late 1972, the communists prepared for another large-scale offensive. Frustrated U.S. negotiators had suspended the Paris Peace Talks in March until the communists decided to return for serious discussions. Second only to Tet in 1968, the new attack was launched at the end of March 1972 using mass troops as well as conventional armor and surface-to-air missiles (SAMs) never seen so far south to date. The offensive was not a guerrilla struggle against the Saigon regime. It was clearly nothing short of an actual conventional invasion by Northern troops into South Vietnam, having all the elements of a Nazi blitzkrieg, minus air superiority. It was called the Easter Offensive.[4]

On 2 April, three days after the offensive began, a specially-equipped U.S. Air Force EB-66 electronic warfare jet received a direct hit from a SAM. The aircraft and a sister EB-66 had been escorting three B-52 bombers on a mission near the DMZ. One man was known to have escaped the aircraft as it went down: Lieutenant Colonel Iceal Hambleton, an Electronic Warfare Officer (EWO) aboard the stricken craft. Under parachute canopy, he was able to contact an OV-10 spotter plane, which assisted in pinpointing his location once he landed on the ground. Hambleton had landed deep inside enemy-held territory along the Song Mieu Giang River in I Corps. The NVA wasted no time in surrounding his position but was unable to grab him immediately. Air Force A1E Skyriders began dropping ordnance in support of a large rescue effort. A group of four army UH-IH helos entered the area to attempt a pickup, but received heavy fire. One crashed, killing all on-board. Another made an emergency landing on a beach south of Quang Tri.

Hambleton was in a very tight position. The air force dropped a mine field around his location, and the NVA could not touch him. However, the NVA was also interested in using him for bait. Whenever rescue aircraft entered the area, they received extremely heavy antiaircraft fire. Two OV-10 spotter planes were shot down, as well as a large HH-53 rescue helo, while attempting a pickup. There were now several crewmen dead and others unaccounted for on the ground. Between 2 and 13 April, while the Easter Offensive raged in the surrounding province, the air force launched a massive effort to get Hambleton and others out. It was soon learned that Hambleton had spent time working in the Air Forces Strategic Air Command. The knowledge he retained on the U.S. ballistic missile system was considerable. If the NVA and their Soviet allies had ever hoped to get their hands on a prize captive, it was one such as he. U.S. military leaders were just as determined to get him out. While plans were being made in the rear, the fifty-three-year-old Hambleton hung on for dear life. There was considerable concern that he couldn't survive on minimal water for so long. The batteries to his survival radio had to be nursed with care as he maintained contact with spotter planes overhead.

It was at this point that Lieutenant Thomas Norris, on temporary duty from SEAL Team Two to SEAL Team One, entered the scene. The young SEAL officer was part of a detachment, known as the Strategic Technical Directorate Assistance Team (STDAT) 158, which was assigned to advise the Vietnamese. It was during the month of April 1972 that MACV-SOG was disestablished and STDAT commissioned to replace it. It was for just such a rescue mission, when all the technology and heavy machinery of war could not complete the job, that a small team of highly-trained men could provide useful alternatives. Just as Vietnamization was becoming a reality in SOG and now STDAT, the U.S. was forced to return many Americans into the direct line of fire.

On the night of the 10th, Norris led a five-man team two thousand meters into NVA-controlled territory and rescued one of the missing OV-10 crewmen just before dawn. The team was able to evade to a forward operating base (FOB) and safety. After the FOB came under heavy attack, Norris led a three-man team into the bush twice on the 11th to try to get to Hambleton, but he was unsuccessful (see Map 2). A new approach was needed. Norris and a Vietnamese LDNN, Nguyen Van Kiet, dressed as peasants and paddled upriver to a pickup point on the night of the 12th. Hambleton had been vectored to that point over a period of several days by aircraft laiden with special electronics. Norris and Kiet located Hambleton and helped him into their small sampan, covering him with banana leaves for concealment. The linkup was quiet and uneventful, but the ride home was not. Carefully picking their way with frequent stops to evade NVA patrols, the three men traveled downriver, hugging the bank. Several times, the SEAL called in air strikes on positions directly in their path. After more than three hours, they neared their objective. Just before returning to the FOB, they came under heavy automatic weapons fire. The air force was standing by and delivered an equally heavy lot of ordnance. The team was covered long enough to reach the FOB.[5]

The rescue mission, the most intensive of the Vietnam War, was a success, but it had been very costly. It would remain a fact of the mentality of U.S. military planners that small units like the SEALs were oftentimes forgotten or called upon only as a last resort when the large military machine could not do the job. Under such conditions, special operations units often meet the worst possible mission circumstances. Consideration for employment and possible advance positioning very early in a crisis situation almost always places special operations units in a better position if called upon. For his daring action and relentless efforts in the rescue, Lieutenant Norris became the second SEAL in the history of Naval Special Warfare to be awarded the Medal of Honor. Nguyen Van Kiet, who volunteered to guide Norris deep into enemy controlled territory, became the only Vietnamese of the war to be awarded the Navy Cross.[6]

With heavy U.S. air support, the South Vietnamese counterattacked the communist offensive and were victorious. As the Easter Offensive ground to a halt, the pull-out of U.S. forces continued. On 21 April, the last two advisors in Detachment Echo in Danang were called home without relief.[7] While MACV-SOG was dissolved and its advisors sent home, others remained under STDAT and performed similar functions.

The Nixon administration responded to the Easter Offensive with a heavy bombing campaign in North Vietnam. Called Linebacker 1, the operation also included the mining of Haiphong and other North Vietnamese harbors, effectively cutting the supply of military equipment from communist bloc countries. The North Vietnamese would now begin to feel the serious pressure of a nation who wished to disengage. Their Easter Offensive would not only be stopped, it would be answered. At the same time, U.S. political overtures to communist China would make the Hanoi leadership sweat.

In late May and early June, preparations were made to conduct a classified maritime operation in Vietnam. The *Grayback* was once again called into action, and Lieutenant Melvin Dry's Alfa platoon from Okinawa was required for the mission. Before the operation could be fully conducted, Lieutenant Dry and others had to link up with the forces at hand. It was during the link-up process in the Gulf of Tonkin that a tragic accident occured, killing the young SEAL Team One officer and injuring others. On 6 June, Lieutenant Dry, known as Spence to his colleagues, became the final Special Warfare fatality of the war. He was buried with full military honors at Arlington National Cemetery.[8]

The war overseas was never forgotten by those who had been there. Although the vast majority of frogmen in the teams were no longer active participants, there were always reminders that the war was still being fought. On 6 July, SEAL Team One boxed and sent a shipment of old combat uniforms and jungle boots to their Vietnamese brothers in the LDNN.[9] At the end of the month, the commanding officer of SEAL Team One served as the official escort to Brigadier General Lon Nol of the Khmer Republic during his visit in the San Diego area.

During the latter part of the year, Danang continued to be plagued by rocket attacks. Intelligence had plotted an actual belt from which the missiles always seemed to originate. Two U.S. SEAL advisors, one officer and one enlisted, led a Vietnamese team in an operation to locate the rocket crews on 18 October. The SEALs were part of the STDAT 158 advisors that remained actively assisting the Vietnamese in special operations in I Corps. The men established an observation point along a river which intelligence believed the enemy forces were using to transport the rockets. Taken under fire, they were able to complete their operation, the results of which helped neutralize the effects of the communist rocket crews.[10] By the end of October, Henry Kissinger had announced that peace was at hand. The presidential election was around the corner and the war seemed all but over. However, every day in the field held the same danger for the SEALs left in the country.

On 31 October, a five-man team was working deep within I Corps. Two of the men were U.S. SEALs; Lieutenant Tom Norris, the man who rescued two U.S. airmen during the Easter Offensive earlier in the year, and Engineman Second Class Michael Thornton, his assistant, from SEAL Team One. With them were three Vietnamese LDNN. The mission of the group, which was based out of Cat Lai, was to capture an NVA prisoner and gather intelligence on the Cua Viet Naval River Base (see Map 2). The base had been previously owned by the South Vietnamese before the Easter Offensive disrupted Quang Tri Province.

The small team set out in an IBS from a Vietnamese navy junk in the predawn hours. It landed on the beach at about 0400 hours and hid the craft. All was quiet; the landing had not been detected. The team patrolled inland through the sand dunes for the next two hours to close on their target. Things seemed to be going well until just after dawn. The team was notified at that time that it had been inserted too far to the north of the intended landing point. Among the nondescript dunes, it was hard to find a known reference point to pin down an exact location. Without an accurate position, the group would not be able to receive gunfire support if it ran into trouble. Since the team was deep in enemy territory, it could waste no time. It turned back toward the beach to contact the junk and get a better fix.

As the men reached the last few dunes, their luck ran out. Two NVA soldiers spotted them and a skirmish broke out. Ten other enemy soldiers immediately appeared and joined the firefight. The frogmen set up a defensive perimeter while Norris attempted to make radio contact with supporting forces and call in naval gunfire. After several minutes of fighting, the enemy soldiers were all killed or wounded, but the fight had just begun. An estimated forty to sixty NVA were seen just beyond the dunes, making a fast approach to encircle the team.

The next forty-five minutes saw a fierce firefight, including grenade attacks and naval gunfire from offshore. Despite the ferocious fighting, the NVA moved to within twenty-five yards of the SEALs. One of the LDNN was hit in the hip, and Thornton had shrapnel wounds in both legs. There was no place to run. Badly outnumbered and low on ammunition, Norris ordered the men to the last cover before the open beach and the ocean. He and one LDNN stayed behind to cover the "leapfrog" maneuver. Thornton and the other two LDNNs sprinted through gunfire, 125 yards back to the last dune. Before long, the final LDNN made it to the position and told Thornton that Norris was dead. He had sustained a head wound while trying to fire his final light anti-armor weapon. Thornton believed the words of the LDNN, but he refused to leave the officer's body to the enemy. He immediately sprinted back through a hail of small-arms fire to Norris' position. As he came upon the area, two NVA soldiers were overrunning the site. Thornton immediately attacked and quickly killed them both. He found the lieutenant critically wounded and unconscious, but still alive. Wasting no time, he picked him up and slung him over his shoulder, sprinting back to the LDNNs at the last dune line through heavy weapons fire. The NVA now believed they had the men trapped and pressed forward to storm the position.

Thornton and the LDNN relied on their training and experience and took the only way out. They turned for the water and fought their way to the surf. It was 250 meters across the open beach, and the exhausted Thornton ran and crawled with Norris on his back. Laden with his combat gear, he swam the team leader out through a four-foot surf and inflated his UDT life jacket. They swam hard until they were outside of small-arms range. Thornton then gave the wounded officer first-aid treatment and tied Norris' hands together. Draping the officer's hands around his neck, Thornton continued to tow him seaward for the next two hours. The Vietnamese junk that had dropped them off at the beginning of the mission now picked them up at about 1130. Shortly after, they were transferred to the USS *Newport News* for medical treatment.[11] Norris survived the mission and recovered remarkably well from the critical wound after extensive medical treatment. For his nearly superhuman display, EN2 Thornton became the third frogman in Naval Special Warfare history to win the Medal of Honor.

The year had been one of little engagement for the few SEAL advisors remaining in the South, but it was during the operations of 1972 that the quality of the individual frogmen became clearly evident. Through all the offensives and counteroffensives and the massive use of the technological war machine, there were still those moments when the skill and daring of a few individuals made the difference. No longer in the direct-action mode, the Special Warfare men proved their high value as advisors once again, as they had at the beginning of the war.

In December, the Nixon administration had finally had enough. With presidential approval, Operation Linebacker II was launched before Christmas. The heavy day and night bombing of military and industrial targets in the north finally brought the communists to the negotiating table with a serious attitude. After only a few days, the U.S. bombers were meeting little resistance over the north. Because of the mining of their harbors the previous spring, the communists were unable to resupply their missile and antiaircraft forces. They chose to sign a cease-fire in order to buy time and regroup. One way or another, the world sensed that the end of the long struggle was near.

Notes

1. SA LDNN 180010Z Jan 72.

2. Unclassified command history for SEAL Team One for the year 1972, Enclosure 1(b), p. 1.

3. Unclassified command history for SEAL Team Two for the year 1972, Enclosure 1(b), p. 3.

4. For details of the Easter Offensive, see Col. G.H. Turley, *The Easter Offensive* (Novato, California, 1985).

5. William C. Anderson, *BAT-21* (Englewood Cliffs, New Jersey, 1980); Alexander Jason, *Heroes* (Pinole, California, 1979), p. 174; *All Hands* (April 1976), p. 17.

6. *The Navy Cross, Vietnam* (Forest Ranch, California, 1987), pp. 332-333.

7. Unclassified command history for SEAL Team One for the year 1972, Enclosure 1(b), p. 1.

8. Ibid., p. 2; ADMIN COMNAVFORV 171320Z Jun 72.

9. Unclassified command history for SEAL Team One for the year 1972, Enclosure 1(b), p. 2.

10. Letter of Commendation from Col. William W. Hoover, USAF, to STDAT 158, dated 27 October 1972.

11. Jason, *Heroes*, p. 233; *All Hands* (January 1974), pp. 19-21.

CHAPTER TEN

The Years After
(1973–1975)

In the years following the cease-fire signed in January 1973, the war became a memory. For some in the teams, it was a nightmare to be forgotten, but one that always remained. For others, it had been some of the best years of their lives when the outside world didn't exist and friendships were unshakable. It was the Vietnam war years that really built the foundation of the modern Special Warfare reputation, a reputation that would not soon be forgotten. However, the end of the Vietnam involvement had not come yet, and there would always be the reminders.

The Naval Advisory Group and Marine Corps Advisory Unit received a Navy Unit Commendation following the cease-fire for their action from 10 May 1965 to 28 March 1973. As a small but important part of that advisory effort, SEALs and UDTs had advised, assisted, and even led South Vietnamese forces on countless combat operations to help stem the flow of the insurgency. Although their many successes in enemy-held territory could be readily counted, it was on the political side that the final outcome of the war was being decided. On 11 January 1973, the entire LDNN team from Dong Tam was ambushed on the Bo De River. Two LDNN were killed and eight wounded. Without the support of their U.S. SEAL advisors, the Vietnamese frogmen would find the communist forces taking the offensive.[1]

On 12 March 1973, STDAT 158 was disestablished, and the final U.S. advisors, including a handful of SEALs, were sent home to Conus.[2] As part of the cease-fire agreement, the United States swept and disarmed mines that had been dropped into North Vietnamese waters to isolate Haiphong and other harbors in the 1972 Linebacker campaigns. One particular SEAL, trained extensively in explosive ordnance disposal, was assigned to the EOD detachment, which helped in the mine clearance. He had volunteered for the duty in hopes of winning an informal bet with another SEAL. Each man wished to be the last active duty SEAL assigned to Vietnam. After so many years of considering Haiphong and other waters in North Vietnam deeply denied areas, it was strange to stay in a Haiphong hotel during the work. He had never guessed he would see the North from that perspective.[3]

Such competition was not unusual for many of the SEALs who thrived on the operations they conducted during the war. As highly trained professionals, they were far from the unfeeling, unemotional men they were often made out to be. They lived hard, and they played hard. They entered their professional community through personal determination and strength. One pair of SEALs assigned to the same platoon competed for the dubious honor of participating in the most missions during a single six-month deployment. The platoon had split into two squads, each conducting a mission every other night in order to double platoon efforts, yet keep men fresh. The two betting SEALs went out each night, growing a little more weary each day, but unwilling to let the other get ahead. Finally, after several months, one of the pair claimed he had had enough. He took a week's leave and packed off to Saigon for a little R & R. The other SEAL, elated at his victory, went on one more operation before taking a well-deserved rest at their base. The tour eventually ended after six months, and the platoon rotated home. It was then that the settlement of the bet occurred. It was at this point that the SEAL who went to Saigon revealed that he hadn't really gone on leave after all. He had travelled to another base and run missions for a week with another platoon in another province. When the story was corroborated by the other SEAL platoon, the loser was beside himself.

One SEAL officer related a different feeling. After two tours with SEAL platoons in Vietnam, he had compiled an impressive record. His platoons performed well in combat, and he became a highly experienced and decorated officer. Speaking years later, he was proud of his accomplishments, but it was clear the war had deeply affected him, as it had countless other veterans. He explained that experiencing the incredible carnage of war became nearly unbearable by the time the war ended. He turned to other matters within the community and was ready to serve his country again, if the need arose. However, the sustained combat of years in Vietnam would never be forgotten.

During the early part of 1974, SEAL Team Two was awarded its second and final Presidential Unit Citation. Its exemplary performance on numerous operations, including prisoner rescues, was clearly evident.[4] Nearly a year later, on 9 January 1975, SEAL Team One received its third and final Presidential Unit Citation. Their operations amply demonstrated the quality of the many men who comprised the various Team One detachments from 1 January 1970 to 7 December 1971.[5]

In the desert east of San Diego, the SEALs of Team One constructed an isolated training base near the Salton Sea. Named at that time for the young SEAL officer who first won the Medal of Honor, Camp Kerrey became the site for all SEAL platoons conducting live demolition and weapons training. Much later, it would be renamed for the first SEAL killed in Vietnam, Billy Machen. On 4 April 1974, Alfa platoon from Team One concluded the first phase of a training program at the site for twelve Cambodian naval officers. The men would return to their country to assist in stemming the communist insurgency, supported by the North Vietnamese, still alive in the Khmer Republic.[6] Between 5 and 11 May, Alfa platoon continued the training at the naval station in Vallejo, California, where harbor defense and port security techniques were taught as part of Hardefex 1-74.[7]

Later in the year, SEAL training of Cambodian naval

personnel continued. From 1 July to 6 September 1974, SEAL Team One's Charlie platoon conducted tactics and diving training for the foreign frogmen in Subic Bay.[8] Team One's Golf platoon took over the training role from 26 November to 5 December.[9] Alfa platoon finished the training during the final week of 5 to 11 December.[10] One report, meanwhile, stated that five SEAL officers served as naval attachés to the American Embassy in Phnom Penh between 1973 and 1975.[11] It was obvious that the Special Warfare men were highly respected for their abilities to prepare others to fight insurgency. Although the United States was disengaging from the Vietnamese war, the government continued to try to assist the pro-U.S. forces against the communists.

The North Vietnamese launched their final offensive on the South after the first of the year in 1975. By the end of April, the communist forces succeeded in conquering the South when the United States Congress refused to intervene. Like Marines and other U.S. forces, elements of UDT 11 and Delta platoon from SEAL Team One stood by for possible contingencies. They were not used in combat. Only days before the fall of Saigon, the capital of Cambodia was captured by the communist Khmer Rouge.

On 12 May 1975, the SS *Mayaguez*, a U.S. cargo container vessel, was captured by communist Cambodian forces. The Khmer Rouge was just then attempting to consolidate their power in the provinces around the country. Cities were being emptied, and people were driven into the countryside in an attempt to bring the country back to the year zero. On the islands along the coast, the Khmer Rouge was fortifying every small possession in the event of anticipated future border clashes with their Vietnamese communist neighbors. Several ships under various flags had been attacked in early May off the coast of Kampuchea, as Cambodia was now called, as they transited the Gulf of Thailand.[12]

During the next four days, the United States prepared to retake the *Mayaguez* and rescue the crew after all diplomatic initiatives had proven unsuccessful. The ship had been relocated off the island of Koh Tang by the communists, while the crew was believed to be located at an enemy encampment at the northern end of the island (see Map 2). Delta platoon from SEAL Team One was available in Subic Bay for contingency operations. The team was initially alerted and moved to Naval Air Station Cubi Point with ammunition and weaponry. Soon after, the team was ordered to stand down. U.S. Marines were used without Special Warfare support and struck the island using a small armada of CH-53 and HH-53 helicopters on the morning of 15 May. Even as they attempted to land, the leathernecks immediately became heavily engaged. A full day of fierce fighting erupted on the island. The crew was released early in the day by the communists, having been set free on a boat coming from the mainland, and the rest of the operation was spent attempting to disengage and recover the marines on Koh Tang. Recovery of the ship, abandoned by the communists, was easily accomplished during the early phase of the mission, and it was towed to sea while the island fighting raged.

On the island, the Cambodians were much more heavily armed and entrenched than originally believed. In the end, the marines suffered fifteen killed, three missing, and a large number wounded. Almost all of the fourteen helicopters utilized were literally shot to pieces. Delta platoon was brought forward, and a plan was then proposed in the aftermath by conventional staffers for the SEALs to go ashore unarmed and recover some of the U.S. bodies and equipment left behind in the fighting. A leaflet drop would indicate to the communists that the frogmen were there on a humanitarian mission, and a request would be made to allow them to work freely. In light of the attitude of the communists during the previous days, the plan was scrapped as unsound.[13]

No SEAL or UDT element was used for a clandestine reconnaissance of the island prior to the assault, as is characteristic of most amphibious operations. Such a mission is completely within the design and charter of UDT/SEAL teams. A small reconnaissance party of combat swimmers might well have been able to discover that the captured crew was not on the island. At the very least, they would most likely have been able to notify planners of the heavily fortified bunkers and weaponry the Khmer Rouge had on line. At times it seems hard for the United States to temper its conventional military response through special operations. Small teams of highly trained men, at the right place, at the right time, can oftentimes make the critical difference, whether they are the main assaulting force or in support of others.

In the final analysis, the small role played by UDT/SEAL units in the Vietnam War was just as typical. Although they were highly successful in their own districts and provinces throughout the Delta, their full potential was never really fully understood or tapped. Most of their operations, especially early in the war, were nothing more than small-unit infantry tactics in a swamp environment. During the early years of the war and into early 1967, they were not only unknown in most military arenas, but they were seldom understood. They were posted throughout the Ca Mau Peninsula and only gained attention as a product of their operational results. The early squads generally sat in all-night riverine ambushes or blindly stalked the swamps in hopes of running into a large enemy force. Their daring and aggressiveness gained more attention from most conventional planners than their true skills and capabilities. By the middle of 1967, they were able to develop their own intelligence nets in their assigned areas, which were successfully cultivated and produced significant dividends. Each platoon passed on its experience and intelligence nets to newly arriving teammates, who would carry on the fight for another tour. While the United States had a tremendous potential with the UDT/SEAL submarines, they were never really fully employed to assist in striking heavily into North Vietnam. Although the SEAL squads matured in their operations in the Delta over the years using helicopter, fixed-wing, and naval support, they were rarely used in more than small raids and ambushes. As advisors, they proved invaluable from the early years of the conflict until the very end. Their leadership and training ability carried the LDNN program a long way. Their parachuting capabilities were never really employed, as was typical of U.S. Army Airborne forces also. Their scuba diving skills were only utilized on a small level and then mostly for administrative rather than operational missions. Most of all, their full potential in special operations was never fully integrated in the overall military strategy and goals of the war. They were never really viewed as anything more than a local tactical asset.

Fourteen men from the United States Navy won the Medal of Honor during the Vietnam War. Three were SEALs, all from SEAL Team One. Seven frogmen won the Navy Cross, three from Team One, two from Team Two, and two from UDT 12. One South Vietnamese was also awarded that honor. Over fifty Silver Stars and several hundred Bronze Stars were also awarded to frogmen who served in Vietnam.

For both SEAL Teams, what remained was a distinguished combat record. However, teams also lost a lot of men. At the time of the cease-fire, there were over 2,500 Americans missing or otherwise unaccounted for. Some had been seen alive in communist hands, yet never came home. Some were lost in combat operations. Others were lost through the accidents inherent in a war zone. Yet none of the missing were from the ranks of UDT/SEALs. In all the deep penetration strikes, the operations in enemy-controlled territory, no UDT frogman or SEAL ever failed to return. For those who died, their teammates carried their remains back every time. It was a feat unmatched by any special operations unit of similar involvement. Of the forty-eight men who died in Vietnam assigned to Naval Special Warfare units, thirty-four were from SEAL Team One, nine from SEAL Team Two, three from UDT 13, one from UDT 12, and one detached from NAVSPECWARGRUPAC (Naval Special Warfare Group, Pacific) and assigned to SEAL Team One Det Golf.

A more important statistic involved prisoner rescues. Throughout the war, and especially toward the end, SEALs stood ready to strike any suspected prisoner-of-war camp in the hopes of saving others. These were the type of special operations that truly employed the talents of SEALs. Ninety-eight total rescue operations were mounted by U.S. forces throughout the war, the most famous being the Son Tay raid. Only twenty of those missions succeeded in recovering prisoners, and 318 South Vietnamese were freed in those twenty operations.[14] Of the six major successful rescues in which SEALs participated, 152 Vietnamese captives were freed, accounting for 48 percent of the POWs freed during the war. Unfortunately, and much to the frustration of the maritime raiders, no Americans were ever found in the Mekong Delta, although numerous hot leads were followed.

The most important lesson identified by this example is that true special operations are extremely intelligence-dependent. The information to plan and conduct a successful mission must be detailed and, above all, timely. This lesson is as valid today as it has been in any previous conflict. For men such as the SEALs, target data is never sufficient enough. Planners must also be provided with an accurate picture of environmental and maritime intelligence. As was seen in Vietnam, the teams must always fight two enemies to succeed: the enemy force and Mother Nature.

The number of enemy casualties caused by U.S. naval frogmen during the conflict will never be officially detailed; the records remain too complex to attempt the arithmetic. Officially, the navy claims the teams had a confirmed kill numbering 580, with over 300 probable. The figure is inaccurate and very low. Official records show that the SEAL direct-action platoons alone held the following statistics:

Killed in Action	Confirmed	Probable
SEAL Team One	1000	370
SEAL Team Two	1026	419[15]

The number of enemy captured by these units nearly equaled the number killed. Additionally, it must be remembered that these statistics are for the direct-action platoons alone, which ran more than four thousand missions. They do not consider the numbers accounted for through SEAL-led LDNN and PRU operations, nor do they account for those from MACV-SOG missions. At the same time, none of the numbers involve enemy forces caught by close air support or naval gunfire directed by frogmen. Lastly, none of the statistics include the forces killed or captured by UDT operations. The data to compile these additional points is either lost, scattered, inaccessible, or incomplete, but the point made by the known statistics can be readily digested. Men with the extensive training of the SEALs or UDTs can produce results far beyond expectations for their numbers.

Death in war is the frightening reality. It is only through violent struggle that political goals can be met. One SEAL said it best. When asked about the numbers of enemy killed officially disclosed by the navy, he stated that the navy probably figured the teams could only receive the type of attention that would taint their image if the full results were ever compiled. Their job was to capture and kill the enemy and destroy his areas of basing. The teams did just that with tremendous effect; perhaps too well for some. Body counts, all-important recordings at one point in the war of attrition, at the end seemed almost a repugnant statistic following so many years of combat on both sides.

Of the men from the teams who served in Vietnam, enough has not been written. Many were discharged after their time elapsed in the service. Others remained and continue to serve even today. Many of those who remained lived to teach younger frogmen the meaning of lessons learned in combat. Of those awarded the Medal of Honor, EN2 Thornton was such a man. He became an instructor at the BUD/S course and later became an officer. Lieutenant Tom Norris was retired from the Navy in the mid-1970s and went on to lead a distinguished career with the Federal Bureau of Investigation.

Lieutenant (JG) Joseph Kerrey had a difficult return. Pulled from the SEAL operation on that night in March 1969, he was put into the medical evacuation system. The lower part of his right leg was destroyed and lost from the grenade that exploded at his feet. It took many long, hard months of rehabilitation to come home. In many ways, he felt the bitterness of many Vietnam veterans once back in the States. A year after the combat operation that wounded him, he was awarded the Medal of Honor, but it didn't end at that. To fully adjust took time—a lot of time. Joseph Kerrey went on with his life as best he could. The movie and media stereotype of the half-crazed Vietnam veterans did not help him or others. He eventually rose to become the governor of Nebraska, a tremendous tribute to both his own recovery and symbolic of those veterans who proved the stereotype wrong.

In 1983, the term Underwater Demolition Team was erased from the active duty navy rolls. All the teams are now SEAL Teams. Their mission remains very similar to that of the UDTs and SEALs who served in Vietnam. Today they support fleet operations worldwide in amphibious and special operations. Even today, they look to the lessons of the past and to those men who have acquired experience. Experience itself is the best teacher of all, and they fully realize they have a strong reputation to uphold.

Notes

1. Navy Unit Commendation for the Naval Advisory Group, Vietnam and Marine Corps Advisory Unit, Vietnam.

2. Shelby Stanton, *Green Berets At War* (Novato, California, 1985), p. 278.

3. Interview with BMCM James Finley by author, 21 August 1987, Virginia Beach, Virginia.

4. Presidential Unit Citation for SEAL Team Two, second award.

5. Presidential Unit Citation for SEAL Team One, third award.

6. Unclassified command history for SEAL Team One for the year 1974, Enclosure 1(b), p. 2.

7. Ibid., p. 3.

8. Ibid., Enclosure 3(b)2.

9. Ibid., Enclosure 3(b)10.

10. Ibid., Enclosure 3(b).

11. *New York Times*, 11 August 1975.

12. For details of the Mayaguez Incident, see Roy Rowen, *The Four Days of the Mayaguez* (New York, 1975).

13. Drew Middleton, *Air War—Vietnam* (New York, 1978); Interview with CDR Thomas Coulter by author, 21 August 1987, Virginia Beach, Virginia.

14. Benjamin Schemmer, *The Raid* (New York, 1976), pp. 237-238.

15. Statistics compiled by the author from the command histories for SEAL Teams One and Two.

APPENDIX A

Naval Special Warfare Breast Insignia

APPENDIX B

Navy Special Warfare Personnel Killed in Vietnam

RANK	NAME	UNIT	DATE	LOCATION; INCIDENT
1. CDR	Robert J. Fay	SOG	28 Oct 65	Danang; Mortar attack
2. RD2	Billy W. Machen	ST-1	19 Aug 66	RSSZ; Ambush
3. LT	Daniel M. Mann	ST-1	7 Apr 67	RSSZ; River ambush
4. IC3	Donald E. Boston	ST-1	7 Apr 67	RSSZ; River ambush
5. RM3	Robert K. Neal	ST-1	7 Apr 67	RSSZ; River ambush
6. SM3	Leslie H. Funk	ST-1	6 Oct 67	RSSZ; Drowned
7. SN	Frank G. Anthone	ST-1	23 Dec 67	RSSZ; Small arms
8. SN	Roy B. Keith	ST-1	11 Jan 68	Ba Xuyen; Small arms
9. GMG1	Arthur G. Williams	ST-2	18 Jan 68	Mekong; Small arms
10. LCDR	Robert E. Condon	UDT12	18 Jan 68	Mekong; River ambush
11. ADR2	Eugene T. Fraley	ST-2	21 Jan 68	Mekong; Booby trap
12. AMG3	Clarence T. Risher	ST-2	31 Jan 68	Chau Doc; Small arms
13. BM1	Walter G. Pope	ST-1	29 Apr 68	Kien Hoa; Nonhostile
14. SFP2	David E. Devine	ST-1	6 May 68	Kien Hoa; Drowned
15. SK2	Donald H. Zillgitt	ST-1	12 May 68	Vinh Binh; Small arms
16. CS1	Donnie L. Patrick	ST-1	15 May 68	Vinh Long; Explosion
17. EMC	Gordon C. Brown	ST-1	19 May 68	Kien Giang; Booby trap
18. MM1	Joseph A. Albrecht	ST-2	2 Aug 68	Chau Doc; Booby trap
19. SK1	Robert K. Wagner	ST-1	15 Aug 68	Vinh Binh; Booby trap
20. WO1	Eugene S. Tinnin	ST-1	20 Aug 68	Vinh Long; Ambush
21. LT	Fredrick E. Trani	ST-2	14 Sep 68	Mekong; Booby trap
22. ABH2	Roberto Ramos	ST-2	29 Oct 68	Long Xuyen; Small arms
23. ETN3	James K. Sanders	ST-1	22 Nov 68	Saigon; Nonhostile
24. SM1	David A. Wilson	ST-1	14 Jan 69	Vinh Long; Booby trap
25. GMG1	Harry A. Mattingly	ST-2	16 Jan 69	Mekong; Small arms
26. HMC	Robert L. Worthington	UDT13	12 Apr 69	Duong Keo; River ambush
27. ATN1	Kenneth E. Van Hoy	ST-1	18 May 69	Kien Giang; Mortar round
28. QM2	Ronald E. Pace	ST-1	18 May 69	Kien Giang; Mortar round
29. MM2	Lowell W. Meyer	ST-1	18 May 69	Kien Giang; Mortar round
30. HM1	Lin A. Mahner	ST-1	25 May 69	Kien Giang; Mortar round
31. LTJG	David L. Nicholas	ST-1	17 Oct 69	Nam Can; Small arms
32. HM1	Richard O. Wolfe	ST-1	30 Nov 69	Nam Can; Helo crash
33. AE1	Curtis M. Ashton	ST-2	27 Dec 69	Long An; Grenade

SEALs: UDT/SEAL Operations in Vietnam

RANK	NAME	UNIT	DATE	LOCATION; INCIDENT
34. LTJG	John Brewton	ST-2	11 Jan 70	Mekong; Died of wounds
35. PT1	Douglas E. Hobbs	DET G	16 May 70	Mekong; River ambush
36. BM3	James R. Gore	ST-1	23 Jun 70	Can Tho; Helo crash
37. MM2	Richard J. Solano	ST-1	23 Jun 70	Can Tho; Helo crash
38. SM3	John S. Durlin	ST-1	23 Jun 70	Can Tho; Helo crash
39. RMSN	John J. Donnelly	ST-1	23 Jun 70	Can Tho; Helo crash
40. FN	Toby A. Thomas	ST-1	23 Jun 70	Can Tho; Helo crash
41. SN	Luco W. Palma	UDT13	18 Sep 70	Hai An; Mine
42. HMC	L. C. Williams	UDT13	18 Sep 70	Hai An; Mine
43. EMC	Frank W. Bomar	ST-1	20 Dec 70	Truc Giang; Ambush
44. EM3	J. L. Riter	ST-1	20 Dec 70	Truc Giang; Ambush
45. LT	J. F. Thames	ST-1	19 Jan 71	Nam Can; River ambush
46. FN	Harold E. Birky	ST-1	30 Jan 71	Ben Tre; Small arms
47. LT	Michael Collins	ST-1	4 Mar 71	Kien Hoa; River ambush
48. TM1	Lester J. Moe	ST-1	29 Mar 71	Kien Giang; Mine
49. LT	Melvin S. Dry	ST-1	6 Jun 72	Gulf of Tonkin

APPENDIX C

Excerpt from 2nd Platoon, SEAL Team Two, Vietnam Operations, 30 January to 30 May 1967

Weapons and Equipment

1. Frag grenades can best be carried by putting the spoon behind the web belt and wrapping a rubber band around the lip on the base of the grenade and the spoon. The end of the spoon has to be bent slightly to keep the rubber band on.

2. Grenades proved to be extremely effective and useful weapons. We generally patrolled with 4 frags per man with a few WP and offensive mixed in.

3. There are two types of offensive grenades: one paper coated and one made of plastic. The plastic type is far superior for use on patrols due to its sturdier exterior shell and ability to withstand long immersion in water.

4. CS grenades are not waterproof and must be kept dry if they are taken on patrol.

5. Smoke grenades are unnecessary items on patrol. Other means can be used, such as M-79 flare rounds, MK-13 flares, WP grenades, signal mirror, pamel, etc., which either serve more than one purpose or weigh less and are less bulky.

6. If flare rounds and canister rounds were available for the M-79, the weapon's versatility would be increased tremendously.

7. MK 8 Very pistol rounds can be fired from the M-79.

8. Use of the Stoner LMG is not recommended until the drum magazine becomes available.

9. Use barrel plugs to prevent mud from clogging weapons. Insure all water drains from the barrel if the weapon becomes immersed.

10. Silent weapons were found to be very useful (9MM SMG'S).

11. Magazines should be emptied after every operation to ease tension on the spring. Magazines should be loaded just prior to an operation.

12. Magazines must be wiped clean and oiled after every op. They should be stripped and cleaned after every few operations.

13. .223 ammo should be disposed of after a max of 2 wet operations to eliminate misfires and jams.

14. Ammo must be carried as high as possible on the chest to keep it as clean and dry as possible.

15. The best solution to the problem of keeping ammo clean and dry is a net vest with pockets. It is presently available for 40mm rounds and a similar item could be made for .223 ammo and shotgun rounds.

16. Pistols are not needed other than for use in travel from base to base, around Saigon, etc.

17. Shotguns proved to be extremely effective for close range fighting. Personnel should be thoroughly indoctrinated in the use and care of this weapon.

18. A flash suppressor is needed for the .223 SMG. When fired at night the flash is blinding.

19. 30 round magazines should be issued to all personnel. Normal contact is brief and furious and 30 round magazines would greatly increase the unit's firepower in this situation.

20. A patrol's rate of movement is determined by the radioman. He sinks in the mud at least one foot deeper than any other patrol member. The PRC 25 is too heavy for the above reason. A light walkie talkie type radio with a 5-7 mile range, 1 or 2 freq's, and waterproof at 3′ would be ideal.

21. First aid kits should be waterproofed. Morphine should be carried by several members of every patrol in a container to prevent breakage.

22. Cleaning gear should be part of the individual weapon as is the case with the M-1 rifle.

23. All individual weapons should have slings mounted from the side or top of the weapon rather than underneath. The sling should be on the weapon at all times. This lets the individual, if necessary, use his hands for quieter movement, searching, etc., yet the weapon will stay slung in the firing position. Also if a man is wounded his weapon is less apt to get lost.

24. A small set of fins that can be used for swimming insertions yet not get in your way while patrolling, would be extremely useful.

25. A patrol life jacket is needed that allows quieter movement, is more comfortable and lighter than the UDT type; possibly waist type.

26. Camo uniforms should be made of heavy material and have lots of pockets.

27. Sneaks or coral shoes are better for patrolling in Delta areas than jungle boots. They are easier to get in and out of mud and make less noise doing so. Another advantage is that they don't leave an obvious footprint.

28. SEAL personnel should dress so as not to distinguish themselves from the normal base personnel. This generally means greens with name/US patches only.

29. Extensive practice in snap firing and firing from the hip should be given to in-coming platoons.

30. Encountered difficulty in getting sight picture of moving target at intermediate range (40-100 yds.). A possible solution is an open rear sight.

APPENDIX D

Award Recipients

Medal of Honor

LT(JG) Joseph R. Kerrey   14 Mar. 69   Nha Trang Harbor
ST-1

Led a SEAL squad on a mission to capture important VC cadre on an island in Nha Trang Harbor. The team scaled a 350-foot cliff to get above the VC, then descended into their camp. Kerrey was severely wounded in the ensuing firefight. The mission was a huge success.

LT Thomas R. Norris   10-13 Apr. 72   Quang Tri Province
ST-2/STDAT 158

SEAL advisor attached to STDAT 158. Norris led several patrols into enemy-controlled territory to recover downed U.S. pilots during the Easter Offensive. He succeeded in recovering two men against heavy odds.

EN2 Michael E. Thornton   31 Oct. 72   Quang Tri Province
ST-1/STDAT 158

Assistant advisor on an intelligence-gathering and prisoner capture mission with SEAL officer Norris and three LDNN. Once ashore, patrol became heavily engaged with North Vietnamese forces. Thornton rescued a critically wounded Norris from certain death and led the team in an emergency extraction under fire by swimming to sea.

Navy Cross

ICSC Robert T. Gallagher   13 Mar. 68   Mekong Delta
ST-2/Det Alpha
   Assistant patrol leader for a SEAL squad on a night operation. The patrol penetrated a VC base camp, and Gallagher and two SEALs entered a barracks building. A heavy engagement followed, and Gallagher led the patrol in a running firefight to extract after the patrol leader was severely wounded.

YN3 Gary G. Gallagher   10-11 Oct. 68   Mekong Delta
ST-1/DET Bravo (PRU)
   Led a PRU unit on a prisoner capture mission. After securing several prisoners, the unit became heavily engaged. Gallagher rallied the force and extracted them under fire, carrying one wounded man over eight kilometers.

RM2 Robert J. Thomas   23 Mar. 69   Chau Doc Province
ST-2/Det Alpha
   Aboard a Navy Seawolf helo when it was downed by enemy fire. Although injured, Thomas helped pull two injured crewmen from the flaming wreckage. He shielded them as enemy forces closed in on their position, and he fiercely countered the assault though only lightly armed.

HMC Donel C. Kinnard   20-21 Jan. 70   Mekong Delta
UDT 12/Det Golf
   Kinnard distinguished himself during a sweep-and-clear operation with U.S. Marine forces. Among other events, he was wounded while attacking enemy forces in a fierce firefight. In hand-to-hand combat, he also overpowered an NVA officer who attacked him from behind.

SFC Guy E. Stone   27 Jan. 70   Mekong Delta
UDT 12
   After discovering several enemy soldiers waiting in ambush for his teammates, Stone alerted his men. He then was

instrumental in leading the frogmen's counterattack, resulting in the Vietcong defeat.

GMC Barry W. Enoch   9 Apr. 70   Ba Xuyen Province
ST-1

While leading a combined force into enemy territory, the unit became heavily engaged and surrounded. Enoch deployed the forces and directed the defense, calling in close air support. He then led the men in a fierce break-out and extraction maneuver.

RM2 Harold L. Baker   20 Dec. 70   Mekong Delta
ST-1/Det Golf

Acting as rear security for his SEAL patrol, the unit was ambushed. Baker overcame his own initial shock and initiated a heavy volume of fire to keep the enemy from overrunning the position.

Nguyen Van Kiet   13 Apr. 72   Quang Tri Province
South Vietnamese Navy

Volunteered to act as guide for a clandestine recovery of a U.S. pilot shot down deep inside enemy-controlled territory. Kiet became the sole South Vietnamese recipient of the U.S. Navy Cross.

GLOSSARY

AO

Area of Operation. The normal boundary within which a military unit is assigned to operate.

ARG

Amphibious Ready Group. Small force of naval vessels and units designed as the forward deployed amphibious arm of the various fleets to which they are attached.

ARVN

Army of the Republic of Vietnam. The South Vietnamese army.

BUD/S

Basic Underwater Demolition/SEAL school. The initial training of all navy combat swimmers.

CHIEU HOI

Literally, "Open Arms." Amnesty program that accepted Vietcong who surrendered.

DET

Detachment.

FROGMAN

UDT or SEAL member. Distinguished from other navy divers for their combat role in amphibious operations; formally called a combat swimmer.

HELO
 Common military slang for helicopter.

HOI CHANH
 One who Chieu Hoi'ed.

IBS
 Inflatable Boat, Small. A seven-man, black rubber boat commonly used by Navy Special Warfare throughout the Vietnam conflict. The boats were used for a variety of operations and could be paddled or employed with a small outboard engine.

KCS
 Kit Carson Scouts. Former Vietcong who had defected and worked on missions against their former comrades.

LCM
 Landing Craft, Medium. One of many sized amphibious craft of the intermediate size. Used for beach assaults and riverine operations, it is called a Mike Boat.

LDNN
 Lien Doc Nguoi Nhia, or the "soldiers who fight under the sea." South Vietnamese frogmen.

LSSC
 Light SEAL Support Craft.

MACV
 Military Assistance Command, Vietnam.

MACV-SOG
 Military Assistance Command, Vietnam-Studies and Observation Group.

McQUIRE RIG
 System used early in the war to extract a small team by using a line suspended underneath a helicopter when a landing zone could not be found.

MSSC
 Medium SEAL Support Craft.

NAD

Naval Advisory Detachment. SEALs assigned to MACV-SOG out of Danang worked in the NAD as a cover unit. Their mission included advising LDNN in the conduct of maritime special operations.

NASTY BOAT

High-speed Norwegian "Nasty" class patrol/torpedo boat purchased by the United States and used against coastal targets in North Vietnam.

NAVSPECWAR

Naval Special Warfare.

NCDU

Navy Combat Demolition Unit. Early frogmen of World War II.

NILO

Naval Intelligence Liaison Officer.

NVA

North Vietnamese Army.

OIC

Officer-In-Charge. Term used by frogmen to describe the officer in charge of an operational platoon or patrol.

PBR

River Patrol Boat.

PCF

Patrol Craft, Fast.

PRU

Provincial Reconnaissance Unit. Indigenous mercenaries.

RANGER

Graduate of U.S. Army School, which teaches small-unit dismounted patrolling. Also, a member of a Ranger unit.

RECON

Slang for Reconnaissance.

RSSZ

Rung Sat Special Zone. Large swamp area located southeast of Saigon within easy striking distance of the city. A long-term Vietcong sanctuary, SEAL direct-action platoons conducted their first operations of the war in this area.

SDV

Swimmer Delivery Vehicle, also known as SEAL Delivery Vehicle. Free-flooding submersibles used to transport UDT/SEALs to a target area.

SEAL

Frogman assigned to a Sea, Air, Land Team. During the Vietnam conflict, two SEAL teams were in existence. SEAL Team One was located in San Diego, California. The Team One platoons sent to Vietnam held letter designations. SEAL Team Two was located in Norfolk, Virginia. The platoons from Team Two were numbered to avoid confusion in message traffic and discussions. The platoons were assigned to one of the existing SEAL detachments once in-country. Det Alfa consisted of all the SEAL Team Two direct action platoons. Det Bravo were individual SEALs from both teams assigned to advise Provincial Reconnaissance Units. Det Echo advised LDNN under MACV-SOG. Det Golf consisted of all the SEAL Team One direct action platoons. Det Sierra was formed in the latter stages of the war to advise LDNN under the Vietnamization program.

SLICK

A helicopter with minimal armament used for transporting personnel.

SOP

Standard Operating Procedure. Those procedures specifically designed and practiced by a unit to meet its needs in certain training and combat circumstances.

SPECIAL FORCES

U.S. Army units utilized mainly in guerrilla and counter-guerrilla operations. These versatile units can also conduct a wide variety of special operations. Commonly known as the Green Berets.

SPECWAR
Special Warfare.

STAB
SEAL Team Assault Boat.

SWIFT BOAT
High-speed boat smaller in size than the Nasty boat. Used for a variety of riverine and coastal operations during the Vietnam War.

2IC
Second-In-Charge. Term used by frogmen to describe the second in command of an operational platoon or patrol.

UDT
Underwater Demolition Team. During the Vietnam conflict, UDTs 11, 12, and 13, all located in San Diego, California, served in the Southeast Asian war. Additionally, an element of UDT 21 supplemented UDT 13 during its first WESTPAC cruise. The UDTs deployed on a basic six-month WESTPAC cruise as an entire command. Once in the Far East, the men were split into detachments to support fleet operations. Since only one UDT served in WESTPAC at a time, all the commands lettered their detachments the same. Det Alfa served at Subic Bay in the Philippines as the command headquarters. Det Bravo supported the Far East Phibron (Amphibious Squadron) as the beach reconnaissance group. Det Charlie conducted submarine operations from the available conventional WESTPAC submarine asset. Det Delta conducted operations from a small camp outside Danang. Dets Echo and Foxtrot were embarked as part of the Amphibious Ready Group (ARG). Dets Golf and Hotel were formed during the course of the war in support of riverine operations in the Mekong Delta.

VC
Vietcong. South Vietnamese Communist Guerrillas.

WESTPAC
Western Pacific area of operations.

BIBLIOGRAPHY

Primary Sources

Most of the primary sources can be found at the Naval Historical Center, Washington, D.C.

Unclassified histories of the following U.S. naval commands for the years indicated:

SEAL Team One	1962-1975
SEAL Team Two	1962-1975
UDT 11	1946-1975
UDT 12	1946-1975
UDT 13	1968-1971
USS *Perch*	1960-1967
USS *Tunny*	1967-1970
USS *Grayback*	1970-1973

Historical summary of SEAL Team operations in Vietnam printed by the U.S. Navy (undated).

Monthly Summaries of the Commander U.S. Naval Forces Vietnam (COMUSNAVFORV), 1965-1972.

UDT 11 WESTPAC Cruise Books for the following cruises: 1967, 1968-1969, 1970.

UDT 13 Cruise Book for the year 1969.

Navy Unit Commendation for SEAL Team One.

Three Presidential Unit Citations for SEAL Team One.

Two Presidential Unit Citations for SEAL Team Two.

Three Medal of Honor Citations for SEAL Team personnel.

Seven Navy Cross Citations for NAVSPECWAR Personnel.

One Navy Cross Citation for South Vietnamese LDNN.

Naval Special Warfare Training Handbook 1974.

"UDT Training at Little Creek," *Naval Training Bulletin*, Winter, 1962-1963.

"Navy's Triphibian Teams," *All Hands*, May 1967.

"Frogman Recruits," *All Hands*, March 1969.

"Trained They Are; Clean They're Not," *All Hands*, December 1972.

"NUC to UDT," *All Hands*, July 1967.

"Navy SEALs Special Warriors," *All Hands*, December 1987 (Special issue dedicated to a description of Naval Special Warfare).

Hooper, Edwin B., Dean C. Allard, and Oscar P. Fitzgerald, *The United States Navy in the Vietnam Conflict*, Volume I, Naval Historical Division, Department of the Navy, Washington, D.C., 1976.

Marolda, Edward J., and Oscar P. Fitzgerald, *The United States Navy in the Vietnam Conflict*, Volume II, Naval Historical Center, Department of the Navy, Washington, D.C., 1986.

Stubbe, Ray W., *AARUGAH!*, Report to the Director, Historical Division, Headquarters, Marine Corps, on the History of Specialized and Force-Level Reconnaissance Activities and Units of the United States Marine Corps, 1900-1974, 1981.

Tilford, Earl H., Jr., *Search and Rescue in Southeast Asia*, Office of the U.S. Air Force, Washington, D.C., 1980.

Bibliography

Secondary Sources: Books

Anderson, William C. *Bat 21*. Englewood Cliffs, New Jersey: Prentice-Hall, Inc., 1980.

Ayers, Bradley Earl. *The War that Never Was*. Canoga Park, California: Major Books, 1979.

Berry, Erick. *Underwater Warriors*. New York: David McKay Company, Inc., 1967.

Best, Herbert. *Webfoot Warriors*. New York: The John Day Company, 1962.

Blassingham, Wyatt. *Underwater Warriors*. New York: Random House, 1964.

Fane, Cdr. Francis and Don Moore. *The Naked Warriors*. New York: Appleton-Century-Crofts, Inc., 1956.

Forbes, John and Robert Williams. *Riverine Force*. New York: Bantam Books, Inc., 1987.

Friedman, Norman. *U.S. Small Combatants*. Annapolis, Maryland: Naval Institute Press, 1987.

Generous, Kevin M. *Vietnam: The Secret War*. New York: Gallery Books, 1985.

Hettema, Arthur D. *My Experience with U.D.T. at Luzon and Iwo Jima*. Personally published.

Jason, Alexander. *Heroes*. Pinole, California: Anite Press, 1979.

Marchetti, Victor and John D. Marks. *The CIA and the Cult of Intelligence*. New York: Dell Publishing Company, Inc., 1974.

Middleton, Drew, et al., *Air War—Vietnam*. New York: Bobbs-Merrill Company, Inc., 1978.

Nolan, Keith William. *Battle for Hue: Tet 1968*. Novato, California: Presidio Press, 1983.

Nolan, Keith William. *Into Laos*. Novato, California: Presidio Press, 1986.

Pisor, Robert. *The End of the Line.* New York: Ballantine Books, 1982.

Padden, Ian. *U.S. Navy SEALs.* New York: Bantam Books, 1985.

Prados, John. *Presidents' Secret Wars.* New York: William Morrow and Company, Inc., 1986.

Rowen, Roy. *The Four Days of the Mayaguez*, New York: W.W. Norton & Co., 1975.

Santoli, Al. *Everything We Had.* New York: Random House, 1981.

Schemmer, Benjamin F. *The Raid.* New York: Harper & Row Publishers, 1976.

Sheehan, Neil, Hedrick Smith, E. W. Kenworthy, and Fox Butterfield. *The Pentagon Papers.* New York: Bantam Books, Inc., 1971.

Stanton, Shelby. *Vietnam Order of Battle.* Washington, D.C.: U.S. News Books, 1981.

Stanton, Shelby. *Green Berets at War.* Novato, California: Presidio Press, 1985.

Thompson, Leroy. *US Elite Forces—Vietnam.* Carrollton, Texas: Squadron/Signal Publications, 1985.

Truby, J. David. *Silencers, Snipers, and Assassins.* Boulder, Colorado: Paladin Press, 1972.

Truby, J. David. *The Quiet Killers.* Boulder, Colorado: Paladin Press, 1972.

Turley, Col. G. H. *The Easter Offensive.* Novato, California: Presidio Press, 1985.

Uhlig, Frank, Jr. *Vietnam: The Naval Story.* Annapolis, Maryland: Naval Institute Press, 1986.

Waddell, Bernard. *I Am Somebody.* Boston: Quinlan Press, 1986.

Wilkinson, Burke. *Cry Sabotage!* New York: Dell Publishing Company, Inc., 1972.

The Vietnam Experience. Boston, Massachusetts: Boston Publishing Company, 1981-1987.
This Series includes the following books:

> *Setting The Stage*
> *Passing The Torch*
> *Raising The Stakes*
> *America Takes Over*
> *A Contagion Of War*
> *Nineteen Sixty-Eight*
> *Fighting For Time*
> *Combat Photographer*
> *Thunder From Above*
> *South Vietnam On Trial*
> *A Nation Divided*
> *A Collision Of Cultures*
> *Tools Of War*
> *Rain Of Fire*
> *The False Peace*
> *The Fall Of Saigon*
> *The Aftermath*
> *Images Of War*
> *A War Remembered*
> *The North*
> *Flags Into Battle*

The Navy Cross-Vietnam. Forest Ranch, California: Sharp & Dunnigam, 1987.

The Vietnam War. New York: Crown Publishers, Inc., 1979.

Secondary Sources: Periodicals

Boyd, Ellsworth. "UDT/SEAL; A Fierce Desire to Succeed," *Skin Diver*, June 1974.

Brown, Frank. "The Phoenix Program; A Postmortem," *U.S. Army Military Intelligence Magazine*, April-June 1976.

Brown, Frank. "SEAL Team Operations: Vietnam 1966-1972,"

Sea Combat, April 1979.

Drenkowski, Dana. "The U.S. Navy SEALS," *Soldier of Fortune*, March and April 1979.

Dwyer, John B. "UDTs in Korea," *Soldier of Fortune*, September 1986.

Fleck, Matthew. "Don't Run A Perfect Op," *Gung Ho*, May 1984.

Gray, Robert. "Tough Training For The Navy's Tough Guys," *Boys' Life*, August 1981.

Hill, Richard. "Mean Mothers With Dirty Faces," *Esquire*, May 1974.

Hubbell, John G. "Hell Week At Little Creek," *Reader's Digest*, December 1960.

Hubbell, John G. "Supercommandos of the Wetlands," *Reader's Digest*, June 1967.

Huddleston, Jenny C. "When You Say BUD/S, You've Said It All . . . Almost," *All Hands*, October 1977.

Merrick, LCDR Walt. "Spec War Ops," *Surface Warfare*, April 1979.

Nutall, M. E. "Guerrillas From The Deep," *All Hands*, October 1966.

Polmar, Norman. "The Navy's SEAL Teams," *Navy*, 9 September 1969.

Powers, William E. "Almost Beyond Human Endurance," *U.S. Naval Institute Proceedings*, December 1977.

Randau, John A. "With the Navy's Hit and Kill Saigon Guerrillas," *Bluebook*, February 1968.

Reed, Fred. "Gutting It Out," *The Times Magazine*, 4 September 1978.

Ritter, James. "UDT Comes of Age," *U.S. Naval Institute*

Proceedings, February 1965.

Roscoe, Theodore. "The Navy's Frogmen; Underwater Astronauts," *New York Times Magazine*, 9 August 1959.

Shults, Jim. "So Ya Wanna Be A Frogman," *Gung Ho*, May 1981.

Smith, Murry. "Captain Phil H. Bucklew, Chief of The Navy's Special Operations Branch," *Coinops*, December 1969.

Watts, David and James Ritter. "The Combat Swimmer," *U.S. Naval Institute Proceedings*, May 1965.

White, David F. "Are They The Toughest Men Alive?", *Parade Magazine*, 16 August 1987.

Wood, Michael. "From Tadpole To Professional In 25 Weeks," *All Hands*, April 1979.

"UDT Hell Week-Trial by Sand and Mud," *Pacific Stars and Stripes*, 2 December 1969.

"Unconventional Commandos," *Time*, 12 January 1968.

"Rendezvous With Death," *Gung Ho*, April 1981.

New York Times, 18 December 1966.
18 August 1967.
29 November 1971.

Christian Science Monitor, 10 January 1967.

Pacific Stars and Stripes, 25 April 1965.
5 January 1966.
11 January 1966.
8 April 1966.
19 December 1966.
29 December 1966.
24 January 1967.
21 May 1967.
14 June 1967.
25 June 1967.

21 August 1967.
16 September 1967.
25 October 1967.
22 January 1968.
11 May 1968.
16 June 1968.
 1 August 1968.
29 August 1968.
 8 October 1968.
23 April 1969.
25 April 1969.
14 May 1969.
29 May 1969.
 1 July 1969.
 9 July 1969.
22 August 1969.
 2 December 1969.
22 December 1969.
 8 April 1970.
 1 May 1970.
 3 June 1970.
21 July 1970.
 9 October 1970.
 8 November 1970.
16 November 1970.
23 November 1970.
 3 December 1970.
23 January 1971.
 1 February 1971.
 2 February 1971.
27 May 1973.